May God Bless America

May God Bless America

George W. Bush and Biblical Morality

Joseph J. Martos

May God Bless America: George W. Bush and Biblical Morality

Copyright © 2004 Joseph J. Martos. All rights reserved. No part of this book may be reproduced or retransmitted in any form or by any means without the written permission of the publisher.

Unless otherwise noted, the Scripture quotations contained herein are from the NEW REVISED STANDARD VERSION BIBLE, © 1989, Division of Christian Education of the National Council of the Churches of Christ in the U.S.A., and are used by permission. All rights reserved.

Scripture quotations marked (NIV) are taken from the HOLY BIBLE, NEW INTERNATIONAL VERSION® copyright © 1973, 1978, 1984 by International Bible Society. Used by permission of Zondervan. All rights reserved.

Scripture quotations marked (KJV) are taken from the HOLY BIBLE, AUTHORIZED KING JAMES VERSION, which is in the public domain.

Published by Fenestra Books®
610 East Delano Street, Suite 104
Tucson, Arizona 85705 U.S.A.
www.fenestrabooks.com

Publisher's Cataloging-in-Publication Data
(Provided by Quality Books, Inc.)

Martos, Joseph J., 1943–
   May God bless America : George W. Bush and Biblical morality / by Joseph J. Martos.
   p. cm.
   LCCN 2004104686
   ISBN 1587363313

  1. Bible--Influence. 2. Bush, George W. (George Walker), 1946---Religion. 3. United States--Politics and government. 4. Biblical ethics. 5. Religion and politics--United States. 6. Christianity and politics. I. Title.

BS538.7.M37 2004   261.7'0973
                               QBI33-2016

To the dozens of teachers and ministers
who opened my heart and mind
to the personal and social meaning of the Bible.

And to the hundreds of people
who researched, wrote, published, and posted the information
that helped me to write this book.

Contents

	Introduction	1
1	Principles and Policies	5
2	Environment and Resources	23
3	Poverty and Wealth	51
4	Human Rights	121
5	War and Peace	163
6	Policies and Consequences	213
	Conclusion	235

May God Bless America

Introduction

George W. Bush is a religious man. A *Newsweek* cover story in March 2003 described his religious upbringing, recounted his spiritual conversion, and explained how his faith has guided what he says and does as president of the United States.[1] A more recent book describes his spiritual growth and religious faith in greater detail.[2] There is little doubt that he is sincere.

Yet sincerity is not enough. A person can be sincere and also misguided. A person can be trying to do the right thing and yet be mistaken. A clear conscience is no guarantee of correctness.

The history of Christianity is filled with people who thought they were right at the time. The early centuries are replete with individuals and groups whose sincere beliefs about God and Jesus were eventually judged to be heretical. In the Middle Ages, Christian nobles and knights were convinced that God wanted them to rescue the Holy Land even if they had to kill thousands of Muslims to do it. During the decades following the Reformation, Protestants and Catholics waged war on one another in the name of true religion. For over two hundred years, Christians in the American South believed that slavery was justified by the Bible.

It is always easier to see the mistakes of the past than those of the present. Long after the events, it is not difficult to compare the beliefs and actions of Christians with the teachings and behavior of Christ, whom they claimed to follow. It is much more difficult to do this in our own time and in our own lives. We tend to think that if something feels right, then it is right. We also tend to think that society's approval is a sign of God's approval. Both liberals and conservatives are guilty of this kind of thinking. Nor is this kind of thinking limited to Christians. Everybody does it.

President Bush is no exception. He works hard to understand what America needs, and he tries sincerely to meet those needs. He devotes time to studying international issues, and he uses his best judgment to address those issues. But there is little evidence that the president or his advisors consult the Bible when formulating national and foreign policy. There is little to suggest that before making a decision they ask, "What would Jesus do?"

One reason for the lack of evidence is the separation of church and state mandated by the U.S. Constitution. Although Congressional sessions traditionally open with a prayer by a member of the clergy, neither committee meetings nor cabinet meetings begin with a Scripture reading or a prayer asking for God's guidance. At the very least, it would be quite awkward if a Christian president were to suggest doing this in our pluralistic society. More likely, someone would accuse such behavior of being unconstitutional.

Another reason for the lack of evidence is the people who surround and advise the president. They are not all evangelical Christians, but they represent the religious pluralism in American society. They may be Methodists like the president, but Methodists range from conservative to liberal, and from devout to nonpracticing, as do people of any faith. They may be also Baptists or Lutherans, Episcopalians or Presbyterians, Catholics or Jews, even possibly agnostics or atheists, since religion or the lack of it is not a qualification for public service in America.

It would be difficult for people from such diverse backgrounds to bring religion into government discussions, even if they wanted to do so, which is unlikely. Such discussions instead revolve around factual information, around political and economic realities, around objectives and strategies. If government discussions entail ethics and morality, they are guided by the principles and values that are common to Americans, or at least common to the people in the conversation. And the people who surround and advise the president do not hold in common the heritage of biblical Christianity.

Although the president is a Christian, then, it is unlikely that he is getting Christian advice from the Cabinet and others who today are closest to the White House. With regard to domestic policies, he is most likely getting ideas from national business organizations such as the U.S. Chamber of Commerce, Federal Reserve Chairman Alan Greenspan, longtime confidant Karl Rove, and research organizations such as the American Enterprise Institute. With regard to foreign policy, he is hearing from Secretary of State Colin Powell, National Security Advisor Condoleezza Rice, and research organizations such as the Rand Corporation. With regard to energy policies, he appears to be following the thinking of organizations such as the American Petroleum Institute and the American Coal Council, major oil and coal production companies such as Exxon-Mobil and Peabody, energy supply companies (of which the now defunct Enron was the largest), and American automobile manufacturers (especially General Motors and Ford). With regard to military policy, he appears to be following strategies suggested by Secretary of Defense Donald Rumsfeld, Richard Perle and the Defense Policy Board, Paul Wolfowitz, Elliott Abrams, and others associated with The Project for the New American Century.

There is no doubt that the individuals and institutions just mentioned are political conservatives, commonly referred to since the early days of the French parliament as the right wing or, more simply, the right.* Moreover, for the past quarter century or so, religious conservatives in the United States have also been referred to in this manner, labeling evangelical and other conservative Christians as the religious right or the Christian right. It is often assumed that in America today the two groups overlap and, to some extent, they do. Nevertheless, they are different, for not all political conservatives are evangelical Christians, and not all evangelical Christians (or, as they are sometimes more broadly called, biblical Christians) are political conservatives.

---

* Just before the French Revolution, as tensions mounted between those who supported the traditional monarchy and those who supported the introduction of democracy, the conservatives sat on the right side of the chamber and the liberals sat on the left.

If this is the case, then it is not illogical to suspect that in certain respects there might be a tension or even an opposition between U.S. government policies and what the Bible teaches, especially what the New Testament teaches. Furthermore, to the extent that government policies diverge from biblical morality or the teachings of Jesus, they might reasonably be called unbiblical or unchristian.

Such are the major premises on which this book and its title are based. They are not terribly sophisticated, but they are somewhat disturbing. They are disturbing first of all because many Christians have been led to believe that they should think the way political conservatives think, and that they should want what the right wing wants. They are disturbing secondly because, if there is indeed a disconnect between right-wing policies and biblical morality, and if our country is implementing unchristian policies, then it is difficult to believe that God will bless America.

The format of this book will be fairly straightforward. After an opening chapter on principles and policies, subsequent chapters will do three things: they will look at the policies and practices of the current administration, they will look at principles of moral behavior set forth in the Bible, especially the New Testament, and they will suggest what our government's policies and practices might look like if they were based on biblical principles. Needless to say, a short and inquiring book cannot look at everything. It can hope, however, to raise some questions.

Notes

[1] Howard Fineman, "Bush and God," *Newsweek* (March 10, 2003), pp. 22–30.

[2] Stephen Mansfield, *The Faith of George W. Bush* (J.P. Tarcher, 2003).

1

Principles and Policies*

Where your treasure is, there your heart will be also.
(Matthew 6:21)

People act in accordance with their principles. At least they are supposed to. When they do not, their behavior is said to be inconsistent with their principles.

But what are principles?

Some people equate principles with feelings. Since principles do not get verbalized when we are using them, they can seem like feelings, attitudes, intuitions, even instincts. But they are not. We do not put our knowledge of how to drive a car into words when we're driving, but that does not mean our knowledge is a feeling. You can't pass a driver's test on feelings. In addition, you can't drive well without knowing the principles of good driving.

It is true that we all act and react to some extent on the basis of feelings and attitudes. Sometimes we can't help it: we react before we can think. More often, though, we follow our feelings because we have internalized principles that say it is all right to be spontaneous in certain situations. We know, though, that we have to keep a check on ourselves and behave more thoughtfully in other situations. Our principles help us to decide when to follow our feelings and when not to.

---

* Some readers may find this introductory chapter somewhat abstract. If you prefer to go straight to the issues, please turn to Chapter 2.

Principles can be understood as ideas and values that motivate and guide human behavior. If you accept the idea that people are basically honest, you will tend to trust others. If on the other hand you think the opposite, you will tend to be mistrustful. Trust and mistrust are two principles that guide people's behavior.

Principles don't have to be global and all-encompassing, however. You can trust your family and friends, and be mistrustful of strangers. You can trust Americans but not foreigners, or white people but not black people. You can be mistrustful of others until they prove themselves trustworthy, or you can be trustful of others until they prove themselves to be untrustworthy. Principles can be finely tuned and delicately balanced, but they are no less principles, still motivating and guiding behavior.

When we see people who behave differently than we do—when we see them being dishonest or disrespectful or sexually promiscuous, for example—we may think they have no principles. But they do. It is just that their principles are different from ours. Or maybe they apply their principles differently than we do. As the old adage has it, there is honor even among thieves.

We are not always aware of the principles that guide our behavior, making it more or less consistent. Were it not for our guiding principles, however, our behavior would be completely erratic. One day we would be open and honest, and the next day we would be secretive and deceitful. One hour we would be conscientious and then the next hour we would be lazy. One minute we would be concerned and the next minute we couldn't care less. And vice versa. Consciously or unconsciously, our principles guide our behavior.

This is not to say that our principles are always consistent. We are not robots or computers that are programmed to behave only in certain ways. Especially when we are not aware of the principles out of which we are operating, we can act in accordance with one principle for a while and then unconsciously switch to act in accordance with another principle. We can be friendly toward some people and antagonistic toward others. We can be generous in our family and stingy in church. Very often, other people notice inconsistencies of which we ourselves are unaware. And when we perceive other people being inconsistent, we can think they are being hypocritical.

All the same, the ability to be inconsistent is necessary for human growth and development. If as children we were locked into a limited set of principles, we could never grow into adolescence (often a period of conflicting principles!) and we could never mature into adulthood. As St. Paul notes, "When I was a child, I spoke like a child, I thought like a child, I reasoned like a child; when I became an adult, I put an end to childish ways" (1 Corinthians 13:11).* He recognized that it is possible (and normal, in some respects) to move from one set of principles to another.

When children become teenagers, they often begin departing from family principles and moving into others, trying out new things that are consistent with what they see in the media or hear from their peers. If parents recognize this as part of the normal growth process, they will adapt to this development and begin interacting with their adolescents as young adults rather than as children. If they do not recognize this, they will perceive teenage inconsistency as simple disobedience and they will act according to their parental principles, sometimes with disastrous results.

The ability to be inconsistent is the basis not only of growth but also of human creativity and freedom. The early American essayist Ralph Waldo Emerson declared consistency to be "the hobgoblin of little minds." Creativity means being able to try something new, to be inconsistent with what we have done in the past.

So too with freedom. Since our principles do not determine our behavior with absolute consistency (the way computer programs are supposed to operate), we have the freedom not only to behave in ways that are inconsistent with our principles but even to discard one set of principles and adopt another. We can

---

* Unless otherwise noted, all Scripture quotations are from the New Revised Standard Version (NRSV).

choose to buy something that does not fit our current wardrobe, and we can also accept the challenge of conversion. When we turn our lives over to Christ, we let go of one set of principles and accept another set, no matter how imperfectly at first. In St. Paul's words, we put aside the works of darkness and put on Christ (Romans 13:12–14). Even if our behavior does not suddenly become totally Christ-like, in making a decision for Christ we have decided to exchange one set of principles for another.

There are limits, however, to inconsistency and even to freedom. If we act in a way that is inconsistent with the law of gravity and decide to jump out an open window, we will not have the freedom to fly no matter how hard we flap our arms. If we drink in a way that is inconsistent with sobriety, the alcohol we consume will have its natural effect on our thought processes even if we deny that we have drunk too much. If we exercise our ability to say things that are inconsistent with the truth and tell lies, people will eventually not believe us even when we try to speak the truth. Human nature and God's natural laws always have a way of catching up with us.

Shared Principles

Where do we get our principles?

Some of them come from our own human nature. We have a physical nature that tells us to eat when we are hungry, drink when we are thirsty, and sleep when we are tired. Our bodies know how to grow and mature, how to produce the hormones and enzymes that we need, how to fight infections and restore health. In the words of Psalm 139, we are "wonderfully made" (v. 14). Some of our ideas and values, then, come from experiencing our own bodies and understanding what we should do in order to stay alive and be healthy.

There is also a psychological and emotional dimension to human nature. We experience needs for safety and security, for acceptance and love, for belonging and fellowship, for respect and dignity, and for having a sense of self-identity as well as a good self-concept. Human nature prompts all of us to pursue these values, and for this reason they are common principles of human behavior. If we ignore them, we do so at our own peril.

We also have a spiritual dimension that makes us the unique creatures that we are. Our human nature gives us a thirst for knowledge and truth, a desire for justice, a willingness to show compassion, an ability to invent and create. We can think and reason and learn from our experience. We discover notions of morality and systems of ethics, we pursue philosophy and religion in the hope of finding answers to our deepest questions, and we develop a whole range of sciences to better understand ourselves and the world in which we live.

But our spiritual nature also gives us freedom, and with freedom comes the ability not only to do good but also to sin, to act contrary to what God wants for us and others. Besides being honest we can also be dishonest, besides being loving we can also be hateful, besides being temperate we can also give in to addictions and excess. Other creatures such as animals, which have a physical and psychological nature but not a spiritual nature, are not free. They are bound to behave according to the way God made them; they must obey their instincts. Have you ever seen a deer that did not behave like a deer? Have you ever known a dog or cat to deceive you?

Our sinfulness reveals spiritual needs for forgiveness and salvation that we ultimately cannot meet for ourselves, though not for want of trying. If we are fortunate, we learn there is what twelve-step programs call a Higher Power, which believers call God. If we are Christians, we acknowledge that forgiveness and salvation come through Jesus Christ. "For God has destined us not for wrath but for obtaining salvation through our Lord Jesus Christ" (1 Thessalonians 5:9). If we have turned our life over to Christ, we have to admit that we still do things for which we need to be forgiven by God and others.

Whether we act contrary to our physical nature, our psychological nature, or our spiritual nature, we harm ourselves and others, or at the very least we do no good. We may not experience any negative consequences right away, but that will not prevent them from happening eventually. We may even enjoy what we are doing, and think it's perfectly all right. But whether it is right or not, whether it is good or not, does not depend on what we think. Especially, it does not depend on what we feel. "If it feels good, do it" is not a helpful rule; it is not a sound principle on which to base our behavior. It may feel good, but it could hurt our family, land us in jail, give us AIDS, weaken society, or harm the environment.

The principles based on our human nature are principles we share with all other human beings, whether we know it or not, and whether they know it or not. Our common human nature is what makes us all one family, all children of God. Regardless of our individual or social differences, our ethnicity or nationality, our age or gender, we are all human beings. Regardless of our skin color and other physical characteristics, there is only one race of people on this planet—the human race.

Besides the principles we share with others based on our common human nature, there are principles we share with those who are closest to us. We learn most of our basic beliefs and values from the people we grow up with, our parents and family, even our extended family and the ethnic and cultural groups that they represent. There is an old saying that values are not taught but caught—picked up from the example of others more than from their words. One reason *My Big Fat Greek Wedding* was such a popular movie is that it artfully portrayed the tension between a family's ethnic values and a couple's personal values, showing how (with a little negotiating) both could be satisfied. Even if we are not Greek, many of us could see ourselves in that story.

We pick up other principles from the schools that we attend and, increasingly in today's society, from the media—not only television and radio but also movies and recordings, magazines and newspapers. The title of Robert Fulghum's first best seller, *All I Really Needed to Know I Learned in Kindergarten,* is a tribute to the powerful influence of school, where many of us learn basic principles such as play fair, don't hit others, and clean up your own messes. Whether or not we agree with the materialistic values displayed in today's media, we have to admit that they have a formative influence on what we buy, what we esteem, and even what we think.

Societal and Cultural Principles

Because of their different ideas and ideals, beliefs and values, societies and cultures differ in the principles by which they operate and inculcate in their citizens. Unless we have traveled widely outside the United States, it is difficult to experience this firsthand, and today it is becoming increasingly difficult to experience this even in other countries. The expansion of Western technology (everything from cars to computers), American media (especially films and music), and global franchises (McDonald's and the rest) make airports and hotels, streets and stores look more and more like the ones back home. Beneath the surface, however, cultural differences still abound.

By and large, Asian cultures value social conformity more than Americans do, especially since the 1960s when something like a cultural revolution began upsetting the traditional norms of the U.S. and Europe. Japanese society is much more homogeneous than ours, and foreigners are welcome to visit but not to immigrate. Most Arabic societies value family and religion more than Americans do, and in many places it is still common for parents to pick the spouses for their children. People in sub-Saharan Africa and in the Caribbean (with its many African influences) are generally more expressive than their northern counterparts in Europe and America. The principles of etiquette, family, and government that turn the wheels of daily life in other cultures can sometimes be quite different from our own, despite our common humanity.

When we look back across history, we see the same is true. Part of the fascination of novels and films set in the past is the glimpse they afford us into lives that are organized according to different principles, when life was simpler or harder or more bound by social conventions. Some of us are old enough to remember living through World War II either in real life or in John Wayne movies. We watch Ken Burns' series on the Civil War or the television adaptation of Alex Haley's *Roots*, and we see people who are very much like us but at the same time different: they talk and behave in ways that we do not. In books and movies we can travel back in time to Europe with its monarchies, to the Middle Ages with its code of chivalry, and to the Roman Empire with its armies and conquests. In each period, the principles (that is, the ideas and values) around which life was organized were somewhat the same as, yet somewhat different from, our own.

To simplify our discussion, let us focus on two forms of government and the principles by which they operate: monarchy and democracy. Europe for a long time was governed by monarchies, by governments headed by kings and queens, along with their attendant nobility. The right to rule, both at the top of the social pyramid and at any point below it, was inherited, and it was quite independent of gifts and talents, virtues and vices. History is filled with stories of intelligent monarchs who tried to improve the lot of their subjects, and it is also filled with stories of less than brilliant rulers who made stupid decisions and brought disaster to their countries. Charlemagne, Louis XIV and XVI of France, Isabella and Ferdinand of Spain, Henry VIII and Elizabeth I of England, and Ivan the Terrible and Catherine the Great of Russia are known to us because of the accomplishments and calamities associated with their names.

Monarchs (at least in Europe) were said to rule by divine right, that is, with God's approval, and the monarch's rights could therefore not be questioned. The monarch's rights were also absolute, covering all the property in the realm as well as the lives of all the people. Without the idea of private property, monarchs could in theory confiscate any land they wanted and give it to any subject in the realm, although in practice they took lands mainly from their opponents and gave it to their supporters. There was no concept of human rights since all rights, including the right to life, came from the monarch, who could also therefore take it for any reason deemed appropriate. Kings and queens could pass laws at will, impose taxes at will, and completely rule the lives of their subjects. The principles on which monarchy was based gave them the power and authority to do so without question.

Along came the Enlightenment in eighteenth-century Europe, and things began to change. What changed first were ideas—the idea that the monarch's right is not absolute, that there are basic human rights that come from God, that people have a right to private property, to a trial by their peers, and to some extent to govern themselves. From the perspective of monarchy, these ideas were revolutionary, and in fact two revolutions before the end of the century—one in America and one in France—turned these ideas into reality, one perhaps a little more successfully than the other at the beginning. The United States was founded on a completely different set of principles, the principles of democracy.

Americans are quite familiar with the principles of democracy, enshrined as they are in the two foundational documents of this country, the Declaration of Independence and the United States Constitution. Soon after the founding of the nation, it became evident that some further principles needed to be articulated, and so the Constitution was amended with the Bill of Rights. To these first ten amendments were later added others, clarifying and extending the principles on which the country was founded. These guiding principles govern the creation of all other legislation—from state constitutions and laws to local ordinances—in the sense that they must be in conformity with democratic principles and not violate any constitutional rights.

Since the eighteenth century, the principles of democracy have been adopted and implemented around the world, although not always following the U.S. model of government. Some democracies in Europe and elsewhere retain monarchs with limited rights and primarily ceremonial duties. All have elected representatives, but many have parliaments and prime ministers rather than congresses and presidents. All have freedom of speech, though most place greater limitations on this right than the United States does. All have separation of church and state, though often the separation is not as severe as it has become in our country. The broad and general nature of principles allows the principles of democracy to be implemented in a great variety of equally valid fashions.

At the same time, however, principles are not so vague that they are infinitely flexible. Just because a country calls itself a democracy does not mean it is one. Just because a country has elections does not mean the elections are fair. Just because a country has a legislature does not mean that the lawmakers truly represent the people. The former Soviet Union displayed the trappings of democracy (periodic elections, for example) while remaining a totalitarian system, and the same is true of countries that still call themselves Communist today. For a long time, many Latin American countries had elected legislatures and presidents, even though they were run overtly or covertly by military leaders. The appearance of democracy is not the substance of democracy.

Even though they are very general, principles have a power to effect real changes in the way people live. When the American colonists decided to adopt the principles of democracy, they fought for political freedom and founded an independent country. The Declaration of Independence proclaimed "that all Men are created equal, that they are endowed by their Creator with certain unalienable rights, that among these are Life, Liberty and the Pursuit of Happiness." A few years later, however, the Constitution granted many rights only to those men (that is, human beings) who were white males. But the principles of democracy inspired the abolitionist movement in the nineteenth century to fight for the elimination of slavery and the extension of human rights to people regardless of their skin color. And those same democratic principles motivated women in the twentieth century to win the voting rights and property rights that men had long enjoyed.

In some respects, then, principles are more powerful than bombs and armies, especially when they are principles that are in conformity with human nature and God-given rights.

Religious Principles

Just as governments are based on principles, so too religions have foundational principles. Indeed, every institution in society is based on ideas and values that give it coherence and direction. Hospitals and schools, police and fire departments, businesses and charities are guided by principles that make them what they are and define their purpose. Sometimes these principles are written down in a charter or set of bylaws, and sometimes the purpose is expressed as a mission statement, but smaller institutions often get by without a written document, working with an unwritten consensus about the nature and purpose of the enterprise. The absence of written principles, however, is not evidence for the absence of principles themselves. As with individuals, ideas and values can operate silently, guiding people's behavior without being put into words.

We tend to think of religion as promoting principles rather than as based on principles, but every religion has foundational principles that give it coherence and direction, shaping and guiding the lives of its adherents. The great foundational principle of Judaism is the notion that there is one God and only one God— in contrast to the belief in many gods that was so prevalent in the ancient world. This belief is so important that it is repeated daily by Orthodox Jews in the *Shema*, a prayer whose title comes from its first word in Hebrew: "Hear, O Israel [*Shema Yisrael*]: The Lord our God, the Lord is one" (Deuteronomy 6:4, NIV). This belief is also so important that it is a theme which permeates the entire Old Testament, especially the first five books known as the Pentateuch or Torah, and indeed the first four of the Ten Commandments* concern the honor and worship due to God. From the existence of the one God and his covenant with Abraham and his descendents flow all the particulars of the Jewish law, so that Jesus could summarize the teachings of the Hebrew Bible in two great commandments, love of God and love of neighbor (Matthew 22: 34–40; see also Mark 12:28–31, recounting the same incident, but including the *Shema*).

Contrary to Judaism, one of the foundational beliefs of Hinduism is a belief in the possibility of many gods; another is belief in reincarnation rather than an afterlife. Buddhism articulates its foundational principles in four points: (1) life involves suffering; (2) the cause of suffering is attachment to desires; (3) suffering can be eliminated by eliminating attachments; and (4) attachments can be eliminated through eight spiritual practices. Both of these religions and other eastern religions have such a foundational reverence for life that many of their adherents are vegetarians: because they value all life, they refuse to kill animals for use as food. Islam, like Judaism and Christianity, is a monotheistic religion, and it also has a foundational belief in prophets, people who can speak on God's behalf, such as the prophet Mohammed.

The foundational principles of a religion are often so broad that they cut across sectarian or denominational differences. All Jews, Christians, and Muslims are monotheists, for example, regardless of the different branches of those religions to which they belong. In contrast, all Hindus are polytheists, although no Hindu prays to all the gods; rather, Hindus pray to those gods to which they have a special devotion. Also in a foundational way, all Christians accept the divinity of Christ regardless of the church or denomination to which they belong.

Down through the twenty centuries of Christianity there have been many attempts to formulate its foundational beliefs and values. St. Paul began articulating them in his letters even before

---

* Or the first three, depending on how the commandments are divided. They are not numbered in the original Hebrew, nor in most translations.

the gospels were written, and the four gospels themselves were to some extent attempts to write down what first-century Christians believed about Jesus and his teachings. Much shorter summaries later began appearing in the form of early creeds, the most famous of which is the Nicene Creed, which is recited even today in many churches. The original portion of this creed dates to 325 AD, when the Emperor Constantine gathered church leaders from around the Roman Empire in the town of Nicea, and instructed them to produce a statement of beliefs to which, in the name of religious and political unity, they could all subscribe.

Other historical statements of faith include the Athanasian Creed, attributed to one of the great Fathers of the Church, the Augsburg Confession, setting forth Lutheran beliefs at the outset of the Protestant Reformation, the Thirty-nine Articles, summarizing the early foundations of the Anglican Church, and "The Fundamentals," a series of booklets composed in the early twentieth century to set down the beliefs of American Christians who rejected the religious liberalism of that era.* Much later in the last century, *Baptism, Eucharist and Ministry*, a statement of principles from the World Council of Churches, was crafted as liberally as possible in order to encompass the beliefs of a broad range of Protestant denominations about church membership and practices.

It would be difficult to spell out the Christian principles to which George W. Bush subscribes. On the one hand, he is a Methodist, and Methodists by and large are fairly liberal. On the other hand, he identifies with Evangelicals, and Evangelicals for the most part are conservative. It seems that it would be fair to say that President Bush sees himself as a biblical Christian, but not necessarily a fundamentalist. He accepts the Bible as revealing God's truth, and he is comfortable using biblical language and imagery in his speeches.

---

* Christians who subscribed to these beliefs became known as fundamentalists, but today the term is used to designate any believers (even non-Christians) who base their lives on certain religious fundamentals.

People who call themselves biblical Christians today are somewhat right of center on the American religious spectrum. They are close to Evangelicals in their reverence for the Bible as the word of God, but they are sometimes uncomfortable with positions taken by leaders in the Evangelical movement, especially the more fundamentalist ones such as Jerry Falwell and Pat Robertson. At the same time, they believe strongly in the Lordship of Jesus Christ and the necessity of turning one's life over to Christ in order to call oneself a true follower of Jesus. Very often they are biblical literalists, but they can also be open to the findings of modern scholarship with regard to ancient languages and literature, history and culture, which can nuance the interpretation of biblical texts.

Like other Christians, and indeed like most religious people, biblical Christians believe that their faith should be put into action. They accept that the ideas and values that they find in the Bible should guide the way they live their lives. They do not accept the notion that religious faith is a purely personal matter, something that is for private consumption only, or something that can be reduced to Sunday worship. Biblical Christianity, in other words, implies biblical ethics, a code of morality that is in conformity with the teachings of the Bible. For people who are biblical Christians—whether they are Evangelicals or fundamentalists, Methodists or Lutherans, Pentecostals or charismatics, Catholics or nondenominational, born-again or Spirit-filled—their lives should be based on biblical principles. That is, the ideas and values that they find in the Bible should be the basis of their behavior.

If George W. Bush is a biblical Christian in any of the above senses, one would expect that his life would be based on biblical principles—not only his private life, but his public life as well. That is to say, one would expect him not to abandon his Christian principles when he walks out of his residence and into the west wing of the White House every morning. And by all appearances, he does not. He has supported faith-based initiatives for delivering needed social services, and he has promoted the appointment of pro-life judges to the federal judiciary. His speeches ring with religious phrases not only when he is talking before Christian audiences but also when he is addressing the nation. He has asked for God's blessing not only on those who have suffered from terrorist attacks but also on a war against terrorism. President Bush does seem to be following the same principles consistently throughout his life, in all his behavior.

But perhaps the president would invoke the separation of church and state if one were to point out policies that, on the surface at least, seemed to be unchristian or unbiblical. Perhaps he would say that a vast government bureaucracy cannot be held to the same high moral standards to which he holds himself. Perhaps he would argue that much of what the federal government does is based on policies that were in place long before he came into office, and so he cannot be thought responsible for them.

This does not seem to be what Mr. Bush would say, but even if it were, a citizen would still be entitled to question his government, and a Christian citizen would be entitled to ask whether or not his government's behavior and policies measured up to biblical principles. In fact, a Christian would be obligated to do so even at the risk of being thought disloyal or called unpatriotic, if he thought his president had chosen a course that ran counter to biblical principles.

Prophetic Dissent

Some of us Americans who call ourselves Christians find ourselves in an uncomfortable position today. We are saddened when we look at the direction in which our country has been moving since January 2001, when Mr. Bush assumed the presidency, for in some respects it seems to be far different from the direction in which God calls us. At the same time, we are aware that many of our Christian brothers and sisters do support the president and his policies, and we are puzzled by this. Is it that they do not always know what their government is doing in their name? Is it that they are not searching the Scriptures for biblical affirmation of their country's behavior? Or is it that both they and the president are being unconsciously inconsistent by operating out of two different sets of principles—one set that is grounded in the Bible and the teachings of Jesus, and another, quite different set that is grounded in the doctrines of political and economic conservatism?

Inconsistency is not a sin. As was pointed out earlier in this chapter, our spiritual ability to be inconsistent is essential to human creativity and freedom. But our God-given freedom does give us the ability to sin, not only by deliberately choosing what we know is wrong but also by mistakenly choosing what we believe is right. It is all too easy for intelligent and free creatures to do the wrong thing for the right reasons, just as it is possible for us to do the right thing for the wrong reasons. What counts in the long run is not whether we think we are doing the right thing, or even whether we are convinced we are doing the right thing, but whether or not we are in fact doing the right thing—what is right in the eyes of God, what is right according to God's law, what is right according to what is revealed in the Bible.

If we suspect that our country is doing wrong, then we have a duty as citizens to examine the issues and to question our government's policies and actions. For democracy means, in Lincoln's famous phrase, "government of the people, by the people, and for the people." In a democracy, we are responsible for what our government does because we have elected it and we have the freedom to challenge it if we disagree with what it is doing. In a representative democracy, our elected representatives, including the president, act in our name, and so if we believe they are acting wrongly, we have a responsibility to speak up and speak out.

As Christians we have a similar responsibility. It is grounded in the biblical principle of prophecy, not prophecy in the sense of foretelling the future but prophecy in the original Hebrew sense of speaking for God, of saying what God would want people to hear. It is prophecy in the sense that Nathan spoke prophetically when he told King David that he had acted wrongly by having Uriah killed in order to take his wife Bathsheba (1 Samuel 12:1–14). It is prophecy in the sense that the prophets spoke out against the sins of Jerusalem (Isaiah 1–5), condemned infidelity to God's covenant (Jeremiah 7–11), and pointed out injustice and idolatry in Israel (Hosea 4–10). The people to whom the prophets spoke—usually the wealthy and those in power—probably thought they were doing just fine, and the prophets felt compelled to say that, despite appearances to the contrary, everything was not all fine.

This principle is found in the New Testament as well, although under different circumstances. Early Christians, as noted in the book of Acts, sometimes said things that those in power found offensive. Not long after Pentecost, for example, the apostles were brought before the authorities—not once but twice—and they were ordered to stop preaching in the name of Jesus. They listened respectfully, but in the end, they disagreed. In their own way, they concluded that they had an obligation to say what they knew in their hearts to be true. In Peter's words, "We must obey God rather than any human authority" (Acts 5:29; see 4:18–20).

Some Christians today have no difficulty following the biblical principle of prophecy with regard to certain issues such as abortion and school prayer. When they believe that federal law runs counter to what God wants, they are willing to speak out and even to demonstrate publicly for change. It is somewhat more difficult to follow this biblical principle, however, when the issues are the policies of a president whom many Christians support. And it is much more difficult to follow this principle when Christians themselves support those policies.

Nevertheless, the principle remains, and those who call themselves biblical Christians can feel obliged to take it seriously even when the issues get difficult.

2

Environment and Resources

The earth is the Lord's and all that is in it. (Psalm 24:1)

For eight years, the Clinton presidency had been marred by ideological divisions and partisan wrangling. Mindful of this history, George W. Bush promised to "change the tone in Washington, D.C." when he spoke to the nation as president-elect on December 20, 2000. "After a difficult election," he said, "we must put politics behind us and work together." He acknowledged that "America wants reconciliation and unity," and he indicated his intention "to find common ground and build consensus."

Yet with regard to environmental and energy policies, Mr. Bush seems to have been operating with a single-mindedness that leaves little room for dialogue and compromise. Exactly one month later, within hours of having been sworn in as president on January 20, 2001, he halted implementation of a recently passed federal policy which would have stopped the building of new roads in almost sixty million acres of national forests in order to preserve them as wilderness areas.[1] In May of the same year, the Bush administration unveiled a national energy plan that was developed without public discussion or consultation with environmental experts, after Vice President Cheney had met privately with representatives of the energy industry.[2] In the months and years since then, the federal government seems to have been pursuing policies of production rather than preservation, and of consumption rather than conservation.

The Public Record

U.S. government policies and decisions with regard to the natural environment and the Earth's resources fall primarily under the jurisdictions of the Department of the Interior, the Department of Energy, the Environmental Protection Agency, and the White House. It is impossible to examine each of these in detail, but something can be learned by looking at who heads them. For example, none of the president's appointees have what environmental groups would call a strong background in ecology. Interior Secretary Gale Norton was once a lawyer for the Mountain States Legal Foundation, an organization that supports private property rights and opposes government regulations that restrict them. Energy Secretary Spencer Abraham had favored increased oil production but not increased fuel efficiency when he was a U.S. Senator from Michigan. When Mr. Bush's first EPA director, Christine Whitman, was governor of New Jersey, she was known primarily for reducing state taxes, but she also reduced state programs for monitoring and fighting pollution. Likewise, Governor Michael Leavitt of Utah, the new EPA nominee, was known as a consensus builder on environmental issues, but he reached more agreements with pollution-producing industries than he did with environmental groups. And of course President Bush himself, prior to being elected governor of Texas, had worked for several companies that were in the oil and gas producing business.

By its own admission, the Bush administration takes a "pro-growth" approach to environmental issues.[3] In other words, policies affecting the natural environment are expected to stimulate the economy and not stifle it, even while they show concern for ecology. Toward this end, government agencies under the leadership of Bush appointees have been revising regulations that prevent economic development in some areas, that slow down expansion in others, and that make businesses vulnerable to legal suits and other challenges from environmentalists who have little appreciation for economic realities.

Environment and Resources 25

President Bush has done many things to promote growth and development, some of which have an impact on ecology.[4] Since January 2001, various departments, agencies and offices have

- sought to increase logging in national forests and to reintroduce offshore drilling for oil and gas in places where it had been banned;
- promoted drilling for oil in the Arctic National Wildlife Refuge and the Alaska National Petroleum Reserve;
- trimmed down government programs that discourage the economic development of rural areas, especially wetlands and farms;
- looked for ways to remove smaller bodies of water from being covered by the Clean Water Act so that the land around them could be freed for economic development;
- attempted to speed up the commercial use of protected lands by streamlining the environmental review process and limiting opportunities for obstructive objections;
- proposed elimination of federal funding to enforce court orders to comply with environmental laws that restrict business or individual rights;
- given little resistance to legal challenges to environmental laws and regulations, thus allowing them to be overturned in favor of business interests;
- reduced access to government information that could be used in suits alleging environmental damage;
- delayed or suspended implementation of government regulations that would reduce pollution but increase business costs;

- favored long-term development of alternative technologies (such as hydrogen fuel cells) over short-term conservation measures (such as increased fuel efficiency) that could hurt the automobile and oil industries;
- changed rules governing aging power plants to enable them to continue to produce cheap electric power without having to introduce expensive new pollution-reduction technologies;
- favored overall reductions in pollution through voluntary compliance and economic incentives instead of forcing every polluter to meet national standards since this could reduce profitability and force some companies out of business;
- extended the use of snowmobiles and jet-skis in national parks to allow time for the development of more environment-friendly machines.[5]

Two Major Issues

Even if they are not conversant with all of these matters, many Americans are familiar with a few of the major stories that have made headlines, such as opening protected areas to oil and gas drilling, developing the FreedomCAR, rejecting the Kyoto agreement and the Clear Skies proposal, and revising sections of the Clean Air Act and Clean Water Act. One reason why these stories make the news is that they all relate to two basic environmental issues that even schoolchildren have heard about and studied: depletion of the earth's resources, and environmental pollution. If we briefly review these two issues, we can better see how the president's initiatives attempt to address them.[6]

Depleting the Earth's Resources

When we stop to think about it, it is clear that we live on a planet with limited resources. All the water that is on the Earth has been on the Earth since its creation. The proportions of fresh water and salt water may change slightly, but the total amount of water remains the same.

Likewise, the coal, oil, and gas that we find in the Earth today have been there for a long time. Once they are taken out of the Earth and used as fuel, however, they are not replaced. They are called nonrenewable resources because once they are used, they cannot be used over again.

For as long as human beings can remember, it has seemed as though the Earth's resources were virtually limitless. We could always drill more wells for water, or cut more trees, or farm more land, or discover more oil. As Americans, we grew up with the idea that we could always push back the frontier, that there was always more to discover. If we ran out of resources on this continent, we could turn to other places and find even more.

In the 1960s and 1970s, however, we began to look at the Earth differently. Photos of our planet taken by NASA astronauts made us begin to think of our world as a more limited place, as a blue and white marble against the darkness of space, as a natural environment with clearly defined boundaries. The experience of Apollo 14 prompted many to start thinking of the world as "Spaceship Earth," a self-contained living environment that could possibly break down with disastrous consequences.

The fact is that we humans have been using and using up the Earth's resources at an enormous pace, and the pace is accelerating. Part of this is due to the population expansion—sometimes called the population explosion—that has been going on since the nineteenth century, when modern medicine made it possible for people to live longer and have more children who survived infancy. The human population was about one billion around 1830, around two billion in 1930, around four billion in 1975, and around six billion in 2000, and it will soon reach eight billion.[7] We are doubling our numbers in shorter and shorter periods of time.

Not all of us use the Earth's resources in equal amounts, however. The rich consume more than the middle class because they can own more houses, buy more cars, dress more elegantly, eat out more often, take more vacations, and so on. Similarly, the middle class consume more than the poor do. Unlike middle class wage earners, poor people often have nearly empty closets and nearly empty refrigerators. And they ride buses and bicycles rather than cars.

Those of us who live in so-called developed or industrialized countries consume more than people in other countries do. Not only do we eat more food per person, we also use more building materials, buy more clothing, own more vehicles, and use more energy than do people in less developed or non-industrialized countries. With only about 20 percent of the world's population, Americans and people in other developed countries annually consume more than 80 percent of the world's production. The two billion people in India and China combined use less oil every year than the 280 million people in the United States.[8]

Americans have become more aware of the benefits of recycling, but we still throw away most of what we use, producing about 240 million tons of garbage (almost a ton per person) annually.[9] It has been estimated that every year we throw away enough aluminum cans, foil, and other products to rebuild the entire fleet of commercial airplanes in the United States. When it comes to nonrenewable energy sources, however, there is no such thing as recycling. Once oil, gas, and coal are used, they are used up for good.

In the 140 years since the first commercial use of oil, human beings have used up about a third of the world's available petroleum, and if we continue to use it at the present rate, the world will run out of oil by the end of this century.[10] Natural gas is usually found near petroleum, so much the same can be said of gas. Coal is much more plentiful, but the fact is that we have used up more coal in the years since World War II than were used in all the previous centuries.[11] Not even the world's coal will last forever.

Pollution of the Environment

A natural consequence of using things is leftovers. We finish eating and the leftovers get saved or thrown in the trash. We build a house and throw the remaining pieces of wood and drywall into the dumpster. Even when things are used up, there are leftovers. When wood and coal burn, they leave ashes. When oil and gas burn, they give off unburned gasses.

In a simpler age, most human leftovers were organic and nature could be expected to absorb them and cleanse itself in the long run. As the human population skyrocketed, however, and as our manufactured products became increasingly inorganic and synthetic, we began to exceed the Earth's capacity to decompose and naturally recycle our waste material. We entered into the era of environmental pollution.

Pollution becomes a problem when it begins to cause harm. The harm may be to human beings, but it may also be to other living things. The harm may be direct and sudden, as when a chemical spill in a river kills millions of fish. But the harm may also be indirect and gradual, as when underground water is contaminated by pesticides, herbicides, and industrial waste. A slow but steady exposure to radiation from nuclear power plants and dumps can cause a slow but steady increase in liver cancer and birth defects. In many ways, the most insidious pollution is the type that goes unnoticed.

People today do not remember that the automobile was once regarded as the solution to a pollution problem. The horseless carriage, as it was called then, was hailed as an invention that would usher in an era of clean streets, unpolluted by horse manure. We realize now, however, that this was only a short-term solution that eventually created a new pollution problem—air pollution—especially in cities.

Other modern inventions were also welcomed as cleaner technologies. Burning coal for heat was more efficient and less polluting than burning wood. Eventually oil replaced coal, and gas replaced oil in most places because it was cheaper and cleaner.

Likewise, electric lights were brighter and less polluting than candles, kerosene lanterns, or gas lamps, and electricity could be used to power machines as well.

Electricity, however, had to be generated in centrally located power plants. The first power-generating plants burned coal, and many of them still do because coal is plentiful and relatively inexpensive when used on a large scale.[12] Later power plants were built to burn oil or gas, and some were even built to use atomic energy, which was first thought to produce no pollution but which was later acknowledged to result in highly radioactive waste material—very toxic leftovers.[13]

When coal, oil (whether fuel oil or gasoline), and gas are burned, they produce air pollution. Although this pollution is often not visible, it is still measurable. And since this pollution is being produced by millions of cars and thousands of power plants, the quantities are significant. Add to this the fact that the automobiles and power plants of other industrialized nations also produce air pollution, and the problem gets larger. And as poorer countries become increasingly able to buy cars and build power plants, the problem becomes worldwide.

As the world's largest and richest industrialized nation, however, the United States also has the distinction of being the world's greatest polluter.[14]

Addressing the Two Issues

In recent years the federal government has taken some initiatives to address these issues, but the current administration has also taken steps to reverse earlier government initiatives, calling them too costly or unfair to American business.[15] Apparently, President Bush favors short-term solutions to energy problems and long-term solutions to pollution problems. To meet U.S. energy needs, he has proposed drilling for more oil and building more power plants, which increase consumption and pollution, rather than proposing greater gasoline efficiency for cars and investing in alternative ways to generate electric power (e.g., wind

Environment and Resources 31

and solar energy), which decrease pollution. At the same time, he has promoted the development of nonpolluting fuel cells to power cars and trucks, but this technology will not be widely available for at least ten years. Critics point out that both of these strategies enable oil companies to increase their profits in the short run without requiring them to spend money to reduce pollution in the long run.

Other criticisms about the ecological impact of the president's policies have also been raised.

- Putting the emphasis on consumption rather than conservation is unfair to future generations that will have no access to the Earth's God-given resources once they are used up.

- The Clear Skies proposal of 2002, while it promises a 70 percent reduction in air pollution over the next fifteen years, is weaker than the current Clean Air Act, which will reduce pollution even further if left unchanged.

- Removing wetlands and smaller bodies of water from government protection will destroy natural habitats for animals and fish, and it may also make water in those areas less safe for drinking and recreation.

- The FreedomCAR (Cooperative Automotive Research) proposal ignores the fact that in developing pollution-free vehicles, power plants will be using pollution-causing technologies to generate the energy needed to produce hydrogen and make fuel cells.

- Continued reliance on fossil fuels means continued damage from acid rain caused mainly by pollution from coal-burning power plants. The chemicals in acid rain damage soil, weaken trees, and sicken fish in lakes and streams.

- Improving the fuel efficiency of cars and trucks would save more oil than the protected areas of Alaska could ever produce—without causing environmental damage—and the oil would still be there if it were ever really needed.

Global Warming

The two major issues just discussed are obviously interrelated. The consumption of nonrenewable energy sources (also known as fossil fuels because they come from plants that lived millions of years ago) is slowly increasing the amount of air pollution on our planet, and it is especially concentrated in large cities. But the increased pollution is also having worldwide effects. One of the most important is global warming.

In the midst of a snowstorm or a prolonged cold spell, it is hard to take global warming seriously. And when environmentalists themselves say that the Earth's average temperature has risen only one degree in the past 100 years, it does not seem to be much of a problem. Nevertheless, scientists see it as a problem, and one that is increasing in intensity.

Global warming is caused by the burning of plant materials (primarily fossil fuels and wood, even in forest fires), which releases so-called greenhouse gases into the atmosphere, mainly carbon dioxide. Carbon is a plentiful element on Earth because it is found in all living creatures, both animals and plants. When plants burn, the carbon in them combines with oxygen in the atmosphere and creates carbon dioxide—one part carbon to two parts oxygen.

Greenhouse gases have been given that name because in the atmosphere they behave like the glass in a greenhouse. Just as a greenhouse gets warm by allowing light in and preventing heat from escaping, greenhouse gases do the same thing all over the planet: they allow light energy from the sun to hit the Earth and warm things up, but they prevent heat energy from radiating back into space.

On the whole, greenhouse gases are good, because without them, our planet would be a much colder place. The problem is

Environment and Resources 33

that since the Industrial Revolution in the nineteenth century, when human beings began burning huge quantities of wood, coal, oil, and gas, the amount of carbon dioxide in the Earth's atmosphere has increased by 30 percent. Fortunately, the Earth's average temperature has not gone up by that amount, but it has gone up about one degree Fahrenheit, and the last two decades have been the warmest in recorded history.[16]

Some indications of global warming are quite visible. For example, the polar icecaps are shrinking and getting thinner. It is now possible to sail to the North Pole in the summer, which used to be covered by about ten feet of ice even in the warmest weather. At the same time, huge blocks of ice are breaking off the Antarctic ice shelf and are floating northward as icebergs. There are predictions that the melting ice caps will cause sea levels to rise one to three feet by the year 2100.[17]

Others indications are not quite so apparent. Populations of penguins and polar bears, which need cold habitats, are slowly decreasing because the places where they live and breed are getting warmer. At the same time, some plants, insects, and birds, which used to be found only in warmer climates, are being increasingly found at higher latitudes as the temperatures there become more moderate.[18]

Further indications of global warming seem to be unrelated to heat. Since heat is a form of energy, heat trapped in the atmosphere increases the total amount of energy in the Earth's weather system. In other words, the more energy in the system, the more energetic the weather will be. So one effect of global warming is more severe weather—more hurricanes and tornadoes, more rain and drought, more extremes of hot and cold—not just warmer weather. And this indeed seems to be happening.[19]

Global warming by definition is a global issue, and so it easily gives rise to concerns about our management of the Earth and its resources. From a biblical perspective, "The Earth is the Lord's and all that is in it" (Psalm 24:1), which means that human beings are the caretakers of God's creation, entrusted to take care of it according to God's will. Does God want the planet's petroleum reserves to be used up for the benefit of those who can afford it, to the detriment of those who cannot pay for it now or in the future? Does God want to increase pollution that causes respiratory disease and shortens people's lives? Does God want human beings to change the planet's weather, making it hotter for some people and more unpredictable for others, changing plants and animals' growing and migration patterns, increasing the likelihood of being hurt and killed by droughts and storms and floods?

A Question of Principles

The idea that we are supposed to be caretakers raises questions about the relationship between human beings and the environment not only with regard to global warming, but also with regard to other ways that we use and use up the Earth's natural resources. The most fundamental question is the question of principles: what principles are we following in our daily lives and in our government policies when we interact with the world around us? Are we following principles of conservation as well as consumption? Are we thinking about others as well as ourselves? Are we following Christian principles as well as business principles?

There are Christians who claim that using the Earth and all that is in it is man's prerogative, that God made human beings the pinnacle of creation and gave them rights over all other animals, all plant life, and even the Earth itself. They point to Genesis 1:28, where God says to Adam and Eve, "Be fruitful and multiply, and fill the Earth and subdue it; and have dominion over the fish of the sea and over the birds of the air and over every living thing that moves upon the earth." They believe that if we have this God-given dominion over all other species, then we can do what we want with them.

Although Christians have seemingly behaved according to this principle for centuries, it was only in 1966 that historian Lynn White brought it out into the open in a now-famous lecture to the

American Association for the Advancement of Science.[20] White charged that Christianity is to blame for today's ecology problems because it is the religion of the Western world, which is where the problems started. The creation story in the Bible portrays man as being made in God's image and likeness, separate from and above the rest of nature, rather than as a creature closely connected with the natural environment. Western science and technology have implemented the biblical command to subdue the Earth—instead of befriending the Earth as other religions might suggest—and in doing so they have created pollution problems of unprecedented magnitude. Western medical research and health care have enabled human beings to increase and multiply to the point that overpopulation has become a serious problem. The world was suffering, according to White, because Christians had taken the Bible to mean that people could use the Earth for their own benefit without regard for the rest of creation.

Christian responses to White have pointed out that while the technology that is exacerbating today's problems was first developed in the West, even pre-Christian civilizations had ecological problems. Archeologists have discovered ancient sites that were apparently abandoned because the inhabitants over-farmed the surrounding land or because they polluted their own drinking water. Moreover, Western scientists and industrialists have never cited Genesis 1:28 as a justification for their work. It seems wrong, then, to blame the Bible for what can be more logically attributed to human thoughtlessness—the tendency we all have not to think about the ultimate consequences of our actions.

Even if White is wrong, however, Christianity is vulnerable to the charge of thoughtlessness about the environment because of its focus on personal salvation. Over a hundred years ago, the philosopher Ludwig Feuerbach wrote, "Nature, the world, has no interest for Christians. The Christian thinks only of himself and the salvation of his soul."[21] If one could compare the number of sermons preached about salvation with the number preached about caring for nature, his comment would seem to be just as true today. More recently, the revival of evangelical Christianity has put renewed emphasis on the Second Coming of Christ, when the world as we know it will pass away. If evangelicals believe that the rapture is coming soon, why would they be concerned with ecology?[22]

Charges of this sort have prompted Christian scholars to reexamine what the Bible says about the natural environment and man's relationship to it. Concern for one's personal salvation, they point out, does not exclude concern for creation. And as for the return of Christ, Jesus himself said that no one but God the Father knows when it will happen,[23] so we cannot presume that it will occur soon. The doctrine of the Second Coming needs to be viewed within the larger context of biblical teaching.

Biblical Principles

Christians believe that the Bible is God's word, that it is God's self-communication to humanity about what is important in life, and that it is an inexhaustible source of wisdom and insight. One reason why personal Bible study is so rewarding is that God keeps speaking to us no matter where we are in our personal journey, once we agree to read the Scriptures for spiritual guidance. The depth of God's revelation in the Bible is so great that it keeps revealing more and more to us as we approach it with new questions and concerns.

For some decades now, Christians with questions about the environment have been rereading the Scriptures to find what God has revealed about the natural world. Not surprisingly, they have not concluded that humans are completely free to do whatever they want with the Earth and its resources, as Lynn White had charged. Nor have they found that being concerned for salvation and expecting the Second Coming excuse Christians from ecological responsibility. Perhaps most significantly, of the dozens of books and hundreds of articles that have been written by Christian thinkers about the environment since 1966 (even those written by evangelical Protestants), not one of them suggests going in the direction of deregulation and growth, as favored by political and economic conservatives.[24]

The broad themes that emerge most clearly from these writings are those of creation and stewardship: the world is something that God created and still loves, and he wants human beings to take care of it in ways that suit his purposes.

The World as God's Creation

According to the Bible, the world is not simply a collection of resources to be used for human benefit. It is not something that simply appeared as the result of the blind forces of cosmic evolution, and on which human beings happen to find themselves. It is not simply what naturalists call the natural world, what materialists call the material world, and what humanists call the nonhuman world. It is first and foremost a created world, for it is the work of a divine Creator.

The very first chapter of Genesis portrays God creating the heavens and the earth, and after each day of creation God sees that what he has made is good. Creation is good in God's eyes even before human beings are created on the sixth day, which is to say that it has worth and value apart from its usefulness to humankind. God creates water and dry land, and the land brings forth all kinds of vegetation. The water and the land and all the species of living things belong to God, and in his eyes they are good. Then God creates the birds of the air, the fish of the sea, and both wild and tame animals. These are all God's creatures, great and small, and they are all good in God's eyes.

This theme echoes in other books throughout the Old Testament, especially the book of Psalms:

> O Lord, how manifold are your works!
> In wisdom you have made them all;
> The earth is full of your creatures.
> (Psalm 104:24)[25]

After the Flood, God makes a covenant not only with Noah and his family but also with all the animals on the ark, and seals it with a rainbow. In the book of Exodus, God declares a Sabbath not only for people, but also for animals and even for the land. In Deuteronomy, God gives the Promised Land—his land—to the Israelites on the condition that they continue to obey his ordinances. In the book of Job, God insists that the natural world is in his hands, not man's.[26]

If this is the case, then people of biblical faith must regard the world and all that is in it as God's creation, not as humanity's possession. If human beings seem to own things, it is only for a while, for they come into the world with nothing and they leave it with nothing. God deigns to share his creation with us; it is not ours by right, and if we destroy it we are ruining someone else's property.

Human Beings as God's Stewards

Creation is good, then, not because it is useful but because it is God's, and because God made it good. With regard to the natural world, therefore, the role of human beings in the biblical scheme of things is to take care of someone else's property—in biblical language, to be a steward.

In the ancient world, most people did not own very much, and the little that they did own tended to be what we would call personal possessions—things we individually wear or carry with us. Land and animals, if owned, were regarded as belonging not to individuals but to families and clans, although rulers and lords could claim ownership through the allegiance that was owed to them. If ownership entails disposing of property according to one's will, most people were not owners but caretakers of property to which others also had a claim.[27]

This is the vision of the world in which the human authors of the Bible lived and wrote. They saw humankind's relationship to creation as parallel to most people's relationship to the property they used but did not ultimately own. This relationship was primarily one of responsibility—responsibility for the family's land or herd, or responsibility for the other items with which they were entrusted. It also entailed responsibility to the ancestors and family from whom the property was received, as well as responsibility to the next generation that would depend on this property for survival and prosperity.

In such a world, the notion of stewardship was natural for people. Everyone was a steward in some sense or another, and a few would have had had the formal occupation of steward, managing a large household for someone else. In this sense, everyone had dominion over some area of responsibility, whether it was the father for maintaining the household, the mother for running it, or the children for doing their chores.

It is in this sense as well that human beings were given dominion over God's creation in the Garden of Eden. Their role was to be one of caretaker or steward, not one of user or abuser. Having dominion is therefore the opposite of dominating; it means rather having a realm or area of responsibility.[28]

Being made in God's image, about which Genesis also speaks, needs to be seen in this light as well. At the point in the creation story when God says, "Let us make humankind in our image, according to our likeness" (Genesis 1:26) the only image of God presented in the Bible is one of someone who brings wonderful things into being and marvels at their goodness. It appears that being made in the likeness of God means being able to create new things and appreciate their goodness.

Being Like God

It may sound presumptuous to say that human beings are supposed to be like God, but the idea is not at all foreign to the Bible. It is true that the transcendence and uniqueness of God are quite prominent in the Scriptures (e.g., Exodus 8:10; 1 Samuel 2:2; Psalm 113:5), for in most ways there is no comparison between God and humanity: God is eternal, almighty, omniscient, omnipotent, and so on. Nevertheless, God has breathed his spirit into man (Genesis 2:7),[29] and God expects human beings to imitate his moral qualities, especially his justice and mercy (e.g., Isaiah 56:1; Psalm 82: 2–5; Amos 5: 14–15; Daniel 4:27). Jesus himself said, "Be merciful, just as your Father is merciful" (Luke 6:36), and even more surprisingly, "Be perfect, therefore, as your heavenly Father is perfect" (Matthew 5:48).

With regard to the world of God's creation, therefore, human beings are to take care of it just as God would, that is, just as God did for all the centuries prior to the rise of cities and empires and modern civilization, and just as God continues to do in the natural world. For the principles that are supposed to govern our behavior are apparent from what has been already said: first, regard the natural world as God's creation, not man's possession; and second, use the natural world and its resources as God's stewards, with a sense of responsibility to God and to other human beings, with a sense of appreciation for goodness and beauty, and with a sense of justice and mercy.

These are the two principles, then, that those of us who call ourselves biblical Christians ought to be following in our relationship to the larger world in which we live, and that those of us who believe in democracy ought to be promoting in our government's policies.

Christian Environmentalism

Some Christians have already taken the initiative to put these biblical principles into practice and to persuade others to do likewise. One such group with a presence on the Internet is Christians for Environmental Stewardship, which is physically located in Brush Prairie, Washington, but which can be found in cyberspace by typing their name into an Internet search engine such as Google or Yahoo!* Their specialty is posting Scripture verses that promote appreciation for God's creation and the practice of environmental stewardship. Closely related to it is the

---

* When searching for organizations on the World Wide Web, be sure to put quotation marks before and after the name (e.g., "Christians for Environmental Stewardship") so that the computer looks precisely for that string of words and not for a random collection of those words.

Fund for Christian Ecology, which serves primarily as a link to other Christian ecology sources of information and inspiration.

The Evangelical Environmental Network is a more ambitious organization, posting a number of Christian resources including a large selection of scripture sources as well as the Evangelical Declaration on the Care of Creation, formulated in 1994 at the instigation of the Theological Commission of the World Evangelical Fellowship and other groups.[30] EEN has published *Creation Care* magazine since 1998 in print and online editions, and it is currently promoting an air pollution awareness campaign against gas-guzzling cars and for alternative forms of transportation, calling it "What Would Jesus Drive?"

WWJD literature points out that the United States, with about 5 percent of the world's population, uses more than a third of the world's transportation energy every year. The majority of people in the world use bicycles or walk to where they need to get. Almost half of the rise in global-warming pollution from personal vehicles since 1990 has come from vans, pickups, and SUVs, which are exempt from automobile pollution standards. Medical costs due to pollution from vehicles are now in excess of $56 billion and are climbing every year. Asthma in children is reaching epidemic proportions, having almost doubled for teenagers since 1980 and having more than doubled for infants in the same length of time. Many of the statistics cited come from information provided by the Environmental Protection Agency.[31]

If these and other disturbing facts are known by the EPA, why isn't the government doing something about them? Clearly the federal government is not listening to the concerns of Christian environmentalists, nor to many of the concerns raised by other environmental groups. While this situation did not originate with the current administration, it does seem to be true that since January 2001 the government is moving backwards and sideways rather than forward, primarily in the name of stimulating the economy through growth and consumption. Unfortunately, however, stimulating the economy is not a biblical principle, nor are growth and consumption. George W. Bush seems to be misled by policy advisors who are guided by business principles that promote profit rather than by biblical principles that promote stewardship.

If the United States government were guided by principles of preserving God's creation and being good stewards of the Earth's resources, one would expect its policies to be moving in directions such as the following:

- Developing programs to reduce air pollution by strengthening emissions standards for vehicles, promoting public transportation and less-polluting forms of personal transportation, and developing power plants that use nonpolluting (solar, wind, hydro, and geothermal) rather than polluting (coal, oil, nuclear) technologies.

- Promoting personal and industrial recycling programs, such as is already done in Europe, in order to reduce waste and pollution, and in order to preserve the Earth's resources for future generations.

- Looking for natural and technological ways to guarantee clean drinking water for all Americans, and to preserve and protect our lakes, rivers, and streams for recreational use as well as for local water consumption.

- Joining with other countries around the world to address problems such as global warming instead of withdrawing from international agreements in order to protect a few American businesses.* The U.S. would bring American ingenuity and leadership to the planet-

---

* Critics of environmental ethics often forget or fail to mention that ecologically sound policies create new jobs in recycling, alternative energy production, and so on. Politically, the problem is that the profits would go to new companies rather than the ones that are benefiting from the present policies.

wide challenge of preventing catastrophic climate change.

- Addressing the global issue of the loss of the world's rainforests, which are being rapidly cut down in order to harvest expensive woods such as mahogany and teak, and in order to graze cattle for meat production, most of which is consumed in the U.S. and other industrialized countries. It is estimated that since 1950, two-thirds of the planet's tropical rainforests have been destroyed, and the destruction is still going on.

- Becoming concerned about biodiversity, or the diversity of the world's plant and animal species, all of which are God's creations. Through the loss of forests and wetlands, the expansion of suburbs, and especially the destruction of rainforests, the Earth is losing an estimated fifty thousand species (different types of plants and animals that cannot be replaced or replicated) every year.

- Responding to the disappearance of fish from the world's oceans. Fully 90 percent of the cod, halibut, tuna, and swordfish that used to roam the seas have disappeared in recent decades—victims of overfishing by industrial fleets. Other edible fish are also endangered, upsetting the oceans' ecology, threatening seafood shortages, and destroying the livelihood of coastal fishing communities.

- Changing the tax structure and providing financial incentives to encourage family farming rather than corporate agribusiness. When individual people rather than huge corporations own farmland, they often take better care of it, causing less ground pollution from fertilizer and pesticide and less erosion of topsoil. This is especially true of organic farming.

- Protecting public lands, which are the natural habitats of many animals and the long-term inheritance of the American people, instead of handing them over to private interests for short-term economic gain.

Conclusion

Thinking about the environment and natural resources in other than business terms is not something that comes easy to economic conservatives.* Conservatives tend to focus on what is good for individuals, but ecology is about everyone. Conservatives stress the importance of personal rights, but ecology is about collective responsibility. Conservatives want to preserve what is theirs, but ecology is about preserving what is God's. Conservatives want to protect private property, but ecology is about protecting the planet. Conservatives think about inheriting wealth from the past, but ecology is about sharing resources with the future.

Given this difference in outlooks, it is not surprising that the conservatives in the Bush administration think more about growth through increased consumption than about how that type of behavior affects the environment. President Bush himself, having been in the oil business, made money by drilling for petroleum and selling it on the free market, so he is familiar with the benefits of turning natural resources into wealth. Understandably, he believes the strategies that created wealth in the past will create prosperity in the future.

---

* Interestingly, economic policies that are called conservative in the United States used to be called liberal, and today's policies that favor multinational corporations are called neoliberal in the rest of the world. The word *liberal* comes from the Latin word meaning free, and economic conservatives want business to be free of regulation, taxation, and other restraints on making profits. Hence their global classification as neoliberals.

The issue, however, is one of sustainability. How long can we continue to use up the Earth's resources? No matter how extensive, they are still limited. No matter how vast, they will not last forever. And how far can we continue to pollute the environment? God made nature capable of cleansing normal amounts of natural waste, but did he make it able to absorb increasing amounts of artificial and toxic waste?

From a Christian perspective, the issue is ownership. The Earth and its resources do not belong to us; they belong to God. We humans are simply the stewards of his creation. From time to time, President Bush has alluded to this, as on Earth Day 2002, when he said, "Good stewardship is a personal responsibility of all of us." But good stewardship for the president seems to mean using resources to create wealth without causing too much short-term environmental damage. Long-term environmental thinking—what God's Earth will look like in the year 2025 or the year 2100—is not something about which the president has spoken.

Stewards and servants are mentioned a number of times in the New Testament. In one famous parable (Matthew 25:14–30), Jesus tells of a rich man who goes on a trip and puts three servants in charge of three amounts of money. Two of them use the money to increase their lord's wealth, and one of them does not. When he returns, the rich man praises the first two servants and scolds the third for laziness. In this parable, the human lord is usually understood to refer to the divine Lord, or God, and the servants are those to whom God has given responsibility in this world.

Since George W. Bush is pursuing environmental policies designed to increase wealth, it might appear that, as the teller of this parable, Jesus would approve—until we ask whose wealth was increased, the servants' or the lord's?

Notes

[1] Bernton, Hal and Craig Welch, "Bush to delay enacting ban on roads, logging," *Seattle Times* (February 6, 2001).

² The names of those consulted have never been disclosed, despite repeated attempts by members of the press and Congress to find out who they were. Vice President Cheney cited executive privilege as the grounds for protecting the identity of his consultants. See CNN Online at www.cnn.com for January 29, 2002: "Bush will withhold task force documents."

³ The fact sheet on United States Global Climate Change Policy issued by the Department of State's Bureau of Oceans and International Environment and Scientific Affairs calls it a "pro-growth, pro-development approach."

⁴ Since the government does not provide a summary of its environmental record, researchers have to rely on information provided by environmentalists. One of the more thorough summaries, complete with dates and some links to news sources, is provided by the Sierra Club at www.sierraclub.org. On the main menu, click first on Politics & Issues, then click on W. Watch for stories that are regularly updated but written from an environmentalist perspective.

⁵ Some environmental organizations have been highly critical of this pattern of changes in government regulations, actions, and policies. For example, in January 2003, the National Resources Defense Council issued a report titled "Rewriting the Rules, Year-End Report 2002," which took fifty-three well-documented pages to detail what it termed "The Bush Administration's Assault on the Environment," available at www.nrdc.org by clicking first on The Bush Record and then looking for the name of the document under Related Reports.

⁶ To do your own research on the Internet, a very helpful website is the Almanac of Policy Issues, which advertises itself as "Comprehensive, unbiased background information and links on major U.S. public policy issues." Go to www.policyalmanac.org and click on Environment or any other area of interest.

⁷ Source: Population Reference Bureau, www.prb.org.

⁸ Actually, India and China together annually use *less* than half as much oil as the United States, according to published statistics.

⁹ EPA estimate for the year 2000. Much of this waste comes from businesses, not just households.

Environment and Resources 47

¹⁰ We sometimes forget that plastics and many other synthetic materials are made out of petroleum. The more synthetic products we use, the more oil we are using up.

¹¹ See *The GAIA Atlas of Planet Management*, edited by Norman Myers (Gaia Books Limited, 1994), pp. 106–107.

¹² More than a billion tons of coal are mined in the United States every year, and 90 percent of it is used in electric power plants. Half of the electricity used in the U.S. comes from burning coal. See the executive summary of the Annual Coal Report published by the Energy Information Administration and available on the Internet at www.eia.doe.gov.

¹³ For this reason, no new nuclear power plants have been built in the United States since the 1979 accident at Three Mile Island. Reliable information about various sources of energy is available from the Pace University Energy Project at www.powerscorecard.org.

¹⁴ "With less than 5 percent of the world's population, the United States is the single largest source of carbon from fossil fuel burning—emitting 24 percent of the world's total. Per person, U.S. emissions are roughly double that of other major industrial nations and 17 times that of India." *Vital Signs 2003: The Environmental Trends That Are Shaping Our Future*, by the Worldwatch Institute (W. W. Norton, 2003), p. 40. This figure is consistent with the fact that the U.S. consumes about a quarter of the oil, coal, and natural gas extracted from the ground every year.

¹⁵ The most famous of these reversals is the 2001 rejection of the Kyoto Protocol to begin implementation of the Framework Convention on Climate Change, a worldwide agreement to reduce air pollution reached in Rio de Janiero and signed in 1992 by 170 countries including the United States. About forty industrialized countries agreed to implement their commitment to reduce pollution to 1990 levels by the year 2010 even though the U.S. did not. News stories about President Bush's reasons for the rejection are available online at www.cnn.com ("Bush firm over Kyoto stance," March 29, 2001) and http://news.bbc.co.uk ("Bush faces up to Kyoto Critics," June 11, 2001).

¹⁶ Quick introductions to global warming can be obtained from the Environmental Protection Agency (www.epa.gov/globalwarming) and from the Natural Resources Defense Council (www.nrdc.org). More

scholarly analysis can be found in books such as *Global Warming: The Complete Briefing* by John T. Houghton (Cambridge University Press, 1997).

[17] See Global Warming In Brief at the NRDC website. For background, read reports from the Intergovernmental Panel on Climate Change, and also "Antarctic Warming: Early Signs of Global Climate Change" (both available on the Internet). For a summary, see *Vital Signs: 2003*, pp. 84–85.

[18] In addition to sources already mentioned, articles by Alex Kirby at BBC News Online provide helpful summaries of developments as they have occurred in recent years. See also *Vital Signs: 2003*, pp. 82–83.

[19] In June 2000, a national assessment on climate change by the U.S. Congress predicted these types of changes in North American weather patterns. Of all the environmental organizations, Greenpeace seems to have the best documentation on this phenomenon. At www.greenpeaceusa.org, click on Media Center, then on Publications, then on Global Warming & Energy, then scroll down to the documents that you want to read. For a quick overview, see *Vital Signs: 2003*, pp. 92–93.

[20] "The Historical Roots of Our Ecological Crisis" by Lynn White, Jr., reprinted in *The Care of Creation: Focusing Concern and Action*, edited by R. J. Berry (InterVarsity Press, 2000), pp. 31–42.

[21] Ludwig Feuerbach, *The Essence of Christianity* (Harper and Row, 1957), p. 287. Originally published in 1841.

[22] This type of thinking can even be found in government officials. Ronald Reagan's secretary of the interior, James Watt, told a Congressional committee, "I do not know how many future generations we can count on before the Lord returns." Watt, an evangelical Christian, was explaining why he was not interested in preserving natural resources for future generations. Cited in *The Greening of Protestant Thought* by Robert Booth Fowler (University of North Carolina Press, 1995), p. 47.

[23] Matthew 24:36. See also 1 Thessalonians 5:2. Readers who want fast access to Scripture texts on the Internet can locate them at www.biblegateway.com.

[24] Besides the books cited elsewhere, the following more recent books are recommended: Lionel Basney, *An Earth-Careful Way of Life: Christian Stewardship and the Environmental Crisis* (Regent College Publishing Co., 2000); Shantilal P. Bhagat, *Creation in Crisis: Responding to God's Covenant* (Brethren Press, 1990); Steven Bouma-Prediger, *For the Beauty of the Earth: A Christian Vision for Creation Care* (Baker Academic Books, 2001); Richard D. Land and Louis A. Moore (eds.), *The Earth Is the Lord's: Christians and the Environment* (Broadman Press, 1992); James A. Nash, *Loving Nature: Ecological Integrity and Christian Responsibility* (Abingdon Press, 1994); Frederick Quinn, *To Heal the Earth: A Theology of Ecology* (Upper Room Books, 1994); Nancy G. Wright and Donald Kill, *Ecological Healing: A Christian Vision* (Orbis Books, 1993). Additional resources can be found in the notes and bibliographies provided in these works.

[25] See also Psalm 24:1–2; 50:10–12; 96:11–13; 104:1–26; 148:1–8.

[26] Genesis 9:8–17; Exodus 23:10-12; Deuteronomy 8:5–20; Job 38:1–39:40.

[27] See Norman K. Gottwald, *The Hebrew Bible in Its Social World and Ours* (SBL Press, 1993); also Victor Harold Matthews and Don C. Benjamin, *Social World of Ancient Israel* (Hendrickson Publishers, 1995).

[28] See "Ruling and Subduing" in *Redeeming Creation: The Biblical Basis of Environmental Stewardship* by Fred Van Dyke, David C. Mahan, Joseph K. Sheldon, and Raymond H. Brand (InterVarsity Press, 1996), pp. 89–100; also D. H. Hall, *Imaging God: Dominion as Stewardship* (Eerdmans, 1986).

[29] In Hebrew, the word for breath is also the word for spirit. See Job 27:3; 33:4.

[30] For more about the Declaration, see Berry, *The Care of Creation*, cited above.

[31] "Transportation is a Moral Issue," *Creation Care* 19 (Fall 2002), p. 6.

3

Poverty and Wealth

How does God's love abide in anyone who has the world's goods and sees a brother or sister in need and yet refuses to help?
(1 John 3:17)

During his campaign for the presidency, George W. Bush repeated a phrase that sounded attractive to conservatives, moderates, and liberals alike. "Compassionate conservatism" is the term he used to describe what he promised would be a unique blend of conservative values and a compassionate response to suffering.

At his inauguration, Mr. Bush echoed this campaign theme in his first address to the nation as president:

> America, at its best, is compassionate. In the quiet of American conscience, we know that deep, persistent poverty is unworthy of our nation's promise.
>
> And whatever our views of its cause, we can agree that children at risk are not at fault. Abandonment and abuse are not acts of God, they are failures of love...
>
> Where there is suffering, there is duty. Americans in need are not strangers, they are citizens, not problems, but priorities. And all of us are diminished when any are hopeless.
>
> Government has great responsibilities for public safety and public health, for civil rights and common schools. Yet compassion is the work of a nation, not just a government...
>
> Many in our country do not know the pain of poverty, but we can listen to those who do.

And I pledge our nation to a goal: When we see that wounded traveler on the road to Jericho, we will not pass to the other side.

It takes time to translate ideals and vision into action, especially legislative action, which is where we must look to find the current administration's attempts to implement the values of compassionate conservatism. During his first two years in office, however, Democrats controlled the U.S. Senate, and Mr. Bush was not able to move much of his legislative agenda through the Congress. Understandably too, the president's attention was suddenly sidetracked by the tragic events of September 11, 2001, and by the military actions that those events precipitated. Even by the third year of the Bush presidency, when this book was being written, there were few major legislative accomplishments.

Fortunately, however, we can discern George W. Bush's values not only in his accomplishments but also in his attempts. That is, we can find the principles governing his administration not only in laws that have been passed but also in legislation that has been proposed, and not only in budgets that have been approved by Congress but also in budget proposals that have been sent to Congress. Indeed, it could be argued that the administration's principles can be found in a purer form in what it sent to Capitol Hill than in what it settled for after congressional debate.

The Public Record

Nearly every law and policy affects people's pocketbooks in one way or another. Not only taxes but also government regulations and programs either cost people money or enrich them, and they sometimes do both. When looking for the current administration's attitudes toward wealth and poverty, it is hard to know where to begin. If one started with the president's full budget for the 2004 fiscal year—all five volumes and 13.5 pounds of it—one would get nowhere fast, bogged down in numbers and details.

Poverty and Wealth

The only way to get a handle on this issue is to look precisely at those proposals that affect people who do not have much money and those who do—primarily programs designed to enrich the lives of the poor on the one hand and to benefit the middle class and the wealthy on the other. The former are social service programs, and the latter are tax reduction programs. Fortunately for the sake of our analysis, the Bush administration has proposed a number of initiatives in both of these areas, some of which have passed into law. The social service programs are for the alleviation of poverty, hunger and homelessness, for the expansion of health care, and for improvement of education. The tax reduction programs are the packages passed in 2001 and 2003.

Faith-Based Initiatives

President Bush is very aware of social problems in the United States. Soon after taking office in January 2001, the White House issued a plan titled "Rallying the Armies of Compassion," in which the president and his staff noted:

- As many as fifteen million young people are at risk of not reaching productive adulthood—falling prey to crime, drugs, and other problems that make it difficult to obtain an education, successfully enter the workforce, or otherwise contribute to society;

- About 1.5 million children have a father or mother in prison;

- More than one out of six American families with children live on an annual income of $17,000 or less.

- Millions of Americans are enslaved to drugs or alcohol. Hundreds of thousands of our precious citizens live on the streets. And despite the many successes of welfare reform, too many families remain dependent on welfare and many of those who have left the rolls can barely make ends meet.[1]

In this plan, the administration proposed making government social programs less rigid and impersonal, partnering with faith-based and community organizations, and adopting a pro-results attitude toward assistance programs. In support of faith-based initiatives, the administration planned to eliminate legal and regulatory barriers between the federal government and faith-based social programs, to stimulate private giving to charitable organizations primarily through tax deductions, and to introduce new federal initiatives to involve faith-based and community groups in programs for the needy. Overseeing the administration's agenda would be a new White House Office of Faith-Based and Community Initiatives, supported by newly mandated Centers for Faith-Based and Community Initiatives in five separate cabinet-level departments (Health and Human Services, Housing and Urban Development, Labor, Justice, and Education).

Since then, the Office and the Centers have been established, and they have a strong presence on the Internet.[2] Moreover, the president has been implementing parts of this vision by executive order in the absence of the legislation originally called for. One reason for the absence of progress on this initiative seems to be that the events of September 11, 2001 drastically shifted the administration's focus from domestic to foreign affairs.

Welfare

In 1996, the United States public welfare program known as Aid to Families with Dependent Children (AFDC) was discontinued and replaced by a program law called Temporary Assistance for Needy Families (TANF). Federal welfare rolls, which had been three million in 1960, had grown to over fourteen million by 1994, and both the Republican Congress and the Democratic president believed that system needed to be changed.[3]

AFDC had been an entitlement program, meaning that under the law, people with little or no income were entitled to financial assistance from the federal government. Although the program had been intended to raise people out of poverty, critics charged that it had become a system that kept people in poverty. Increasing numbers of poor people, especially single mothers with children, had become dependent on their monthly welfare checks and were not motivated to find work and become self-supporting. Families stayed on AFDC for years, and when girls from such families got pregnant and had children of their own, they too often went on welfare instead of seeking work. Because the law would not give assistance to healthy men, fathers who could not find work stayed away from their families so that their children could receive welfare benefits. AFDC seemed to have created a spiral of poverty and dependence that was getting out of control.

The 1996 legislation, appropriately titled the Personal Responsibility and Work Opportunity Reconciliation Act,* tried to fix what was broken. TANF replaced a single federal program with multiple state programs funded mostly by federal taxes. States received block grants from the federal government and, within certain guidelines, each state was free to create a social welfare system that seemed most appropriate to its needs. Two significant guidelines were making recipients work in order to receive assistance and placing a five-year lifetime limit on welfare benefits. The law also sought to promote marriage as a way out of poverty by not favoring single parents and by making married couples eligible for benefits.

For a number of years, TANF seemed to be doing what it was designed to do. In the expanding economy of the 1990s, adults in the program were able to find work that at least partly met their financial needs while they and their children also received other benefits such as health care and food stamps. By 2001, employment of single mothers increased by over 30 percent, their earnings almost doubled, their dependence on welfare income was cut nearly in half, and welfare case loads (the number of family units

---

* Bills with the term *Reconciliation* in them, such as this one, are called such because they are the product of one bill passed by the U.S. Senate and another bill passed by the House of Representatives, after the differences between the two bills have been worked out or reconciled.

on public assistance) dropped to less than half of what it had been in 1996.[4]

Spurred on by this success, President Bush proposed maintaining Temporary Assistance for Needy Families when the program came up for renewal in 2002. Unfortunately, the Republican-controlled House and the Democrat-controlled Senate were not able to agree on a reauthorization bill, and so the terms of the original legislation were temporarily extended without modification. With Republicans gaining control of both houses of Congress in the November 2002 election, there was a greater chance that the president's agenda would be enacted. The administration's reauthorization proposal included:

- maintaining the 1996 spending levels even though the number of welfare recipients has declined, making $16.6 billion per year available to states through block grants for TANF;
- maintaining the 1996 funding level for childcare at $2.7 billion, provided for children whose parents are working;
- reauthorizing $2 billion in contingency funds for use in the event of increased need for financial aid or food stamps;
- gradually increasing the percentage of TANF families who must participate in work-related activities from the current 50 percent to 70 percent;
- requiring able-bodied recipients of aid to engage in work-related activities for a full forty hours per week, at least twenty-four hours of which must be paid or unpaid work, with the rest permitted to be time spent in education and training;
- authorizing about $500 million a year for research and programs to support healthy marriages, promote sexual abstinence education, enforce child support laws,

and help families make the transition from welfare to work.⁵

Most of these recommendations found their way into the House of Representatives bill (H.R. 4, passed on February 13, 2003) reauthorizing TANF through 2008. The bill was strongly endorsed by the Bush administration.⁶

Health Care

The cost of health care in the United States has been increasing steadily in recent decades. From 1960 to 1990, national health expenditures increased by more than 10 percent per year from $26.7 billion to $696 billion. From 1994 to 1999, these expenditures increased by less than 10 percent per year, but beginning in 2000 the rate of increase shot up once again into double digits. In that year, health care in the United States totaled $1.3 trillion, with projections that it would reach almost $2 trillion by 2005.⁷

Americans pay for hospital bills, doctor's bills, and prescription medicines in a variety of ways. Currently, about two hundred million adults and children are covered by private medical insurance, much of which is paid for by employers. This includes government employees whose health insurance costs are paid in part by federal, state, and local governments. Approximately thirty-eight million people are covered by Medicare, an entitlement program that since 1965 has provided health care for the elderly and disabled, and forty-seven million (half of whom are children) are covered by Medicaid, which pays for health services to the poor and unemployed.* Despite all this coverage in a country of 280 million people, about forty-four million people

---

* People who are elderly or disabled on the one hand, and poor on the other hand, can receive benefits under both Medicare and Medicaid. Also, Medicare recipients may have supplemental private health insurance. Thus the total of these three groups plus those without insurance equals more than 282 million. Remember too that people with private health insurance may not be adequately covered.

remain without any form of insurance. To address the needs of children without insurance, the federal government in 1997 created the State Children's Health Insurance Program (SCHIP) and today covers more than five million children, but as of 2002 the number of children without insurance may still have been as high as eleven million.[8] People without any form of insurance in the United States do without medical treatment when they need it, or they pay the full cost of treatment, or they obtain treatment (often in a clinic or hospital emergency room) and never pay for it.

For people who are employed and who can afford to pay for medical insurance, the cost of health care is generally not regarded as a social problem. Rather, it is seen as an economic problem or a cost-containment problem, and solutions such as health maintenance organizations (HMOs) have been created in an effort to slow down the increase in health care costs. Every solution creates new problems, however, and problems created by HMOs are being addressed by additional new solutions such as a proposed Patients' Bill of Rights.[9] Likewise, the problems created when the middle-class uninsured (or underinsured) are hit with enormous medical bills, and the problems created when hospitals and clinics are not reimbursed for emergency treatment given to the poor, are not regarded as large-scale social problems. Therefore, government attention focuses primarily on the large numbers of people who are disabled or too old to work and whose health insurance therefore cannot be covered by an employer, the large numbers of people who are unemployed or whose employers do not offer health insurance as a benefit, and the large numbers of children who are not covered by insurance because their parents cannot afford it.

Since the cost of health care is steadily going up, the cost of government-provided health insurance is also going up. According to the U.S. Census Bureau, Medicare payments for the elderly were $176 billion in 1995 and $214 billion in 2000, and Medicaid payments for the poor were $120 billion in 1995 and $153 billion in 1999, the latest years for which official numbers are available.[10]

The SCHIP budget for 2002 was $3.1 billion, and the program at that time was reaching perhaps a third of the children (eighteen and under) who were legally eligible.[11]

Faced with these escalating costs, the Bush administration has proposed new ways to structure and fund Medicare and Medicaid.

Medicare. To offer more choices in medical insurance, the White House on March 4, 2003, issued a "Framework to Modernize and Improve Medicare" proposing that senior citizens be given three different options. The first option was to remain within the current Medicare program and to receive a 10-to-25 percent discount on prescription drug costs. The second option was to join a new program that offers a variety of private health insurance plans and to select the plan that best suits their individual circumstances. The third option was to join one of a number of managed care (HMO) plans, especially ones that offer benefits that are not offered in the current Medicare program. The second and third options, like the first, offered prescription drug benefits, but the amount of benefits varied according to the particular insurance plan that was chosen.[12]

The federal government's first challenge in redesigning Medicare was to add coverage for prescription drugs. When the program was initiated in 1965, medicines were a relatively small part of health care costs, but over the years they became increasingly important and increasingly expensive. Despite their expense, however, they are much less expensive than hospitalization. Still, under the present system, Medicare covers expensive medical treatments but it does not cover less expensive prescription drugs.

The government's second challenge is rising costs. With the cost of medical care going up every year, with more and more people reaching retirement age and qualifying for Medicare, and with relatively fewer young people entering the job market to pay the taxes that pay for Medicare, Congress and the White House have known for some time that something will have to be done if the system is not to go bankrupt. For years, Democrats have sought to increase Medicare benefits and Republicans have resisted raising taxes to pay for Medicare. President Bush's proposed framework was a straightforward attempt to increase benefits while containing costs to some extent—by privatizing aspects of options two and three, and by the inherent efficiencies of managed care plans.

Nonetheless, the president's budget called for spending $246 billion on Medicare in fiscal year 2004, plus an additional $6 billion in new legislative proposals—an almost 6-percent increase. The Medicare Prescription Drug Improvement and Modernization Act was passed by both houses of Congress and signed by the president in December 2003.[13]

Medicaid and SCHIP. The administration's approach to Medicaid reform has not been publicized in presidential speeches and fact sheets. Nonetheless, it was clearly presented in the 2004 budget proposal for the Department of Health and Human Services.[14] Essentially, the president proposed to transform Medicaid from a federal entitlement program into a federal allotment program. In the transformed program, uninsured Americans would no longer be entitled to health care as individuals, but instead the federal government would give states an annual allotment of funds (also known as a block grant) to help pay for the health care of poor people living in those states. Since the State Children's Health Insurance Program (SCHIP) has been an allotment or block grant program ever since its inception in 1997, the proposed budget treated Medicare and SCHIP together as a single enlarged allotment program.

The rationale for this Medicaid and SCHIP modernization program, as the budget calls it, is that it would

- give states the flexibility to design innovative programs to meet the particular health needs of the poor people in those states;
- make it easier for states to work with the private sector to deliver health care services;

- slow down the growth of state and federal program costs;
- simplify the rules and payment policies for these programs;
- increase accountability to make sure that the programs are succeeding and that the funds are being used for their intended purposes.

The crucial concept in this proposal, from the administration's perspective, was flexibility. In fact, this proposal even gave states the option of staying with the current Medicaid and SCHIP programs or shifting over to a block grant model. The administration seemed confident that, given this choice, all states would eventually opt for the new model because of the benefits it offers them, especially freedom from excessive and confusing federal regulations, and freedom to spend federal tax dollars creatively and effectively. In addition, the administration proposed that states choosing the allotment program would receive more money in the early years than they would have under the entitlement program, and that this amount would increase annually, but not as much as it would have under that program. Thus the states would be persuaded to increase efficiencies and reduce costs over the course of time, and in the long run the federal government would save money by funding state health insurance programs that are increasingly cost-effective.

The budget predicted that this modernization would be cost neutral over ten years; that is, the increased outlays in the early years would be offset by increased savings in the later years, and that after ten years the savings per year would accelerate. Proposed expenditures for the 2004 fiscal year were $182 billion, compared to the $161 billion spent in 2003. The budget also contained proposals to spend an additional $3.4 billion for new initiatives not covered by the existing Medicaid and SCHIP programs. This represented an initial increase of about 15 percent over what would have been spent under the existing programs.[15]

Education

The quality of public education in the United States has been a parental concern for decades, and occasionally it becomes a political concern. Politicians point out that public spending for education goes up every year, including funding by the federal government. Parents and school boards point out that, however much it is, support for public education is never enough, especially for schools in economically depressed urban and rural areas.

In recent years, conservatives have focused attention on the quality of public education, insisting that "throwing money at the problem" will not improve inferior education. Business people have suggested a more entrepreneurial approach such as charter schools that would be exempted from many of the regulations that hamper most public schools. Such schools would operate under a special charter from the state, and their increased autonomy would enable them to develop a high quality curriculum. Catholics and Evangelicals have supported a voucher system in which parents would receive vouchers representing the amount of money that would ordinarily go to public schools for the education of their children. Parents would then take their children and the vouchers to the school of their choosing (whether private or public), the better schools would attract more students and more money, and the poorer schools would be forced to improve or close down. Some supporters of public education have called for a more equal distribution of resources. Instead of local taxes supporting local schools (resulting in excellent schools for wealthy tax districts and inferior schools for poorer tax districts), in their view taxes for education should be centrally collected and distributed fairly around the state.*

---

* All three of these approaches have already been tried. Some states allow charter schools, some states have approved voucher systems, and some states use state revenue to fund local schools.

Soon after George W. Bush took office, he announced support for yet another model for improving the quality of public education. His approach was multifaceted, emphasizing accountability as well as school flexibility and parental choice. Wanting all children to benefit and no child left behind, he secured passage of an education reform bill with bipartisan support by the end of 2001. Termed the No Child Left Behind Act, the bill was signed into law on January 8, 2002:

- required states to set standards in reading and mathematics and to test all students against these standards every year in grades 3 to 8;
- required states to take corrective action with regard to public schools whose students do poorly in standardized tests;
- empowered parents to transfer their children out of failing schools and into better schools;
- invited states to compete for funds to set up innovative programs;
- introduced the Reading First initiative, allowing school districts to compete for funds to develop reading programs that actually work;
- contained funds for charter schools and magnet schools;*
- made more flexible use of funds for teaching English as a second language.[16]

The president's 2004 budget for the Department of Education (apart from student loans) was $53.1 billion, up 5.6 percent over the previous year's expenditures. Additional initiatives included

---

* In contrast to neighborhood schools, magnet schools draw children from a wide geographic area.

more scholarship money for tuition assistance (known as Pell grants) to needy college students, and expanded loan forgiveness for students who teach in poverty areas for at least five years after graduation. The president also proposed changing the federally funded Head Start program for disadvantaged preschool children and making it a block grant program for states to design and operate their own programs to help poor children prepare to enter elementary school.

Biblical Teaching

At first glance, it appears that President Bush's social initiatives are excellent examples of compassionate conservatism and, as such, comply with biblical principles such as love of neighbor and compassion for the poor and the needy. Critics of the Bush administration, however, claim that appearances are deceiving and that the long-term conservative agenda is not compassionate but insensitive. Before looking at those criticisms, it would be good to examine what the Bible says about social ethics.

Scripture scholarship in recent decades has made extensive use of archeology and sociology to reconstruct the social world of the ancient Near East. Readers of the Bible are familiar with the story of the Exodus, the escape of the children of Israel from the injustice of slavery in Egypt. Although it is not obvious from reading the books of Joshua and Judges, the period before the establishment of the Israelite monarchy was characterized by relative social and economic equality. Like the first European colonists in North America, and like the later pioneers moving westward across the continent, the early Israelites in the Promised Land were not rich by later standards, although some people may have been a little better off than others. To some extent the Torah or the Law of Moses reflects what life was like—and how God wanted people to behave—in a society that cherished freedom, equality and opportunity.[17]

After the establishment of the Israelite monarchy under Saul and David, however, and especially during the reign of Solomon, the king and his supporters grew enormously wealthy, and the vast majority of Israelites were reduced to poverty.[18] In time, the unwillingness of people in the north to contribute to Solomon's building projects in the south (most notably the temple in Jerusalem) led ten of Israel's tribes to secede and establish a northern kingdom of Israel with a capital in Samaria, while the kingdom of Judah in the south retained Jerusalem as its capital. Even so, the privileges of the ruling classes continued—now in two kingdoms—while the peasants continued to be economically oppressed. In both the northern and southern kingdoms, a few members of the upper classes spoke out against what they perceived as injustice, condemning it as unfaithfulness to the God who led their ancestors out of slavery. These "spokesmen for God" were called *nebi'im* in Hebrew and *prophétes* in Greek, which is why in English they are called prophets. The four who most clearly articulated a message of what today is called social justice were Amos, Micah, Isaiah and Jeremiah.[19]

Jesus in his own day was called a prophet (Matthew 21:11; Mark 6:15), in part because he preached good news to the poor, proclaiming that captives should be released and that people should be free of oppression (Luke 4: 18-19).[20] He also associated with social outcasts (tax collectors and other sinners),[21] and he had compassion for and even touched people who were regarded as "unclean," especially the diseased and the dead. He taught that people should be personally converted to the ways of God, but his teaching also had a strong social dimension, saying how people ought to behave toward others. His message is recorded in the gospels, and its ethical implications are found in the writings of St. Paul and other epistles.

The main places in the Bible where we find social ethics, therefore, are in the Torah or the Law of Moses, the writings of the prophets, and the New Testament gospels and epistles.

The Law of Moses

It is commonly accepted today among scripture scholars that the Hebrew Bible or the Old Testament was composed, written down, edited, and compiled over a number of centuries.[22] One result of this process is that the Law of Moses, given by God on Mount Sinai (or Horeb) is found in not one book of the Bible but three. Exodus 20–31 begins with the Ten Commandments but goes on to other aspects of social relationships and public worship. The whole book of Leviticus deals with religious rituals, purity before God, and relationships to others. Deuteronomy 5 and 12–26 retells God's giving of the Law to Moses, generally paralleling but sometimes adding to the version presented in Exodus. All three books contain ordinances for dealing with people who are not well off. In general, God commanded that the poor should not be oppressed and that they should be given what they need to improve their lives.

According to the book of Exodus, indentured servants—people who have sold themselves into slavery because they do not have the money to pay their debts—are to be set free after a maximum of six years of work; widows and orphans are to be treated with kindness; poor people are not to be cheated and taken advantage of; fields are to be left fallow every seven years, and in that year poor people may freely take anything that grows there.[23] Typical of God's concern for those who have little was the command not to take interest on a loan to someone who is poor, and "If you take your neighbor's cloak in pawn, you shall return it before the sun goes down; for it may be your neighbor's only clothing to use as cover; in what else shall that person sleep?" But that is not all, for God adds, "And if your neighbor cries out to me, I will listen, for I am compassionate" (Exodus 22:26–27).

Leviticus continues in much the same vein. The Israelites are told to leave some grain in the field and some grapes on the vine so that poor people might collect them after the harvest. They are not to defraud the poor or hold back wages that are owed. They are not to take advantage of people who are physically handicapped. Their legal verdicts must be fair, and their weights and measures must be honest. Every seventh year is to be a Sabbath year in which laborers shall be allowed to rest from work. Moreover, every fiftieth year is to be a jubilee, a year of celebration in which land bought during the previous forty-nine is to be returned to its original owner, so that those who are well-to-do will not acquire too much, and so those who have had hard times and have had to sell their land will not be without a source of livelihood.[24] It is clear that the Israelites are not owners but stewards: "The land shall not be sold in perpetuity, for the land is mine; you are but aliens and tenants" (Leviticus 25:23).

The book of Deuteronomy repeats what was said earlier about the Sabbath year, and adds that when indentured servants are freed in the seventh year, they are to be given ample provisions to make a new start in life. Besides not taking a poor person's only garment as a pledge to repay a loan, Israelites are also not to take something that a person needs for income, such as a millstone. Moreover, poor people are to be treated with respect, even if they have to pawn their belongings. The needy are not to be exploited for their labor, and they are to be paid what they have earned.[25] To sum it up, "Open your hand to the poor and needy neighbor in your land" (Deuteronomy 15:11).

And why should the Israelites behave so generously? Because they have just escaped from years of oppression, and they know what it is like to be treated as expendable. Over and over, they are told, "Remember that you were slaves in Egypt and the Lord your God redeemed you from there. That is why I command you to do this" (Deuteronomy 24:18 NIV).[26]

The Prophets

The situation in the so-called divided kingdom was quite different from what it had been a few centuries before, when the people were first settling in the land of Canaan. The kings of Israel in the north and Judah in the south made alliances with more powerful neighbors such as Assyria and Babylonia to protect themselves against invasion, but in doing so they had to honor the gods of the protectors—roughly equivalent to honoring the national flags of allies today. Such behavior was viewed as idol worship by the prophets, not only because these religious images represented other deities besides the God of Israel (in violation of the First Commandment) but also because they symbolized a political and economic system that was becoming more and more unbalanced. Unlike the earlier egalitarian period, there were increasing disparities between the rich and the poor. The poor paid taxes (sometimes 50–90 percent of their harvest) to maintain the court and the temple in style, to feed the army, and to pay the annual tribute to protector states, while the rich benefited from this oppression and paid little or no taxes. By allowing in the false gods, the prophets charged, the rulers had become unfaithful to the Law of Moses and unjust to God's people.[27]

Amos was one of the earliest writing prophets,* living in the eighth century BC, which was a period of prosperity for both the north and the south—but only for the rich. Those who had property did not share with the less fortunate, as the Law of Moses commanded, and they even charged high interest on loans to their own countrymen, which the Law forbade. When poor farmers could not repay the loans they were thrown off the land, and even their personal possessions were sold to satisfy their debts. Seeing this, Amos cried out in God's name:

> For three transgressions of Israel and for four,
>   I will not revoke the punishment;
> because they sell the righteous for silver,
>   and the needy for a pair of sandals—
> they who trample the head of the poor into the dust of the
>   earth, and push the afflicted out of the way.
>
>   (Amos 2:6–7)

---

* The writing prophets are those whose teachings have been preserved in the Bible. Their words (or summaries of them) were probably recorded by scribes rather than written down by themselves. Earlier prophets in Israel's history are called the non-writing or preaching prophets. The Bible contains stories about Samuel, Nathan, and Elijah, for example, but it does not contain whole books of their prophetic teachings.

Amos saw the rich getting richer and the poor getting poorer. Merchants could not wait for religious holidays to be over—so that they could get back to the business of making money. What's more, they did it by cheating—tampering with the scales, overcharging for their wares, and giving less than was paid for. Wealthy farmers sold every last bit of grain from their fields instead of leaving some of it to be gathered by the poor, as the Law commanded.[28]

The wealthy built larger and more luxurious homes for themselves, while many ordinary Israelites were living in hovels. Reduced to being tenants on land they once owned, the poor were not allowed to raise food to feed their families. Instead they had to raise luxury crops such as grapes and olives for the wine and oil of the wealthy, and they had to raise export crops that could be sold for expensive imports such as ivory and ebony.[29]

The ruling classes used their surplus wealth to decorate the temple and pay for lavish religious ceremonies. They thanked God for their blessings and praised him for his glory. But God, speaking through the prophet, said:

> I hate, I despise your festivals,
>   and I take no delight in your solemn assemblies.
> Even though you offer me your burnt offerings
>   and grain offerings, I will not accept them.
> Take away from me the noise of your songs;
>   I will not listen to the melody of your harps.
> But let justice roll down like waters,
>   and righteousness like an ever-flowing stream.
>   (Amos 5:21–24)[30]

Prophets are commonly known for predicting the future, but most often the future predicted by the prophets of Israel was calamity—death and destruction that a righteous God would surely bring down upon the unsuspecting and self-congratulating oppressors of his people.

> Alas for those who are at ease in Zion,
>   and for those who feel secure on Mount Samaria...

> The Lord God has sworn by himself
> (says the Lord, the God of hosts):
> I abhor the pride of Jacob and hate his strongholds,
> and I will deliver up the city and all that is in it.
> (Amos 6:1, 8)[31]

The northern kingdom, with its capital on Mount Samaria, fell to the armies of Assyria in 722 BC The southern kingdom, with its capital on Mount Zion, fell a little over a century later to the armies of another empire.*

Micah lived in the southern kingdom right around the time that the northern kingdom fell. Although some of his prophesies were directed against Samaria, most of his writings attacked the injustices he saw in Judah. The wealthy were buying up the fields and houses of the peasants, who lost what meager inheritance they had in order to buy food. They extorted high prices for the necessities that the poor had to buy. They bribed judges, perverting justice and encouraging corruption. They lied and cheated their way to wealth, and they protected their ill-gotten gain with violence. The situation was getting so bad that no one could trust anybody any more.[32]

All the while, those in power looked at what happened to their neighbors to the north and said, "It can't happen here. God won't let Jerusalem fall." To make sure it didn't happen, they increased the tax burden on the peasants to pay tribute to Assyria. But Micah, like Amos, saw where all of this was heading: God's

---

* The royalty and landowners of the northern tribes were arrested and dispersed throughout the Assyrian empire, and have come to be known as the ten "lost tribes" of Israel. The leaders and elite of the southern kingdom suffered the same fate 135 years later, but when Babylonia was defeated by Persia less than fifty years after that, their Babylonian captivity was ended and they were allowed to return to Judah (also known as Judea). As inhabitants of Judah, they eventually became known as Jews. Most peasants remained on the land throughout this period, ruled and taxed by whichever government was in power.

Poverty and Wealth

judgment in the form of conquest. Unlike Amos, however, Micah foresaw the possibility of redemption. A faithful remnant would return from exile, having learned the lesson that God wanted to teach them.[33] And the lesson could be put succinctly:

> He has showed you, O man, what is good.
>   And what does the Lord require of you?
> To act justly and to love mercy
>   and to walk humbly with your God.
>   (Micah 6:8 NIV)

Isaiah lived in Jerusalem around the same time as Micah.* Like his contemporary, he described the injustice and oppression that was going on in Judah, and he foresaw that it would be punished by a just and angry God. But he also had a broader vision, for he believed that God's righteous anger would destroy other nations that were just as corrupt and oppressive as his own, and he envisioned a time when God would make morality and fairness rule the earth.

Isaiah predicted that God would punish the perversion of justice that he saw in Judah—greed for land, lust for profits, murder and assassination, bribery in the courts, dishonesty in business, disregard for the poor and powerless, and religious hypocrisy.[34] The prophet spoke in God's name when he said,

> Even though you make many prayers, I will not listen;
>   your hands are full of blood.
> Wash yourselves; make yourselves clean;
>   remove the evil of your doings from my eyes;

---

* The biblical book of Isaiah, according to scripture scholars, is the work of three authors whose prophetic activity spanned more than a hundred years. The first Isaiah was a social critic in the tradition of Amos and Micah (chapters 1–39), the second Isaiah spoke words of comfort to the exiles in Babylonia (chapters 40–55), and the third Isaiah gave words of encouragement to the people who returned to Judah after 539 BC (chapters 56–66). What is said here pertains to the first Isaiah.

> cease to do evil,
> > learn to do good;
> seek justice,
> > rescue the oppressed,
> defend the orphan,
> > plead for the widow. (Isaiah 1:15–17)

Isaiah denounced all sorts of social disorders: pride and arrogance, conspicuous wealth, neighbor fighting neighbor, disrespect for authority, abuse of elders, civic irresponsibility, legalized theft, dressing in finery while the poor suffer, unchecked acquisition of property, continuous drinking and partying, bribing and cheating, calling evil good and good evil, greedy competition, turning a blind eye to corruption, unjust laws and unfair regulations, robbing the poor of their rights, oppressing and ruining the weak, and pretending that God does not see what is really going on.[35]

The prophet recognized that neighboring kingdoms were just as corrupt as his own, so while he envisaged that God would use them to punish Judah for its sins, he also believed that God would not allow their injustice to stand. One by one, he foresaw God's wrath coming down on Assyria, Babylon, Phillistia, Moab, Egypt, Tyre, and other ancient cities and empires.[36] They will eventually be destroyed, he said,

> For the Lord is enraged against all the nations,
> > and furious against all their hordes;
> he has doomed them,
> > has given them over for slaughter. (Isaiah 34:2)

Isaiah believed that, in place of these unjust kingdoms, God will establish a kingdom in which justice will reign. On that day, people will renounce what they have idolized and ask God to teach them his ways. God will give them a leader, a messiah[*] who

---

[*] The word *messiah* is derived from the Hebrew word *moshiach*, meaning one who is anointed. When social conditions in Israel and Judah deteriorated, and then again during the exile and return, those who were

will know right from wrong, who will choose what is good and avoid doing evil. People will be satisfied with owning just what they need. God's anointed leader will secure peace in the land through justice and righteousness. This messiah will be filled with God's spirit, he will be knowledgeable and wise, and he will judge with integrity, render fair verdicts for the powerless, and smite the wicked. He will bring peace—not the absence of war but a true *shalom* in which all live in harmony and do no harm to one another.[37]

> He shall judge between the nations,
>   and shall arbitrate for many peoples;
> they shall beat their swords into plowshares,
>   and their spears into pruning hooks;
> nation shall not lift up sword against nation,
>   neither shall they learn war any more. (Isaiah 2:4)

Jeremiah picked up, as it were, where Isaiah left off. Born in the seventh century BC, he lived through the fall of Judah in 587 and the destruction of Solomon's temple in Jerusalem, the west foundation of which became known as the Wailing Wall. Early in his career he spoke out against idolatry, and he apparently supported the religious reforms that were carried out under King Josiah. When Josiah's successors proved to be tyrants, Jeremiah again took up the cause of speaking out for God.

Jeremiah's prophetic language tended to be more generic and symbolic than that of his predecessors, denouncing the worship of false gods and the abandonment of God's law rather than particular instances of corruption and injustice. Still, he did point out that the wealthy were robbing the poor, judges were not being fair, no

---

oppressed began hoping for an "anointed one," someone with special gifts and powers who would overthrow the unjust regime and restore the proper social order envisioned by the Law of Moses. Until the time of Jesus, most Jews expected that the messiah would be an extraordinary military leader such King David had been. Isaiah here is saying that God's messiah will be even better than David.

one was defending the rights of the needy, false prophets were telling the rulers what they wanted to hear, the powerful were committing perjury and murder, the powerless were being exploited, and lying and deceit were rampant, as were fraud and corruption, the net result being that the wicked prospered and the upright were oppressed. He even publicly exposed the fact that the king did not pay the workmen who were forced to build him a lavish new palace—not the only instance of royal dishonesty.[38]

More often, though, Jeremiah accused the king and ruling classes of worshipping idols instead of the one true God.[39] Far from being a concern about religious practices, however, this was one of Jeremiah's ways of talking about social justice. True worship of the Lord entailed keeping the covenant that the Israelites had made with God after escaping from Egypt, and keeping the covenant meant obeying the Law that Moses had received from God on the mountain. The idols of permissiveness, security and prosperity that the wealthy worshipped did not demand ethical behavior, but the God of Israel did.[40]

Like many religious people, the ruling classes thought that if they participated in public worship, God would bless them. Jeremiah told them in no uncertain terms that this was a bad mistake. Speaking as the voice of God, Jeremiah cried out,

> Here you are, trusting in deceptive words to no avail. Will you steal, murder, commit adultery, swear falsely, make offerings to Baal, and go after other gods that you have not known, and then come and stand before me in this house, which is called by my name, and say, "We are safe!"—only to go on doing all these abominations? (Jeremiah 7:8-10)

When he railed against violations of the covenant, what Jeremiah had in mind were the social precepts that had been set out in the books of Exodus, Leviticus, and Deuteronomy. This is clear from Jeremiah's denunciation of something that happened during the reign of King Zedekiah. Following the provisions of the law regarding the Sabbath year, the wealthy who held indentured servants were supposed to free them after six years in servitude. One year, after the king's proclamation, the upper classes did this—but then they recaptured those whom they had just released and forced them back into being slaves.[41]

> Therefore, thus says the Lord: You have not obeyed me by granting a release to your neighbors and friends; I am going to grant a release to you, says the Lord—a release to the sword, to pestilence, and to famine. I will make you a horror to all the kingdoms of the earth. (Jeremiah 34:17)

Jeremiah is often pictured as a prophet of doom, and not without reason. Much of the book that bears his name contains predictions of disasters that will befall Judah if the government remains corrupt and pays no attention to the welfare of the people. Even in the last years of the declining kingdom, Jeremiah declared that obeying God's law while living under Babylonian control was preferable to independence maintained by oppression, and he promised God's wrath if the ruling classes continued their unethical behavior.[42] For trying to speak the truth, Jeremiah was rewarded with imprisonment and death threats, but he lived to see the day when his prediction was fulfilled. Jerusalem and its temple were leveled, the fleeing king was captured and blinded, his sons were murdered, and the nobles and artisans of Judah were deported to Babylon.[43]

The prophets' prediction that social injustice leads to social disaster is one that has remained true since biblical times. And it is still relevant today.

The Gospels

The social teaching of Jesus is spelled out in great detail in the New Testament books of Matthew, Mark, and Luke, called the synoptic gospels because they share a common viewpoint. In John's gospel, the details in the synoptics get telescoped into a single command: Love one another.

In the Sermon on the Mount, Jesus says that he has not come to abolish the Law and the prophets but to fulfill them (Matthew 5:17), in other words, to practice what they preach. And quite clearly, he does practice the compassion for the poor and the concern for justice that inform the social ethics of the Hebrew scriptures. He goes out of his way to heal the sick, to cure the infirm, to comfort the sorrowful and to encourage the downtrodden, not only preaching but also demonstrating the good news that God's kingdom (about which Isaiah had spoken) is at hand. All the people that the powerful ignore and the wealthy belittle, he touches with his words and his hands and his heart.[44]

Christians today insist on the necessity of accepting Jesus as Lord. This certainly has a basis in the Bible,[45] but the more common biblical way of talking about following Jesus is discipleship. In the gospels, Jesus invites people to be his disciples, seventy or so are referred to as his disciples, and among these there are twelve who are also called apostles. The word *disciple* comes from the Latin *discipulus*, which was used to translate the Greek word *mathétés*, which means a student. So in calling people to be his disciples, Jesus was calling them to be his students, to learn from him, and to put his teachings into practice. As Jesus himself said, "Not everyone who says to me, 'Lord, Lord,' will enter the kingdom of heaven, but only the one who does the will of my Father in heaven" (Matthew 7:21).[46]

And what is God's will? Certainly at the very least it means keeping the commandments, as expressed in the Law of Moses. Thus when Jesus was asked which was the greatest of the commandments, he replied that there are two: love of God and love of neighbor.[47] And when asked who should be considered a neighbor, Jesus replied with the parable of the good Samaritan, teaching in effect that anyone in need is a neighbor, even if that person is someone you hate.[48] Another way to say it is, "In everything do to others as you would have them do to you; for this is the law and the prophets" (Matthew 7:12).

It is said that the gospels were written by disciples for disciples (that is, to teach believers rather than to convert the unbelieving), which is why they contain such a wealth of teaching material. Among other things, Jesus in the synoptic gospels teaches that his followers should not accumulate wealth, and that they should instead give money to the poor. In fact, riches are a danger that prevent a person from entering the kingdom of God, for "No one can serve two masters; . . . you cannot serve God and wealth" (Matthew 6:24).[49]

Both Matthew and Luke portray Jesus prophetically consoling the poor and hungry while blasting the rich and well fed.[50] In Matthew's gospel, Jesus gives the reason why the heartless and uncaring are far from God: it is because love of God and love of the lowly are one and the same. In the dramatic parable of the Last Judgment, the righteous are rewarded for their compassion, but the unrighteous are told by the heavenly judge, "Depart from me into the eternal fire prepared for the devil and his angels; for I was hungry and you gave me no food, I was thirsty and you gave me nothing to drink, I was a stranger and you did not welcome me, naked and you did not give me clothing, sick and in prison and you did not visit me." Surprised to hear this, the unrighteous ask when they ever behaved like this, only to be informed, "Truly I tell you, just as you did not do it to one of the least of these, you did not do it to me" (Matthew 25:31–46).

The gospel according to John, as indicated earlier, does not give many particulars about the social teaching of Jesus. Instead, it summarizes all that the synoptics record Jesus as teaching about relationships toward others in a single word: love. Now, the word *love* in the New Testament translates the Greek word *agâpé*, and *agâpé* does not stand for an emotion, as the English word *love* does. In both its noun and verb forms (just as *love* is both a noun and a verb), *agâpé* describes mental and physical behavior, rather the way that the English word *care* does.[51] So when Jesus gives his disciples the commandment to love one another, he is not telling them how they should feel but what they should do. "Love one another as I have loved you" is better translated as "Care for one another as I have cared for you." Those who call themselves followers of Jesus are to care about and take care of others, even laying down their life for them if need be, just as he did.[52]

What is said here about *agâpé* also applies to the meaning of love in the other three gospels as well. "Love your neighbor as yourself" is better translated as "Take care of others the way you take care of yourself." And "Love God with your whole heart, soul, mind, and strength" should be understood as telling people to care about God and about doing what God wants. Jesus in the fourth gospel says, "If you love me, you will keep my commandments" (John 14:15). In other words, "If you care about me, you will do what I am telling you to do."

The Epistles

Probably the most famous passage about love in the New Testament is 1 Corinthians 13, where St. Paul enumerates the qualities of the love that comes from God and compares it to other spiritual gifts. He is speaking about *agâpé*, and he is clearly not talking about love as a feeling because he says it is patient, kind and trusting, not jealous, selfish, irritable, or resentful, and so on.[53] He is not telling the Corinthians that they should be in love with each other, feel attracted to each other, or even like each other; he is saying that they should care about each other and take care of each other. As he says in another letter, "Love does no wrong to a neighbor; therefore, love is the fulfilling of the law" (Romans 13:10). In other words, if you care about other people, you will be led to do what is morally right.

The Pauline epistles do not have much to say about the particulars of social ethics, and the letters of John, like the gospel of John, talk of social relationships primarily in terms of love, that is, *agâpé*. The author reminds his readers of Christ's command to love one another, and that this love for others is the same as love for God.[54] Therefore,

> Those who say, "I love God," and hate their brothers or sisters, are liars; for those who do not love a brother or sister whom they have seen, cannot love God whom they have not seen. (1 John 4:20)

The most practical-minded of the epistles is the letter of James, which talks about faith and works. The author inveighs against Christians who are "hearers of the word and not doers," and he defines true religion as taking care of the needy rather than behaving like the rest of the world. He upbraids his readers for treating poor people with less respect than they do the rich. He reminds them of the commandment to love your neighbor as yourself. And he asks what good it is to have faith if it is not expressed in caring for others.[55]

> Suppose a brother or sister is without clothes and daily food. If one of you says to him, "Go, I wish you well; keep warm and well fed," but does nothing about his physical needs, what good is it? In the same way, faith by itself, if it is not accompanied by action, is dead. (James 2:15-17 NIV)

Conclusions

In some respects, the Bible is fairly consistent in its social ethics. The Law and the prophets, the gospels and the epistles, all tell Christians who respect the Bible as God's word that they should be fair and just toward others, especially the needy and the helpless. At the same time, however, there is some noticeable development in the Bible's teaching from the earlier to the later books. The Torah envisages a situation in which most people are moderately well off, so most of the Law deals with right relationships to God and one another, but some of it (the part on which we focused) deals with doing right in relation to those who are not well off. The prophets speak to a situation which is rather different, one in which there is a growing gap between the rich and poor, and one in which the wealthy benefit from a social system that distributes benefits unfairly. It looks unfair from

God's perspective—which is the perspective from which the prophets speak—because in God's eyes all people are equal, all are created in God's image, and all are children of God. Well, not quite, for the Law and the prophets still assume there is a distinction between Israelites and pagans, between Jews and gentiles, for in the Old Testament justice and mercy are to be shown mainly toward the chosen people.

In the New Testament, this horizon is expanded. Jesus himself went beyond the tradition of caring just for Jews by healing non-Jews and telling his listeners to be a neighbor (that is, be caring) to anyone who is in need, even an enemy.* The good news of God's love—both the news that God loves everyone and that everyone can love the way God loves—quickly spread beyond the Jewish world and into the Roman Empire. Paul, born a Jew and observant of the Law of Moses, carried this central teaching of Jesus to the pagan gentiles, arguing with them and with the Jewish Christians in Jerusalem that faith in Christ and the love of God (*agâpé* toward others) were sufficient for salvation.[56] Scripture scholars tell us that 1 Corinthians, cited above, was written before any of the gospels were written down—evidence to some extent that the message of Jesus about caring for others was taken very early to apply to Jews and non-Jews alike. Those who called themselves followers of Jesus were supposed to care about everyone.

For biblical Christians, then, social ethics entails both compassion and justice. In the Law of Moses and the gospels, the emphasis seems to be on compassion. The newly arrived Israelites in the Holy Land are told to have compassion for the stranger and the alien, for they should remember what it was like in Egypt, where they had nothing and were treated harshly. This compassion is

---

* Samaritans were regarded as enemies in Jesus' day, and so it is plausible that if Jesus wanted to make this point in Israel today he would have told the parable of the Good Palestinian. Likewise, during the Cold War it would have been the parable of the Good Communist, and these days in the U.S. it would be the parable of the Good Terrorist.

not an option, however, because it is given the force of law. The prophets understand this quite well, and in a society rife with injustice they insist that the ruling classes obey God's law and stop oppressing the poor. Jesus in the synoptic gospels seems to put the emphasis once again on compassion, on caring for the disadvantaged, but in more than a few places he gives compassion the force of law. Jesus in the fourth gospel simplifies the matter and makes *agâpé* the law of Christ. Paul says pretty much the same thing in a letter sent before the gospels were written down, and James much later equates lack of caring with lack of faith, that is, infidelity to Christ.

For biblical Christians, then, compassion is not an option. It is the law.

Biblical Principles and Justice

In traditional ethics, justice is a virtue, a habit of mind, and an ability to act in a way that is fair rather than self-serving. In this sense, it is a principle of human behavior.

Commutative justice is the technical term for fair exchange: giving fair value for what is received. This is the simplest type of justice. It is the justice of the marketplace, of trading, of buying and selling. Theft, forgery, and many other crimes are morally wrong because they violate the principle of commutative justice. Thieves, forgers, and other criminals are unethical or morally bad because they do not practice the virtue of justice; they take more than they give.

In the Bible, the commandments in the Law of Moses dealing with restitution and retribution (as well as some others) are based on commutative justice. The rule "an eye for an eye and a tooth for a tooth" is an example of commutative justice.[57]

Distributive justice is the technical term for fair distribution: fairly dividing the goods available among those who are supposed to receive them. This is a more complicated type of justice, for it is not a matter of equal distribution but of fair distribution. A mother practices distributive justice at the dinner table when she gives her older children larger portions than she gives the younger children because the older children need more to be healthy and to grow. A company practices distributive justice when it makes different health plans available to employees with different needs. A government practices distributive justice when it fairly apportions educational resources to children, adolescents, and adults, to the able-bodied and the handicapped, to the socially advantaged and the disadvantaged, and so on. Favoritism in the family, in business, or in government is morally wrong because it violates the principle of distributive justice. Prejudicial and biased behavior is ethically bad because some people get more than they need while others get less than they need, perhaps even being harmed as a result, and this maldistribution leads to social unrest.

The prophets of Israel and Judah did not have a technical name for it, but what they were describing and objecting to was the breakdown of distributive justice in their society, and the hardship that this caused for some while others felt no pain at all. The letter of James insists that Christians should distribute their wealth to relieve the suffering of the poor, as does the Last Judgment scene in Matthew 25 and the story of the rich man and Lazarus in Luke 16.

Social justice is the technical term for fair systems of commutative and distributive justice. It is the most complicated form of justice and was not recognized by ethicists until the twentieth century.[58] Social justice is not a virtue that is practiced in families nor a principle that governs the running of a business. It is something that is found (or is lacking) only in large societies such as cities, states, countries, and the world.

Put simply, social justice is present when a society provides enough commutative and distributive justice for people to live decently and with dignity. If law and order break down so that there is an excessive amount of crime, there is less commutative justice because there is no longer a fair exchange of goods; rather, criminals are benefiting and victims are losing. The fact that people cannot do anything to right the situation points to the lack of social justice in that society. When people are paid less than they need to live decently and with dignity (think of mining towns and sweatshops in the past, or migrant farm workers and *maquiladoras* in the present), commutative justice is lacking because there is not a fair exchange between labor and wages. But social justice is also missing if workers cannot organize to improve their situation (for example, if people are fired for trying to start a union) and if government does not protect them.

Similarly, there can be a lack of distributive justice in a society. If some parts of a city get good police and fire protection while others do not, there is a lack of distributive justice. But if this imbalance cannot be righted (say, because of the way that voting districts are gerrymandered, or because some members of the city council are being paid off), there is also a lack of social justice in that city. If schools in the suburbs are excellent while those in the inner city and rural areas are underfunded, the principle of distributive justice is being violated. And again, if the citizens who have children in the poor school districts cannot do anything to improve the situation, the principle of social justice is also being violated. When the Supreme Court in 1954 ruled that laws providing for "separate but equal" education for whites and blacks were actually preserving distributive injustice in the United States, it struck down the segregation laws as unjust and unconstitutional.*
In doing this, the Court was exercising the virtue of social justice and attempting to provide better distributive justice in American education.

It is clear that the prophets were directing their message of justice to the ruling classes of Israel and Judah, for only the ruling classes had the power to change the social situation and institute more fair systems of commutative and distributive justice. What

---

* The U.S. Constitution, because it sets forth principles governing the exercise of commutative and distributive justice in the states and in the nation, can be thought of as being written at the level of social justice.

God was demanding through the voice of the prophets was therefore social justice, even though the Hebrew language did not have a word for social justice at the time. Nonetheless, the prophets perceived what was wrong with the social situation in their day and they spoke out strongly against it.[59]

The New Testament does not clearly insist on social justice, perhaps because neither the gospels nor the epistles were written for Christians who were in government at the time. (During the first century, when these scriptures were being written, Christianity was not even a legal religion in the Roman Empire.) Jesus's insistence on the law of *agâpé*, however, makes distributive justice clearly imperative for his followers. Christian families and businesses should be run fairly, and Christian communities should care about the least in their midst. The gospel insistence on distributive justice is the ethical foundation of Christian congregations taking care of their members who are in need, and it is the principle on which churches set up nonprofit organizations as small as a local food bank and as large as Catholic Charities to care for those in need regardless of their religious affiliation. Because Christians have taken this injunction seriously, there are thousands of faith-based organizations helping people in America today.

But what of government? And what of Christians in government? Is it enough that they support faith-based and secular organizations that distribute help to the needy? Such an attitude might have been acceptable twenty or thirty years ago, before Evangelicals began mobilizing to promote Christian values through government action, values such as the unborn child's right to life, the right of religious expression in schools and other public places, and the right of parents to protect their children from pornography. Evangelical support of presidential candidates from Jimmy Carter to George W. Bush, however, shows that Christians realize that Christian principles need to be carried into government and enshrined in law.

In their support of writing Christian principles into law, Evangelicals and other conservative Christians take a place in a long line of Christian activism in the United States. The abolitionist movement to free the slaves before the Civil War was largely a religious movement based on biblical principles. Some of the leaders in the women's suffrage movement drew inspiration from the Bible's clear insistence on distributive justice, which gave them courage to insist that women as well as men should have the right to vote. In the early twentieth century, the movement to end child labor and to give workers basic legal rights was championed by conservative Catholics and liberal Protestants. In the mid-twentieth century, black Protestants led the fight for civil rights that had long been denied them, and their cause was taken up by white Christians of many churches and denominations. In all these struggles, Christians were working to embody Judeo-Christian principles in U.S. law. They wanted to change the legal system so that the values of commutative justice and distributive justice would shine more clearly in American society. In other words, they were pursuing social justice.[60]

Until now, however, Evangelicals and other conservative Christians have not thought through the social justice implications of God's revelation in the Bible. With few exceptions, they have focused on biblical prohibitions against certain types of behavior by individuals (for example, abortion and homosexuality), or they have followed the lead of conservatives who either are not Christians or who have little concern for distributive justice. Political conservatives tend to focus on individual rights, such as the right to be free of government constraint, the right to private property, and the right to bear arms. Economic conservatives tend to focus on commutative justice, insisting that people have a right to the money they earn, and that the rules of the market place should determine the fair value of work and investment. It is true that the Bible does talk about commutative justice and individual rights, especially in the Old Testament books that present the Law of Moses. But as we have seen, the Bible also talks about distributive and social justice. For Christians who claim to read the Bible literally—as many conservatives and Evangelicals do—this appears to be a significant oversight.

If Christians agree that biblical principles should guide the formation of law, the laws proposed by the Bush administration should be examined to see to what extent they are guided by considerations of social justice and how well they embody biblical principles of distributive justice.

Social Legislation

Although the recent legislative proposals made by the Bush administration appear to be good examples of compassionate conservatism, many nonprofit and social justice organizations are opposed to them. Why is this?

The general reason that they give is that the administration is cutting back on social spending. Despite the appearance of increasing assistance to the needy, such assistance is either actually decreasing, or it is being redistributed while remaining the same, or it is being scheduled to decrease in the future. In some instances, although assistance is increasing, the proposed increases are less than is necessary to meet the need.

Faith-Based Initiatives

Three and a half years after President Bush invited faith-based organizations to become more deeply involved in administering federally-funded social services, not much has happened. Service agencies in the five affected cabinet departments have been told to be more receptive to requests from faith-based programs, but no additional funds have been allocated to fill those requests. The Pew Forum on Religion and Public Life reported in 2002 that the White House office was understaffed and underfunded,[61] and little seems to have changed since then.

The main reason is that legislation has been stalled in Congress by concerns raised by both liberals and conservatives. On the left, there are organizations such as Americans United for the

Separation of Church and State, which looks askance at any attempt to lower the "wall of separation" between religious activity and government funding. On the right, there are Evangelical Christians who object to the possibility of federal money going to charitable organizations sponsored by non-Christians, especially Black Muslims.[62] In the middle are those who question whether community nonprofits and religious charities are large enough to handle huge social problems. Some even wonder whether federal funding for faith-based initiatives wouldn't rob from Peter to pay Paul, taking money from established civic organizations in order to give it to new religious organizations.[63]

In an effort to move things forward, the Senate in April 2003 passed a bipartisan Charity, Aid, Recovery and Empowerment (CARE) Act to provide a $1.4 billion increase in social services in a two-year block grant, and the House of Representatives passed a similar measure called the Charitable Giving Act in September of that year. As of March 2004, the two bills had not been reconciled and passed by the Congress, perhaps because recent studies have shown that faith-based programs are not necessarily more effective than others, and that after five years of "Charitable Choice" programs in Texas inaugurated by the then Governor Bush, negative results seem to balance out the positive ones.[64] In any event, apart from the funding that has yet to be approved, the proposed federal legislation is not designed to increase government support for the needy; instead, it rearranges part of the overall system that is currently delivering inadequate support.[65]

In terms of the principle of distributive justice, approving faith-based initiatives alters the distribution but it does not increase the just distribution of help to those who need it.

Welfare

Temporary Assistance to Needy Families (TANF), the federal welfare program in effect since 1996, has helped reduce dependence on government assistance, but it has done little to reduce poverty. Instead, it has shifted the problem from welfare dependence to working poverty. When the expansion of the 1990s was replaced by the recession of 2001, the number of low-paying jobs dwindled and employers could offer even less pay to do the jobs that remained. Working poverty was no longer an option, but many were not able to return to the welfare rolls. Instead, they just dropped out of the system. One reason why welfare reform saves money, therefore, is that TANF does not reach all the people it is supposed to help.[66]

Census figures for 2001 show that poverty in the U.S. was up 3.5 percent over the previous year, to about 33 million people—almost 12 percent of the people in the richest country in the world. For government purposes, poverty in 2001 was defined as less than $9,214 income for a single person and $17,960 for a family of two adults and two children.[67] That is $768 a month for a single person and $1,497 a month for a family—income levels that many social agencies call completely unrealistic. Given the cost of basic necessities such as housing and food, it takes much more than that to live in many parts of the United States. Even with the poverty level set unrealistically low, 11.7 million children were counted as living in poverty, of whom four million were under six years old—almost one in five preschoolers in America.[68]

Contrary to popular belief, TANF does not provide relief from poverty. Even before the reforms of 1996, welfare assistance was going down. States had reduced their typical AFDC assistance for a family of three by almost 50 percent since 1970, and TANF was designed to save money. Today, welfare assistance including food stamps is below the poverty level in every state, and the median TANF benefit for a family of three (a mother and two children) is between a third and a half of the official poverty level, depending on the state.[69] The reforms of 1996 also denied public assistance to noncitizens, but since 78 percent of the children of immigrants are born here, the law in effect denies federal help to children who are in fact U.S. citizens.[70]

Statistics tell only part of the story. As unemployment goes up (including underemployment, such as working only part time or working only part of the year) so do personal problems and social ills. People who are poor experience more stress and more depression, and they have higher suicide rates. They are more prone to alcoholism and drug abuse. Women and children suffer from more emotional and physical abuse. Children do less well in school. Families have their utilities cut off, they get evicted, and they go homeless or have to live with relatives. They go without food, and they go without medical care.[71]

Still, statistics tell a lot. Most people do not believe that hunger is a problem in the United States, but for the thirty-three million American poor, it certainly is. The U.S. Department of Agriculture estimates that thirteen million children and twenty million adults go through periods of hunger or regularly live on the edge of hunger. The new term for this is food insecurity, meaning that people don't know where their next meal is coming from. Like poverty, food insecurity rose between 1999 and 2001. Today there are 180 food banks providing food to about sixty-five thousand soup kitchens around the United States serving meals to people who cannot afford to buy their own food. The nineteen million people who receive food stamps survive on eighty cents a day for food. Children who are fed one meal a day through federal school lunch programs do not get that meal when school is out. Still, children go hungry less than adults do because their parents skip meals or reduce their portions so that the kids can have what little there is. In the United States, food insecurity does not mean starvation; it means being undernourished and malnourished.[72]

The brief recession of 2001 is past, but the economy is recovering slowly in some sectors and not at all in others. The national unemployment rate climbed to over six percent and has not dropped much below that, in what has been called a jobless recovery. Despite extensions by Congress, over a million unemployed workers have run out of unemployment benefits at the same time that states are cutting programs for low-income households due to budget restraints.[73] People who were living from paycheck to paycheck went to living from unemployment check to unemployment check, and now that too is gone. If they have children, they can qualify for TANF and food stamps; if they don't, they are out of luck. Even with food stamps, however, they can still run out of food and find themselves at the local food pantry or soup kitchen. This happens every day, but especially toward the end of the month.

Not having money to pay the rent can lead to eviction, and if renting something cheaper or moving in with relatives is not an option, there is always homelessness. On any given night in America, anywhere from seven hundred thousand to two million people have no place to call home. They seek refuge in homeless shelters, they sleep in cars, they sleep in doorways, they sleep in fields, they sleep under bridges, they sleep anywhere they can. In 2001 over three million people were homeless for at least part of the year. About a million of these were children living with one or both parents.[74]

America had not seen widespread homelessness since the Great Depression until the 1980s, after government reforms closed down institutions for the mentally disabled and then failed to provide other housing for them. Today only 22 percent of adults who are homeless suffer from persistent mental illness, but both the ill and the normal suffer from a lack of affordable housing. Urban renewal in the 1970s, cutbacks in public housing and subsidized housing in the 1980s, and the prosperity of the 1990s led to the demolition of many low-cost apartments and the remodeling of many others into places that the poor could not afford. During the years of the Reagan administration, the need for homeless shelters tripled in 182 cities surveyed, and it is still going up. According to the U.S. Conference of Mayors, requests for emergency shelter were 19 percent higher in 2002 than in 2001, paralleling the 18 percent rise in requests for food assistance.[75]

Almost half of the homeless adults in the United States work for a living, but they do not make enough to be able to afford a place to live. The minimum wage in the United States is $5.15 an hour before taxes and other deductions are taken out, and it has not been raised since 1997 even though the cost of food has gone up 15 percent and the cost of housing has gone up 18 percent since then.[76] A single mother with two children working forty hours a week all year makes $3,000 less than the poverty line, and two parents each working a full-time job barely make it out of poverty if they have three children—again before payroll deductions are taken out. Working people at the lower end of the pay scale need two jobs just to make ends meet. Although the public impression is that most minimum-wage earners are teenagers, the fact is that 68 percent are adults—about 4.8 million people trying to make it on their own with less than $5.00 an hour take-home pay.[77]

In 1996, Temporary Assistance for Needy Families was supposed to solve the welfare problem for the federal government. It did that by shifting the burden of providing services to the states, by forcing adults into low-end or non-paying ("workfare") jobs, by reducing the number of people eligible for benefits, and by financing it with block grants to the states. It worked for the federal government, and it worked for the states while the economy was booming and jobs were being created. Since January 2001, however, the United States has lost an average of sixty-nine thousand jobs a month, and states are facing huge deficits. Unlike the federal government, which can borrow huge amounts of money to cover shortages in tax income, most states are constitutionally mandated to balance their budgets. Anticipated deficits must therefore be covered by increased taxes (never a popular idea) or by cutting programs and reducing services. And since poor people living in the United States are no longer entitled to help, they increasingly do not receive it from the states and cities in which they live.

Yes, welfare reform solved a problem for the federal government, but it did not solve the problem of poverty in the United States. Moreover, after five years it does not matter how poor you are. The United States will not help you.

Health Care

Interestingly, the same overall solution to the welfare problem has been proposed by the Bush administration for the problem of health care for the needy: convert medical assistance from being an entitlement program to being an allotment program.

Critics of the administration claim that, far from increasing Medicaid and SCHIP funding by 15 percent in 2004, the president's budget actually called for a 3 percent decrease in spending.[78] Regardless of how one counts the numbers, though, the intent was clear—to reduce federal spending on health care for poor adults and children—so the long-term effect would be that fewer federal dollars would go for medical assistance to the poor. The attraction to states is that initially they would receive more money in a block grant than they would receive in entitlement funds, even though in the long run the states would be receiving less per year than they could expect to receive if the Medicaid program remained in place. This was what is meant by saying that the president's proposal is "cost neutral"—the federal government would spend the same amount of money in ten years under the president's proposal as it would under the present program. After ten years, however, the federal government would save money every year. In other words, the proposal made the administration look generous at the beginning, while over time it was planning to give less and less assistance to the poor.

In the name of modernization and flexibility, states would be given more discretion over who is covered by state medical plans, making it possible for states to reduce coverage during hard economic times that reduce state tax revenues. Under the Bush proposal, Americans would no longer be entitled to health care; rather, the states would decide which of their residents has that entitlement, and under which conditions. People in wealthy states would receive better health care than those in poor states, and state legislatures could always reduce access to medical treatment if the state treasury was running out of money.

Under Medicaid, the more states spend on health care for the needy, the more they receive from the federal government. Under the Bush proposal, this incentive would be removed and states would receive their allotment regardless of how much of their own money they spend or fail to spend. This has already happened with the TANF block grant program, with some states ending the fiscal year with unspent allotments while others go begging.[79]

The SCHIP program is already a block grant program, and after five years of operation it fails to reach an estimated two-thirds of the children it is supposed to cover. It experiences, in other words, the same difficulty that TANF does in identifying and enrolling needy recipients.[80]

The Bush administration has been less callous toward the elderly on Medicare—perhaps, as critics suggest, because they belong to the American Association of Retired People,* and because so many of them vote. Rather than relegating elderly assistance to block grants, the president has proposed to privatize it to the extent that older Americans might prefer private to government coverage. While privatization would save money for the government, it might not offer better service to the people who depend on it. Under the first option offered, seniors would receive a small discount for prescription drugs. Critics charged that the savings would be negligible, and that people on a fixed income would continue to have to choose between medicine and meals, or between the drugs they need and paying the rent. Under the second option, seniors would be able to choose from among a group of private plans, which offer varying amounts of prescription drug coverage. Critics pointed out that for many Medicare beneficiaries this would offer no real choice, because the rural areas in which they live are served by few private insurance companies, and sometimes by only one. Under the third option, seniors would be able to enroll in a health maintenance organization that could offer them more benefits for the same amount of money that Medicare is costing. Critics argued that HMOs are not the answer because they limit people's choice of doctors and, like private insurance plans, they are not universally available.[81]

---

* The AARP has a powerful lobby on Capitol Hill.

Once again it appears that President Bush's social legislation was not proposed with people in mind, but with the government in mind, especially a government bent on reducing services for the poor and needy. This neoconservative or ultra-conservative attitude has led some more traditional conservatives to call for universal health care such as that enjoyed by citizens of most developed countries in the world today.[82] A single-payer government plan could be cheaper and could reach all Americans, while leaving the well-to-do free to spend money on additional medical care or insurance as they see fit. But "socialized medicine" is a bad word in Washington, even though most Americans believe that it is a good for the public to pay for schools and universities, police and fire protection, streets and roads, parks and recreation areas, and many utilities such as water, sewers and electricity. In most other countries of the world, taxes also pay for public hospitals and public clinics.

From a biblical perspective, however, the issue is not whether health care is privatized or socialized, but whether it is justly distributed or not. If a private system can deliver adequate health care to all the people, it satisfies the criterion of distributive justice. Unfortunately, however, the conservatives in government today do not appear to be motivated by concerns for justice. This was not always true of conservatives, which is one reason why the Bush administration is receiving criticism from conservatives as well as liberals these days. Traditional conservatives were and are concerned for what philosophers call the common good or the general welfare of the people, which is achieved by implementing the principle of distributive justice. To the extent that today's conservatives do not act according to the principle of distributive justice, they are not being biblical and they are not being Christian. And according to the prophets, a socially unjust society will be punished by God.

Education

The name of the President's major education proposal—the No Child Left Behind Act—sounds as though it is concerned with distributive justice but, as mentioned above, it is primarily concerned with the quality of education. Leaving aside questions that have been raised about the standardized testing mandated by the act,[83] let us look rather at the president's budget and ask whether there is sufficient funding to distribute quality education to all of the public school children in America. Now, parents and teachers always complain of insufficient funding for public schools, especially in poorer districts, but that issue is too complex to be treated here. To be fair to the president, therefore, we should look only at what has been added to or taken out of the Department of Education budget.

Unfortunately, even with such a restricted focus, the administration does not appear to be dealing fairly with the schools and children of America. The 2003 federal education budget was 6 percent higher than that of the previous year, but only because Congress insisted on funding programs that the president wanted to cut.[84] Seeking again to save money, the president's proposed 2004 budget for the No Child Left Behind Act* was about 5 percent less than was appropriated by Congress the previous year.[85] Perhaps more significantly, it was $11 billion less than was originally authorized in the president's own No Child Left Behind Act. Among other things, twenty-seven provisions of the original act were left unfunded in the president's budget proposal—including funds for school improvement and reform, dropout prevention programs, school leadership improvement, writing education, technology training, school counseling, foreign language assistance, physical education, art education, parental assistance, community technology centers, alcohol abuse reduction, and rural education.[86]

The federal underfunding of the No Child Left Behind Act is being perceived as imposing a heavy burden on state and local school boards. Considering the dire financial straits that most

---

* Also known as the annually funded Elementary and Secondary Education Act, usually referred to as ESEA in government documents.

states are in, the act's demand for uniform testing of all students is being called redundant (in those states that already test students) and an unfunded mandate—a charge that is usually leveled by Republicans against regulations imposed by the federal government.[87]

The additional Pell Grant money, mentioned earlier in this chapter, turned out to be money that was needed to pay for an earlier shortfall in the program, and the amount of the maximum grant remained frozen at $4,000 for the third year in a row, despite significant increases in the cost of higher education.[88] Moreover, the president's proposal to turn Head Start from a federal program for disadvantaged children into a block grant for states has drawn the same criticism that his proposal for Medicaid has done. Children's advocates fear that unless this successful early education program is mandated and paid for by the federal government, children will suffer when states run short of money and look for ways to trim their budgets.[89] After all, most of the federal social programs in place today were put there because the states had failed to provide for their own residents. Turning money back over to the states seems to be a formula for turning back the clock.

Once again, therefore, we find that the president's words have not matched the administration's actions. There has been much talk about caring for the needy, but at the same time, major proposals would get the federal government out of caring for the needy. The emphasis seems to be on saving money rather than on helping children, especially the children who need help the most. The underlying principle seems to be conservative economics rather than distributive justice.

Tax Reform

Although many Americans are unaware of President Bush's proposals on social legislation, almost everyone has heard and read about his proposals for tax reform, primarily reductions in the income tax for individuals. The first tax reduction package was introduced in 2001, when the government was running a surplus and there seemed to be a possibility of paying off the national debt. The rationale at that time was that the federal government had more money than it needed, so some of it should be returned to the people from whom it was taken. The second tax reduction package was introduced two years later, when the government was running a deficit and the national debt was again rapidly increasing. The rationale this time was that the economy needed to be stimulated, and tax reductions were the best way to fight the recession, create jobs, and ultimately increase revenues in the future. The rationale for the first tax cut was arguably based on commutative justice: give back to the people from whom money had been taken, and give more to those who had been taxed more. The rationale for the second tax cut was not based on fairness but on economic forecasting. The net result of both tax cuts, however, will be the disabling of federal social legislation in the future.

Given the increasing revenues from the expanding economy of the late 1990s, it was difficult to argue against the president's first request for $1.3 trillion dollars in tax cuts spread over ten years. Although there was some talk of paying down the national debt instead of reducing taxes, there was virtually no discussion of using the increased revenue to reduce the burden of poverty at home or abroad. In other words, the biblical principle of care for the underprivileged did not even enter the discussion at the time. Those in favor of the tax cut talked as though the reductions would be fairly distributed to everyone who pays taxes, but an analysis of the law signed by President Bush reveals something quite different. Although the tax reductions were to be phased in over ten years, 80 percent of Americans got most of their tax break in just one year, that is, they saw most of their benefits show up on their 2001 income tax forms. The richest 20 percent received about a third of their benefits the first year, with the remaining two-thirds to come in the next nine years. But for the wealthiest 1 percent in America, 94 percent of their tax cuts were scheduled to take effect after 2001. Not a very equal distribution, it would seem.[90]

The same pattern was also found in the tax legislation that was passed in 2003. Again, after being told that all taxpayers would benefit from the proposed legislation, critics of the additional tax cuts discovered that a third of the nation's tax filers—about 42 million individuals and married couples—would receive no benefit from the law that had just been signed into effect by the president. The administration countered by pointing out that many of these are working class families who do not pay federal income taxes (even though they do pay other taxes), but further analysis by independent research organizations showed that at least eight million low-income people who do pay over $250 in income tax would receive no tax reductions under the new law.[91]

Further complicating the matter is the title given to the 2003 bill. The president and the White House website continually referred to the proposed $726 billion reduction in income taxes as a "jobs and growth plan," claiming that its purpose was to stimulate the economy by putting money in people's pockets and creating new jobs. More than four hundred economists, including ten Nobel Prize winners, pointed out that the proposal would not have any immediate stimulating effect and warned that it would put Social Security and other programs in danger.[92] Nevertheless, Congress passed a $350 billion tax reduction law that kept the proposed reductions for the richest Americans but scaled back reductions for middle-income taxpayers. Moreover, like the 2001 tax reduction, the more recent law will spread reductions over ten years, making it unlikely to have much immediate impact on the economy.[93]

Various analyses of the original proposal and of the law signed by the president have been published, but they all show that the wealthy will receive the most generous tax relief. According to Citizens for Tax Justice, an independent research organization in Washington, D.C.,

- The typical tax cut for the median income taxpayer will be $600 a year.

- For the seventy-eight million taxpayers in the lowest 60 percent of the income scale, the tax cut will average $347 a year.

- In contrast, at the top of the income scale, the average tax cut will be $53,000 annually—virtually identical to the $54,000 annual tax cut proposed by the president.[94]

A further benefit to the rich is the gradual reduction and elimination of the estate tax, originally enacted to reduce the tendency of wealth to concentrate in fewer and fewer hands, and so to keep America a land with greater equality between the rich and ordinary citizens. Republicans dubbed it the "death tax" as though it was paid by the survivors of everyone who died, but in fact estate taxes were paid by only the wealthiest heirs. Before President Bush, estates valued at more than $675,000 were taxed at 55 percent with provisions for trusts and other tax shelters that reduced the actual tax paid in most cases. Over ten years the exempt amount increases to $3.5 million and the tax rate drops to 45 percent, and in 2010 the estate tax disappears altogether. The new law also lowers the tax rates on capital gains (business profits) and stock dividends (regular payments to stockholders), two provisions that benefit primarily the wealthy.[95]

One effect of these tax reductions for the wealthy is that the rich get richer and the poor get poorer—something that the Old Testament prophets were quite familiar with, and against which they spoke out loudly. Conservative economic theory claims that if wealthy people are able to keep more of their own money, they will invest it in ways that produce jobs and increase income, thus increasing income taxes in the long run. Unfortunately, the revisions in the tax law were not designed to do that, as they might have been if tax credits had been given for investing in American companies. Instead, the wealthy can spend the money they save on taxes in any way they want, including trips abroad and luxury import items. Another strategy to stimulate the economy might have been to give more money to lower income groups, who spend all their money at home, thus increasing demand for the goods and services that Americans supply. But since the designers of the new tax laws did not have distributive justice in mind, it did not happen that way.[96]

One effect that the revised tax laws will certainly have is a reduction in federal revenue—about one and a half trillion dollars over the next ten years—for reducing taxes certainly does that, if nothing else. But if revenue is reduced, the federal government will have less money to spend, and the cuts are most likely to come in social programs because those programs serve people who often do not vote. This seems to be one reason why the Bush administration is eager to transfer responsibility for social programs to the states: in ten years, if all goes according to plan, the federal government will be so strapped for cash that it will not be able to fund entitlement programs.

This prediction comes from conservatives as well as liberals. Peter Peterson, secretary of commerce in the Nixon administration, believes that the ultimate purpose of the tax cuts is to reduce the size of government, that is, to reduce the number of programs funded by the federal government. The next generation of Americans will have to expect less of their government or face the disagreeable task of raising taxes on themselves.[97]

It is quite possible that George W. Bush does not comprehend the long-range implications of the tax reforms long sought by economic and political conservatives. It is quite possible that he believes the advisors who tell him that the best way to help the poor is to put money in the pockets of the rich, who will invest it and grow the economy. It is quite possible that he was sincere when in 1999 he criticized the Republicans in Congress by saying, "I don't think they ought to balance the budget on the backs of the poor."[98] But it is not possible that conservatives on Capitol Hill and in the White House are unaware of this. They must know what is going on, even if the president does not.

Christian Responses

Most people associate Evangelicals with conservatives—religious, political, and economic conservatives. As we saw in the previous chapter, however, not all Evangelicals think like conservatives when it comes to social issues. Because of the negative connotations that have come to be associated with the word *liberal*, however, these evangelicals tend to call themselves progressives.

The largest and most widely known progressive Evangelical organization is Sojourners in Washington, D.C. Founded by students at Trinity Evangelical Divinity School in Deerfield, Illinois in the early 1970s, the group moved to the nation's capital in 1975, organized themselves into an intentional Christian community, and founded *Sojourners* magazine, devoted to bringing biblical principles to bear on social issues—at that time, primarily the war in Vietnam, civil rights, and poverty. The biblical name that they adopted reflected their belief that Christians in the world today, like the Israelites in Egypt, are residents in but are not committed to the kingdom of this world. And like the Israelites in the desert, they are working hard to reach the promised land that the gospels call the kingdom of God—a place where God's justice and peace reign.

Over the years, members of Sojourners developed a neighborhood community center and engaged in a variety of local and outreach ministries. One of its founding members, Jim Wallis, is very much in demand as a public speaker, but others too engage in preaching and teaching about faith and justice; they do public witnessing (demonstrations, etc.) and community organizing, and they offer internships in social ministry. For a number of years, Sojourners has supported an award-winning website (www.sojo.net) and it is connected to like-minded Christians across the United States and around the world through its Call to Renewal network, which operates a website as well (www.calltorenewal.com). As they say of themselves on the Internet, "Rooted in the solid ground of prophetic biblical tradition, Sojourners is a progressive Christian voice that preaches not political correctness but compassion, community, and commitment. We refuse to separate personal faith from social justice, prayer from peacemaking, contemplation from action, or spirituality from politics."

With regard to the social issues examined in this chapter, Sojourners makes the following assessments:

- A truly faith-based initiative promoted by the government would require budget and tax priorities that benefit the poor.
- The president's TANF proposals are unrealistic and unjust.
- The administration's budget neglects the needs of low-income people.
- From a moral standpoint, the president's budget priorities are misguided.
- The Growth and Jobs Plan violates the biblical principles of justice and compassion.[99]

As was said in chapter 1, people act according to principles whether they realize it or not. One way to get to know what a person's principles are is to look at what he does, to see what his priorities are. Here is what Sojourners has to say about the president's priorities.[100]

> To gain a true understanding of where the President's priorities lie, consider that when President Bush first came into office, he proposed a package of charitable giving tax cuts costing $90 billion over 10 years. Now, the number is down to $20 billion.
>
> The President's 2004 budget includes a $15.3 billion increase in defense spending. Note what this amount of money could do:

Provide basic health and food to the world's poor:	$12 billion
Rebuild America's public schools over 10 years:	$12 billion
Reduce class size for grades 1–3 to 15 students per class:	$11 billion
Reduce debts of impoverished nations:	$10 billion
Provide health insurance to all uninsured American kids:	$6 billion
Increase federal funding for clean energy and energy effciency:	$6 billion
Public financing of all federal elections:	$1 billion
Fully fund Head Start	$2 billion

For many years, Evangelicals such as Sojourners have been a prophetic voice in a country prone to wear religion on its sleeve while neglecting biblical principles of justice and compassion. But this may be beginning to change. In 2003, Governor Bob Riley of Alabama proposed a very different type of tax reform from the ones proposed by President Bush. The new tax code "shifts a significant amount of the state's tax burden from the poor to wealthy individuals and corporations. And he has framed the issue in starkly moral terms, arguing that the current Alabama tax system violates biblical teachings because Christians are prohibited from oppressing the poor."[101]

Governor Riley was influenced in part by an article that appeared in the *Alabama Law Review* titled "An Argument for Tax Reform Based on Judeo-Christian Ethics." The author, Susan Pace Hamill, holds degrees in both law and divinity, and she teaches tax law at the University of Alabama. Much as this chapter has done (but with even more extensive documentation), Professor Hamill compared the situation in her state with the moral teachings found in scripture and concluded that the current Alabama tax structure is unethical by biblical standards because it places an oppressive burden on people who are poor. In addition, she notes that "the Old Testament imposes on persons empowered with political or spiritual authority . . . a substantially greater moral obligation to maintain the general well-being of the community, especially a duty to protect the poor from economic oppression and to ensure that they enjoy at least a minimum opportunity to improve their economic circumstances."[102] People in public office who take the Bible seriously, then, need to be mindful of this responsibility that is uniquely theirs.

To the extent that government officials value social justice, they see to it that the principles of commutative justice and distributive justice are written into laws and regulations. And to the extent that they value what the Bible says about care and compassion, they see to it that those with the greatest needs are given priority in the distribution of goods and services.

If the United States government were guided by such principles, therefore, one would expect its policies to be moving in directions such as the following:

- Supporting faith-based initiatives in caring for the needy without subtracting support for those organizations that have traditionally provided for this care.

- Improving the ability of states, local governments and private organizations to offer assistance to needy families and individuals, with sufficient safeguards to protect against abuses of the system, but without punishing people (especially the children of parents) who are truly not able to provide for themselves.

- Seeing that the hungry are fed, especially children.

- Seeing that no one goes homeless, and that decent housing is affordable to people of all income levels.

- Ensuring that everyone in the country has access to good basic health care, including medicines and drugs, at a price they can afford.

- Providing high-quality public education for all of the children in America, and affordable educational opportunities for all adults.
- Changing the tax laws so that the wealthy contribute proportionately more to the common good, and so that the country's wealth is distributed more equitably among its citizens.

Conclusion

If compassionate conservatism is to be more than an election slogan, conservatives need to do more than talk about compassion; they need to show compassion toward those who are less well off in our society.

Conservatism extols the virtues of the free market, but compassion is a virtue that cares for those who do not benefit from the free market. Conservatism emphasizes the right of individuals to amass wealth, but compassion is the ability to share wealth. Conservatism wants to reduce the size of government, but compassion is concerned about reducing the suffering of people. Compassionate conservatism must therefore mean balancing the needs of people and the needs of government. Compassionate conservatism must mean balancing the needs of the poor and the wants of the wealthy. Compassionate conservatism must mean encouraging the fortunate to care for the less fortunate. Compassionate conservatism must mean practicing the virtue of social justice.

From a biblical perspective, compassion is truly conservative. Compassion in the biblical sense—caring about others and taking care of others—conserves the fabric of society and insures that it does not tear apart. God is compassionate, which is why he sent Moses to free the Israelites from slavery in Egypt, and why he sent Jesus to free humanity from the slavery of sin. Jesus in his public ministry was compassionate, which is why he healed the sick and the lame, and why he commissioned his disciples to heal others in his name. Jesus also instructed his followers, "Be merciful, just as your Father is merciful" (Luke 6:36), which can also be translated "Be compassionate, just as your Father is compassionate."[103]

But God is also just, and God demands justice of human beings.[104] Before they entered the Promised Land, God charged the Israelites: "Follow justice and justice alone, so that you may live and possess the land the Lord your God is giving you" (Deuteronomy 16:20 NIV). For by being just and fair with one another, and by making sure that no one suffered at someone else's expense, Israelite society would be preserved and the land would be free from internal dissention. Moreover, they would stand against external enemies, for they would have a strong interest in preserving a society from which they all benefited.

God especially expects leaders and rulers to be just.[105] They should be fair and impartial in their dealings with others, and they should see to it that fairness and impartiality are found throughout the land. In more modern terms, they must practice distributive justice, and they must follow principles of social justice. And leaders can do this because God will grant them the virtue of justice if they truly desire it.[106]

Every child who attends Sunday school knows the story of how Solomon became wise. God appeared to the young king in a dream and asked what he desired, and Solomon asked for "an understanding mind to govern your people, able to discern between good and evil." God was pleased that the king did not ask for riches or a long life, so God granted his wish and gave him not only great wisdom but splendid riches and a long life as well. Shortly after, in 1 Kings 3, there follows the story of how Solomon wisely discerned the true mother of a child that was claimed by two women.

Unfortunately, Solomon did not continue to use the wisdom that God gave him. Evidence in the Bible and elsewhere has led to an understanding of his reign that is very different from the picture we may have gotten in Sunday school.[107] Solomon increased his wealth by taxing caravans passing through Israel and by selling arms to the rulers of nearby states. He also forced the farmers in his own country to raise export crops that could be sold for luxury items that could not be found in Israel, especially exotic timber and metals for his building projects, and sumptuous foods for his lavish banquets. He built the great temple in Jerusalem and also a palace that was larger than the temple. Obsessed with the need for military might, he expanded the army and forced his own subjects into work gangs to build fortifications. Centralizing the command structure in the kingdom, he created a large bureaucracy and expanded the ruling class. Instead of presiding over an economic surplus as in the days of his father, King David, Solomon found himself going into greater and greater debt. But this did not affect the wealthy who dined in the palace; it affected the peasants whose oppressive taxes paid the interest on the king's loans.

Long before the end of Solomon's reign, many Israelites were chafing under the injustice of the situation. On the surface, Israel was becoming a wealthy kingdom that greatly impressed visitors, but beneath the surface, rebellion was brewing. After Solomon died, the overburdened tribes of the north successfully fought to secede from the kingdom and establish the "true" kingdom of Israel— which ultimately proved to be just as oppressive as the southern kingdom (eventually called Judah or Judea) with its temple in Jerusalem.

For not using his wisdom to exercise justice, and for not having compassion on his own people, Solomon lost what God had given to his father, David—a unified kingdom in the Promised Land. In other words, he did not conserve his patrimony. Had Solomon been more compassionate, he might have been more conservative, and Israel's future might have been very different from the history of division and downfall, exile and suffering that it turned out to be.

Notes

[1] This document is available at www.whitehouse.gov, but it is more easily accessed by typing "Rallying the Armies of Compassion" into a search engine. It is best to use quotation marks around this title and any other titles entered into Google, Yahoo! and other search engines.

[2] Most of these can be reached by typing "Faith-Based and Community Initiatives" into a search engine. A website offering assistance is located at www.faithbasedcommunityinitiatives.org, but access to the site is available only through payment of a user fee.

[3] Much of the publicly available information about the U.S. welfare system and other matters of government policy can be accessed through the Almanac of Policy Issues, an Internet portal with links to a wide range of government and non-government sources of information. Go to www.policyalmanac.org and click on Social Welfare, Health, Education, or any other area of interest.

[4] Earnings here include earned income tax credits of up to $4,000 for which low-income wage earners can apply when they file their annual income taxes. These figures were taken from President Bush's February 2002 welfare proposal titled "Working Toward Independence," pp. 5–7.

[5] See "Working Toward Independence," pp. 12–27.

[6] As of March 2004, TANF had not yet been reauthorized by the U.S. Senate. See the Finance Project report, "TANF Reauthorization," at www.financeprojectinfo.org/tanf. For analysis, see also Sharon Parrott and Shawn Fremstad, "The Senate Finance Committee's TANF Reauthorization Bill," a report of the Center on Budget and Policy Priorities, available at www.cbpp.org; click on All Reports by Date, then on 2003, then scroll down to the title at 9/22/03.

[7] Source: Centers for Medicare and Medicaid Services, with statistics from the Department of Health and Human Services, available at www.cms.hhs.gov.

[8] Figures taken primarily from *Statistical Abstract of the United States: 2002*, U.S. Census Bureau, Washington, DC, pp. 98–102, with supplemental data from the Kaiser Family Foundation and the Families USA Foundation, and with statistics from recent news reports.

[9] Both the U.S. Senate and the House of Representatives have passed Patients' Bill of Rights legislation, but the differing bills were never reconciled or signed into law. Republican and Democratic views on this issue can be easily accessed by typing "Patients' Bill of Rights" into an Internet search engine.

[10] *Statistical Abstract of the United States: 2002*, Tables 128 and 132.

[11] Federal Register, Vol. 66, No. 208, October 26, 2001, Notices for Department of Health and Human Services, p. 54250.

[12] See the Executive Summary of the "Framework To Modernize And Improve Medicare," available through www.whitehouse.gov. A fast way to find this document and others is to type the title (in quotation marks) into a search engine.

[13] See "President Signs Medicare Legislation" at www.white house.gov/news > More Issues > Strengthening Healthcare > President Signs Medicare Legislation, or type the full title into a search engine. For sample responses, see "Medicare Changes," a transcript from the December 8, 2003 PBS NewsHour available at www.pbs.org/newshour; click on newshourindex/search, then type Medicare Changes in the Search line. Also look at the information provided by the American Association of Retired Persons at www.aarp.org/prescriptiondrugs.

[14] Available at www.whitehouse.gov/omb/budget/fy2004, or by typing "Budget of the United States Government, Fiscal Year 2004" into a search engine. The introductory document for the Department of Health and Human Services outlines the administration's proposals for Medicare, Medicaid, and SCHIP in a budgetary context.

[15] The revised budget was finally approved and released in February 2004. See "Summary" available at www.whitehouse.gov; click on OMB, then enter "Budget 2004" in the Site Search line.

[16] See the proposed budget for the Department of Education available at the website mentioned above. For an overview of the original legislation, go to www.policyalmanac.org and search for "Executive Summary: No Child Left Behind Act of 2001."

[17] The first scholar to use the available evidence to develop this interpretation of the early history of Israel was Norman K. Gottwald. See his

books, *The Tribes of Yahweh: A Sociology of the Religion of Liberated Israel 1250–1050 BCE* (Orbis Books, 1979), and *The Hebrew Bible: A Socio-Literary Introduction* (Fortress Press, 1985).

[18] See Bruce V. Malchow, *Social Justice in the Hebrew Bible* (Liturgical Press, 1996), pp. 8–12. For an evangelical approach to ethics in the Old Testament, see the works of Christopher J. H. Wright, especially *An Eye for An Eye: The Place of Old Testament Ethics Today* (InterVarsity Press, 1983) and *Walking in the Ways of the Lord: The Ethical Authority of the Old Testament* (InterVarsity Press, 1995).

[19] For a summary, see Malchow, pp. 31–34. For a more thorough treatment, see Joseph Blenkinsopp, *A History of Prophesy in Ancient Israel* (Westminster John Knox Press, 1986), especially the chapters on those four prophets.

[20] Jesus, in speaking about himself, cites a passage from the prophet Isaiah (61: 1–2), thus identifying himself as a prophet. See also Matthew 13:57 and Mark 6:15.

[21] Jewish tax collectors were despised because they were agents of Rome, the oppressive foreign power that occupied Palestine at the time. People who fell short of obeying the Law of Moses (Torah) in any way were regarded as sinners by more observant Jews. Poor people did not have the means to observe the Law strictly, especially its religious obligations, so they were often looked upon as sinners. Sinners may have included people who had a reputation for being criminals or socially disreputable, but not necessarily.

[22] The development of the Jewish scriptures is described in most college textbooks on the subject, such as *The Old Testament: An Introduction to the Hebrew Bible* by Stephen L. Harris and Robert L. Platzner (McGraw Hill, 2003).

[23] Exodus 21:2; 22:22–24; 23:6–8; 23:10–11.

[24] Leviticus 19:9–15, 35–36; 25:8–55.

[25] Deuteronomy 15:1–3, 7–11; 24:6, 10–22.

[26] See also Exodus 22:21; 25:9; Leviticus 19:33–34; Deuteronomy 5:15; 6:21; 15:15; 24:22.

²⁷ See Anthony R. Ceresko, *Introduction to the Old Testament: A Liberation Perspective* (Orbis Books, 1992), especially chapters 15–18.

²⁸ See Amos 3:9–10; 4:1; 8:4–6.

²⁹ See Amos 3:15; 5:7; 5:10–13; 6:4–6.

³⁰ See also Amos 4:4–5; 8:9–10.

³¹ See also Amos 3:1–2; 3:9–12; 5:1–3; 5:16–20; 6:8–14; 8:1–9:4.

³² See Micah 2:1–4; 2:10–11; 3:9–11; 6:10–12; 7:2–6.

³³ See Micah 2:6–7; 3:1–4; 3:11–12; 4:6–13; 5:7–15.

³⁴ Read especially Isaiah 1:2–4, 11–15, 21–23.

³⁵ See Isaiah 2:11–17; 3:5–8; 3:14–26; 5:8–12; 5:20–23; 9:20–21; 10:1–2; 13:11; 16:4; 29:15.

³⁶ See Isaiah 10:5–19; 13:1–22; 14:24–32; and much in chapters 15–23.

³⁷ See Isaiah 2:1–22; 7:13–25; 9:1–7; 11:1–9.

³⁸ See Jeremiah 5:26–31; 7:5–9; 9:1–6; 12:1–3; 22:13–17; also more generally 5:1–5 and 8:11–12.

³⁹ See Jeremiah 1:16; 2:8–11; 2:28; 4:1–2; 5:7; 5:19; 7:18; 7:30; 8:19; 11:10–13; 16:11; 19:4; 22:9; 25:6 and elsewhere. Note that in some translations, idols are referred to as abominations, and foreign gods are referred to as strangers.

⁴⁰ See Jeremiah 7:3–7; 7:21–28; 8:8; 9:23; 11:1–13; 32:23; 44:23.

⁴¹ See Jeremiah 34:8–22.

⁴² See Jeremiah 25:1–13; 27:1–15.

⁴³ See Jeremiah chapters 26, 36–38, 52.

⁴⁴ Luke's gospel has the clearest and the most consistent social message, and Luke describes Jesus beginning his public ministry by reading from the prophet Isaiah and saying that his mission is to fulfill the prophet's words (Luke 4:16–21). Mark's gospel, being short and action-oriented, best illustrates how Jesus fulfilled the Law and the prophets by caring for the sick and infirm (1:21–45; 2:1–12; 3:1–12; 5:1–43; 7:24–37; 8:22–26; 9:14–

29), by feeding the hungry (6:30–44; 8:1–10), and by valuing ethical concerns over religious concerns (2:23–28; 7:1–23; 11:15–19; 12:28–34).

[45] See Romans 10:9–10.

[46] For an introduction to the notion of the kingdom (or reign) of God, see Glen H. Stassen, "The Marks of the Kingdom and the Four Dimensions of Jesus' Justice," posted at www.fuller.edu/sot/faculty/stassen. Click on Kingdom of God and Jesus' Justice.

[47] See Matthew 22:34–40; Mark 12:28–31.

[48] The Samaritans were hated by the Jews because both groups claimed to be descendents of Abraham, but the Samaritans, as a remnant of the northern kingdom of Israel, did not worship at the Temple in Jerusalem. See Luke 10:29–37. The irony in this parable is that the "good guy" in the story is someone Jesus's listeners would have considered a "bad guy," and his listeners were forced to admit that someone they hated could be good.

[49] See Matthew 6:1–4; 6:19–21; 19:21; Mark 10:21–27; Luke 12:16–21; 14:28–33; 18:24–27.

[50] See Matthew 5:1–12; Luke 6:20–26; 16:19–31.

[51] For a thorough treatment, see Morton T. Kelsey, *Caring: How Can We Love One Another?* (Paulist Press, 1981). For a comparison between *agápe* and other Greek words for love, see C. S. Lewis, *The Four Loves* (Harcourt Brace, 1960).

[52] See John 13:34–35; 14:21–24; 15:9–14.

[53] See 1 Corinthians 13:4–7.

[54] See 1 John 2:3–7; 3:14–24; 4:7–13.

[55] See James 1:22–27; 2:1–26.

[56] Paul's account of his confrontation with the leaders in Jerusalem is found in Galatians 2:1–10; but see also 2:11–21 and 3:23–29. This meeting is also recounted in Acts 15:1–29.

[57] See Exodus 21:18–35; 22:5–17.

[58] See Vernon J. Bourke, *Ethics: A Textbook in Moral Philosophy* (Macmillan, 1966), p. 332; Austin Fagothey, *Right and Reason: Ethics in Theory and*

Practice (Fifth Edition, C. V. Mosby, 1972), p. 179. Some philosophers define social justice more broadly, so as to include relations between business and society. See Jacques Thiroux, *Ethics: Theory and Practice* (Fifth Edition, Prentice Hall, 1995), p. 413.

[59] This is not to say the prophets did not also condemn violations of the principles of commutative and distributive justice. Their denunciation of dishonesty in the market place, and their insistence that the Israelites should give God his due worship, shows that they cared about commutative justice. Their denunciation of the gross disparity between the luxurious lives of the rich and the subsistence existence of the poor shows that they valued distributive justice.

[60] For information on these topics, see Douglas Strong, *Perfectionist Politics: Abolitionism and Religious Tensions in American Democracy* (Syracuse University Press, 1999); Geoffrey C. Ward, *Not For Ourselves Alone: The Story of Elizabeth Cady Stanton and Susan B. Anthony* (Alfred A. Knopf, 1999); Ronald C. White and C. Howard Hopkins, *The Social Gospel: Religion and Reform in Changing America* (Temple University Press, 1976); Robert Weisbrot, *Freedom Bound: The Story of America's Civil Rights Movement* (W. W. Norton, 1990).

[61] See the Pew Trust report, "Can an Office Change a Country?" by Karen Dunn Tenpas, February 2002, available at http://pewforum.org. For a summary by the National Housing Initiative, see "Running on Faith," *Shelterforce Online*, Issue 122 (March/April 2002) at www.nhi.org.

[62] See "Prophesies of faith-based initiatives' critics are being fulfilled" by J.R. Labbe, *Fort Worth Star-Telegram* (February 27, 2001).

[63] It seems that this has already begun to happen. In January 2003, *The Boston Globe* reported that homeless shelters in Massachusetts were losing funds to faith-based shelters in other parts of the country. See "State veterans shelters losing faith" by David Abel (January 13, 2003). For a more comprehensive review, go to http://pewforum.org, click on Events, and scroll down to "The Faith-Based Initiative Two Years Later: Examining its Potential, Progress and Problems," which is a transcript of a two-hour discussion held at the Brookings Institution on March 5, 2003.

[64] See "The Texas Faith-Based Initiative at Five Years," a report issued by the Texas Freedom Network available at www.tfn.org.

⁶⁵ For a critical review of faith-based initiatives since their inception, see Bill Berkowitz, "Bush's Faith-Based Finagling" available at www.dissidentvoice.org or by typing the name of the article in a search engine.

⁶⁶ See "Government Data Show Welfare Reform Failure," a July 2002 news release of the NOW Legal Defense Fund available at www.nowldef.org. For additional documentation, click on Welfare & Poverty under the heading, Issues. See also "Welfare to What? Early Findings on Family Hardship and Well-Being" published in 1998 by the Children's Defense Fund and the National Coalition for the Homeless; and "Welfare to What? Part II" published by the National Coalition for the Homeless and the Los Angeles Coalition to End Hunger and Homelessness in 2002. Both reports are most easily accessed on the Internet by typing the name of the article into a search engine.

⁶⁷ See "Poverty in the United States: 2001" published by the U.S. Census Bureau and available on the Internet. For a short analysis, see the Center on Budget and Policy Priorities report, "Census Data Show Increases in Extent and Severity of Poverty and Decline in Household Income," available at www.cbpp.org. The U.S. Department of Health and Human Services used similar poverty guidelines for 2003: $8,980 for a single person and $18,400 for a family of four. See Federal Register, Vol. 68, No. 26 (February 7, 2003), pp. 6456–6458.

⁶⁸ See "Who was poor in 2001?" and ""How many children are poor?" under Frequently Asked Questions on the home page of the Institute for Research on Poverty at the University of Wisconsin, at www.ssc.wisc.edu/irp. For information about children in poverty, consult the National Center for Children in Poverty at www.nccp.org and click on Fact Sheets. Also visit the Children's Defense Fund at www.childrensdefense.org and click on Data.

⁶⁹ See Mark Greenberg and Jim Baumohl, "Income Maintenance: Little Help Now, Less on the Way," in *Homelessness in America* (Oryx Press, 1996), cited in "Why Are People Homeless?" a fact sheet published by the National Coalition for the Homeless, 2002.

⁷⁰ See "Welfare Reform: After Five Years, Is It Working?" a report of the NOW Legal Defense Fund, available at www.nldf.org. Click on Issues, then on Welfare & Poverty.

⁷¹ See Heather Boushey and Bethney Gundersen, "When Work Just Isn't Enough," a briefing paper of the Economic Policy Institute, available at www.epinet.org, available online or for purchase under Publications. See also other EPI publications such as "Inequality at the Starting Gate," about the effects of poverty on children's mental ability. For life stories of the working poor, read Barbara Ehrenreich, *Nickel and Dimed: On (Not) Getting By in America* (Henry Holt, 2001).

⁷² A good summary of the national picture was provided on NPR's Morning Edition on National Hunger Awareness Day, June 5, 2003, archived as "Experts: Hunger Still a Problem in America." For more detailed information, see the websites of the Economic Research Service of the U.S. Department of Agriculture (www.ers.usda.gov), the World Hunger Education Service (www.worldhunger.org), the Center on Hunger and Poverty (www.centeronhunger.org), the Food Research and Action Center (www.frac.org), and Food First (www.foodfirst.org). For personal stories, read Loretta Schwartz-Nobel, *Growing Up Empty: The Hunger Epidemic in America* (Harper Collins, 2002).

⁷³ For information, go to www.unemployedworkers.org, click on Helpful Statistics, then on National Statistics.

⁷⁴ The estimate of the Urban Institute (www.urban.org) is higher: 3.5 million overall, of whom 1.35 million are children. Most figures are based on surveys of homeless shelters, but not all homeless people live in shelters, and some rely on them only periodically. Two good sources of information on homelessness in America are the National Coalition for the Homeless (www.nationalhomeless.org) and the National Law Center on Homelessness and Poverty (www.nlchp.org).

⁷⁵ See Martha Burt, "Causes of the Growth of Homelessness during the 1980s," in *Understanding Homelessness: New Policy and Research Perspectives* (Fanny Mae Foundation, 1991). Information on homelessness in cities can be found in the annual report of the U.S. Conference of Mayors (www.usmayors.org).

⁷⁶ Source: U.S. Department of Labor, Bureau of Labor Statistics Consumer Price Index, available at www.bls.gov/cpi.

⁷⁷ More detailed information is available from the Economic Policy Institute (www.epinet.org > Employment and Wages > Minimum Wage),

and the Coalition on Human Needs (www.chn.org > Issues > Employment > Minimum Wage).

[78] See, for example, Laura D'Andrea Tyson, "Medicaid: Washington Rolls Out a Trojan Horse," *Business Week* (March 24, 2003), p. 26. Also "Slashing Medicaid: The Hidden Effects of the President's Block Grant Proposal," a special report from the Families USA Foundation, available at www.familiesusa.org; click on Medicaid and Children's Health under Issues. For how it is possible for the administration and its critics to make conflicting claims, see Richard Kogan and Iris J. Lav, "President's Claim of Nine Percent Increase in Aid to States is Highly Misleading," a report dated March 1, 2003 from the Center on Budget and Policy Priorities, available at www.cbpp.org under All Reports by Date.

[79] Unspent allotments are more likely to accrue in economically good years. See, for example, Steve Levin, "State, activists at odds over unspent U.S. welfare funds," *Pittsburgh Post-Gazette* (February 24, 2000).

[80] The Update, "Government Data Show Welfare Reform Failure," noted above and available at www.nowldef.org, cites "Indicators of Welfare Dependence" submitted to Congress on June 3, 2002, saying "The data reflect a massive decline in the participation rate—the percentage of families who are eligible for welfare that actually receive benefits. Since welfare reform was enacted, the participation rate has plummeted from 84% in 1995 to 52% in 1999." See also "Radical Administration Medicaid Proposal Threatens Nearly 40 Years of Health Care Progress for Low-Income Children," a fact sheet of the Children's Defense Fund, available at www.cdfactioncouncil.org.

[81] See Laura D'Andrea Tyson, "Why Bush's Plan Threatens Medicare As We Know It," *Business Week* (February 17, 2003), p. 22. Also, "Private Plans: A Bad Choice for Medicare," a fact sheet of the Families USA Foundation, available at www.familiesusa.org; click on Medicare under Issues for this and other analyses of proposals by President Bush and the House of Representatives. In support, see "Study Finds that Bush Medicare 'Reform' Plan Will Limit Iowa Seniors' Choice of Doctors," a press release of Public Citizen, available at www.citizen.org, but more easily accessible by typing the title into a search engine.

[82] See Donald W. Light, "A Conservative Call for Universal Access to Health Care," *Center for Bioethics Newsletter*, Vol. 9, No. 4 (Spring 2002),

pp. 4-6. Available at www.med.upenn.edu/bioethic/newsletter.shtml. See also James H. Rankin, "Bush Health Care Proposal Is A Defective Remedy," *Horizons* (June 2002), available at www.gmpiu.org or by typing the title into an Internet search engine.

[83] For a good review of the NCLB Act, see Greg Toppo, "Most states lag far behind 'No Child Left Behind' law" in *USA Today*, February 28, 2003; available at www.usatoday.com/news but more easily accessed by typing the title into a search engine.

[84] See "Congress boosts federal education budget 6 percent," a Washington Update of the New York State School Board Association, available at www.nyssba.org under School Board News.

[85] Figures from "ESEA Funding Fiscal Year 2002, Fiscal Year 2003, Proposed Fiscal Year 2004," an analysis done by Joel Parker for the National Education Association and available on request from that source.

[86] The $11 billion figure and list of program cuts comes from the NEA's analysis, mentioned in the previous footnote. In other analyses reported in the news, the range is $7–11 billion, but it is always a shortfall.

[87] See the article by Greg Toppo cited above.

[88] See "White House Unveils 2004 Budget Proposal" in *Higher Education and National Affairs*, Vol. 52, No. 3 (February 17, 2003), available online at www.acenet.edu/hena; click on Past Issues.

[89] See "Head Start: A formula for success for disadvantaged children threatened by Bush experiment," a Children's Defense Fund report that is available from the Oregon Head Start Association at www.ohsa.net; click on Talking Points, then on the title of the article.

[90] See "Post-2001 Tax Cuts Offer Little to Most Americans," a report of Citizens for Tax Justice, available at www.ctj.org by scrolling down the home page and clicking on the title. This analysis is very similar to that of the congressional Joint Committee on Taxation, a summary of whose report is available at the same website. See also the more recent report, "Year-by-Year Analysis of the Bush Tax Cuts Shows Growing Tilt to the Very Rich," at the same website.

[91] See "Bush 2003 Tax Plan a Big Fat Zero for a Third of Nation's Taxpayers" at the Citizens for Tax Justice website mentioned above. Also "Tax Cut Leaves Out 8 Million Filers Who Pay Income Taxes," a report of the Center on Budget and Policy Priorities, available at www.cbpp.org; click on Federal Tax, then scroll down to find the title.

[92] See "Economists' Statement Opposing the Bush Tax Cuts" at www.economicpolicyinstitute.org/newsroom/stmt or by typing the title into a search engine.

[93] See "Final Tax Plan Tilts Even More Toward the Richest," a report of Citizens for Tax Justice at www.ctj.org. Also, "Bush Tax Cut Unfair, Won't Help Economy," analysis prepared for United for a Fair Economy, available at www.ufenet.org; click on Research Library, then on Taxes, then on title. For the president's side of the debate, go to www.whitehouse.gov and click on Economic Security.

[94] See "Final Version of Bush Tax Plan Keeps High-End Tax Cuts, Adds to Long-Term Cost," a report of Citizens for Tax Justice, available at www.ctj.org by scrolling down the home page and clicking on the title. See also Laura D'Andrea Tyson, "Tax Cuts for the Rich Are Even More Wrong Today, *Business Week* (July 8, 2002) and available at *Business Week* Online, www.businessweek.com; click on Search & Browse, then type in the author's name. Also, "Comment: Bushonomics" in *The New Yorker*, Vol. 79, No. 11 (May 12, 2003), pp. 37–38.

[95] Information on estate taxes is available at www.estateplancenter.com; click on Estate Tax. Information on changes in the tax laws is available at www.cliftoncpa.com; scroll down to 2003 Tax Law Summary.

[96] See Albert B. Crenshaw, "Gap Between Rich and Poor Grows," *Washington Post* (January 23, 2003), p. E1, available at www.washingtonpost.com, but for a fee; click on Archives, then enter the author's name and the date range for the article. See also Derrick Z. Jackson, "A tax cut for the selfish" in the *Boston Globe* (June 4, 2003) available at www.boston.com/globe; click on Archives, then enter the author's name and the date of the article.

[97] See Peter G. Peterson, "Deficits and Dysfunction" in the Louisville *Courier-Journal* (June 22, 2003), p. D1. This article originally appeared in the *New York Times*. See also Albert B. Crenshaw, "Bush Budget Would

Shrink Federal Revenue: Impact of Tax-Preferred Savings Plans and Other Proposals Could Snowball," *Washington Post* (February 4, 2003), p. A5. For a liberal perspective, see Anne Curtis, "The True Face of Compassionate Conservatism" in *Connection*, the newsletter of NETWORK for May–June 2003, pp. 3–5.

[98] See Juliet Eilperin and Eric Pianin, "Bush Criticism of GOP Surprised House," *Washington Post* (October 2, 1999), p. A1.

[99] For position papers, go to www.calltorenewal.com and click on Public Policy.

[100] See "The Administration's 2004 Budget Neglects the Needs of Low-Income People," available at www.calltorenewal.com > Public Policy > 2004 Federal Budget.

[101] See "What Would Jesus Do? Alabama Republican governor says tax reform," Louisville *Courier-Journal* (June 23, 2003), p. D1. The article originally appeared as an editorial in the *New York Times* on June 10.

[102] Susan Pace Hamill, "An Argument for Tax Reform Based on Judeo-Christian Ethics," *Alabama Law Review*, Vol. 54, No. 1 (Fall 2002), p. 59. For a summary of this lengthy article, go to the University of Alabama Law School website, www.law.ua.edu, then go to Faculty and Staff Directory > Law School Faculty > Susan Pace Hamill. At Professor Hamill's faculty page, click on "Alabamians Professing Faith in God Have a Moral Duty to Support Tax Reform." Or more simply, type the name of the author or the title into a search engine.

[103] See, for example, this passage in the New Jerusalem Bible and the New Living Translation. The Greek word *oiktirmos* can be translated as either merciful or compassionate. See also Exodus 34:6; 2 Chronicles 30:9; Nehemiah 9:17; Psalms 51:1 and 116:5; Joel 2:13; Jonah 3:10 and 4:2; 2 Corinthians 1:3.

[104] See Deuteronomy 32:4; Isaiah 5:16 and 30:18; Luke 18:7; Romans 3:25 and 9:14; 2 Thessalonians 1:6; Revelation 16:7.

[105] See 1 Kings 10:9; 2 Chronicles 9:8 and 19:7; Hosea 12:6; Amos 5:15; Luke 11:42.

[106] See 1 Kings 3:11 and 28; Psalm 72:1. In some translations, the word for justice is translated as righteousness or discernment (of what is right and wrong).

[107] See, for example, Norman K. Gottwald, *The Hebrew Bible: A Socio-Literary Introduction* (Fortress Press, 1985), pp. 321–323.

4

Human Rights

"Do to others as you would have them do to you." (Luke 6:31)

President George W. Bush speaks highly of the values of life and liberty. On the first anniversary of the tragic events of September 11, he said in a televised speech,

> The attack on our nation was also an attack on the ideals that make us a nation. Our deepest national conviction is that every life is precious, because every life is the gift of a creator who intended us to live in liberty and equality. More than anything else, this separates us from the enemy we fight. We value every life; our enemies value none—not even the innocent, not even their own. And we seek the freedom and opportunity that give meaning and value to life.

Life, liberty, equality, freedom—these are the words that appear most often when President Bush speaks about human rights. In his brief speech at the site of a former slave-trading outpost in Senegal, Africa, he spoke of freedom and liberty ten times directly, and indirectly many more times in his eloquent condemnation of slavery.[1] Moreover, he noted that "freedom is not the possession of one race," nor is it the possession of one nation, but it is one of the "natural rights of man." Mr. Bush also acknowledged that the destiny of the human race is "liberty and justice for all," and that the challenges to peace can be overcome "because history moves in the direction of justice."

These are sentiments with which biblical Christians can certainly agree. They express principles that derive from our Judeo-Christian heritage, that motivated the Pilgrims to seek refuge in the New World, and that are enshrined in the U.S. Constitution. At the same time, however, they are sentiments that give biblical Christians pause for reflection. For while some policies and actions of the current administration seem to uphold these principles, others seem to tear them down.

The Public Record

In some areas of public policy, Christian conservatives can find no fault with George W. Bush. He has defended every unborn infant's right to life, he made a difficult and nuanced decision with regard to research with human stem cells, he has championed freedom of religion at home and abroad, he has appointed judges who share his Christian values, and he has promoted faith-based responses to social problems. In one area, however, administration policies run counter to the teachings of the Bible, and neither the president nor his Christian supporters seem to be aware of this. This is the area of arrest and detention, especially of innocent people.

Immigrants and Refugees

The terrorist attacks on the Pentagon and the World Trade Center on September 11, 2001, were perpetrated by men from other countries who took advantage of American hospitality and openness to cause the first major losses of life on United States soil since the attack on Pearl Harbor. Understandably, President Bush interpreted this sinister and coordinated assault as an act of war, and in return he declared a war on terrorism. In his address to a joint session of Congress on September 20, he declared, "Our nation has been put on notice: we are not immune to attack. We will take defensive measures against terrorism to protect Americans."

Fearing additional hijackings, the U.S. government suspended air traffic over American soil for several days after September 11, then cautiously allowed it to resume. Members of the public willing to fly for personal reasons or having to fly on business found themselves subjected to intensive scrutiny that reassured some air travelers and annoyed others. But the government recognized that terrorists could penetrate the United States on land as well as in the air, so automobile travelers and truck drivers crossing the Canadian and Mexican borders into the U.S. were questioned and searched as never before. Long lines at border crossings delayed vacations and slowed commercial transportation. Similar precautions were taken at seaports and ocean resort areas. Moreover, the hijackers had been foreigners, so the government took measures to deal with citizens of other countries who might be a threat to the United States. Among the specific actions taken were:

- Immediate suspension of all immigration into the United States, including refugees whose status had already been approved.

- Locating and questioning individuals from Arab and Muslim countries to determine whether they had any connection to terrorist organizations.[2]

- Passage in October 2001 of the USA PATRIOT (Uniting and Strengthening America by Providing Appropriate Tools Required to Intercept and Obstruct Terrorism) Act, giving the government broad new powers to gather information and detain individuals suspected of being or aiding terrorists. For example, the government could detain noncitizens suspected of possible involvement in terrorism for up to seven days without charging them with a crime or violation of immigration laws, and longer than seven days under certain conditions.[3]

- Creation of the Department of Homeland Security, combining 170,000 federal employees in twenty-two different agencies (including the Coast Guard, the Border Patrol, and the Immigration and Naturalization Service) under a single cabinet member and charged with protecting the nation against further terrorist attacks.[4]

Attorney General John Ashcroft put the matter bluntly when he said, "Let the terrorists among us be warned. If you overstay your visa—even by one day—we will arrest you. If you violate a local law, you will be put in jail and kept in custody as long as possible." The trouble is that none of the hundreds of people who were arrested and jailed—whether or not they had violated any laws—were ever found guilty of terrorism.[5]

Detainees from Afghanistan

Very quickly, U.S. intelligence agencies determined that the fatal attacks of September 11 had been perpetrated by a radical Islamist organization based in Afghanistan and protected by the fundamentalist Taliban government in that country. Al Qaeda (meaning The Base or The Foundation) had for years operated terrorist training camps in Afghanistan, and it was headed by Osama bin Laden, a wealthy Saudi Arabian exile. Bin Laden was angry with his own government for its alliance with the United States and for its having allowed non-Muslim forces on sacred Saudi territory during the 1992 Gulf War against Iraq. He also wanted to retaliate against the United States for what he perceived as crimes against Arabs and Muslims, especially U.S. support of Israel in its oppression of Palestinians.[6]

After giving the Afghan government an ultimatum to surrender the Al Qaeda leaders in its territory, a coalition of forces headed by the United States went to war against the Taliban and very quickly overthrew that government, capturing many Al Qaeda members in the process. More than six hundred of these were sent to a hastily constructed detention center in Guantanamo

Bay, Cuba, where the U.S. has had a military base since before the days of the Castro government. At the detention center, called Camp X-Ray because its occupants were held in see-through cages, the prisoners were isolated from one another and were subjected to intensive questioning. Other captives of the war were kept at the Bagram air base in Afghanistan or were turned over to Arab governments friendly to the United States for special interrogation. In addition, thousands of suspected Al Qaeda operatives and sympathizers were arrested and held in other countries with American assistance.[7]

Even though the president had declared a war on terrorism, and even though the United States went to war against Afghanistan, the U.S. refused to acknowledge that its captured Taliban and Al Qaeda forces were prisoners of war, calling them enemy combatants instead. By use of this simple verbal maneuver, the U.S. government was able to avoid acknowledging that the captives might have rights to humane treatment guaranteed by the Geneva Convention on the conduct of war, to which the United States is a signatory.[8] By not bringing captives into the United States, the government was able to avoid granting them any rights that might be accorded foreign citizens by U.S. law.[9] And by sending some captives to other countries known for unethical interrogation methods, the government was able to avoid being accused under the international Convention Against Torture.[10]

Not only this, but some of the captives turned out to be innocent—picked up and detained during the chaos of war, but not combatants at all. Some were even children.[11]

Prisoners in the United States

The detention of innocent persons for terrorism brings to mind the growing number of people who have been freed from U.S. prisons because they were discovered to be innocent. Since 1976, the year that the death penalty was reinstated, more than one hundred individuals on death row have been exonerated and set free, mainly due to new forensic techniques and DNA evidence that can prove that the crime was committed by someone else. During the same period, more than 750 people were executed in the United States, and some of these may also have been innocent.[12]

One reason for such high numbers is that the United States leads the world in incarcerating its own people. With less than 5 percent of the world's population, the U.S. holds a quarter of the world's prisoners, and now surpasses even Russia with 702 prisoners per 100,000 population compared to Russia's 665. In terms of raw numbers, there are more individuals behind bars in America than there are in Communist China with its population of over a billion people. "On a per capita basis, according to the best available figures, the United States has three times more prisoners than Iran, four times more than Poland, five times more than Tanzania, and seven times more than Germany."[13] About two million residents of the U.S. are in jails and prisons, and another 4.5 million are on probation or parole, with the result that one in every thirty-two adults in America is under the supervision of the criminal justice system.[14]

It was not always this way. From after World War II to the early 1970s, the state and federal prison population remained steady at around two hundred thousand. Then, during the Nixon administration, the nation began to respond to the growing problem of drug abuse by incarcerating users as well as sellers of illegal substances, which themselves were growing in variety and potency. Today about two-thirds of those behind bars are nonviolent offenders, convicted mainly of drug-related crimes. "Crimes that in other countries would usually lead to community service, fines, or drug treatment—or would not be considered crimes at all—in the United States now lead to a prison term, by far the most expensive form of punishment."[15]

Consider also the following:

> About 70 percent of the prison inmates in the United States are illiterate. Perhaps 200,000 of the country's inmates suffer from a serious mental illness. A generation ago such people

> were handled primarily by the mental-health, not the criminal-justice, system. Sixty to 80 percent of the American inmate population has a history of substance abuse. Meanwhile, the number of drug-treatment slots in American prisons has declined by more than half since 1993. Drug treatment is now available to just one in ten of the inmates who need it. . . . Of the 80,000 women now imprisoned, about 70 percent are nonviolent offenders. About 75 percent have children.[16]

At least two justice issues are at stake here. The first is a matter of commutative justice: Are the people in American prisons getting what they deserve, or are they getting more (i.e., worse) than they deserve? The second is a matter of distributive justice: Should more and more of our tax dollars be used for incarceration rather than for education and drug prevention, rehabilitation, and drug treatment, rather than for increasingly expensive prisons?

Further, our jails and prisons are increasingly overcrowded. No matter how quickly they are built, no matter how large they are built, they are too small as soon as they are opened.[17] Since America for thirty years has put the emphasis on punishment rather than rehabilitation, most inmates walk out with no more ability to get a job and cope with society than they had when they went into prison. What this means is that prisoners do not serve their time and then return to society. Instead, most of them serve their time, get out for a while (either on parole or having completed their sentence), and then do something (either a parole violation or another offense) that gets them locked up again.[18] As a result, unlike previous decades when the prison population remained more or less stable, in recent decades it has been going up and up, with fewer staying out and more coming in every year. The system seems to be out of control, consuming not just billions of tax dollars but literally millions of lives.

Not only is this a matter of social justice at a systemic level, but it also raises questions for Christians: Is this how God wants people to live? Does God want a society where millions of people waste their lives doing nothing? Does God want human beings to be punished for their sins? If he does, what if punishment in America makes people worse rather than better? Is this the kind of punishment that God wants?

Biblical Teaching

The signers of the Declaration of Independence in 1776 proclaimed that all men are created equal and are endowed by their creator with certain unalienable rights. One reason for their confidence in this assertion is that they all knew their Bible. Although the Scriptures do not talk about human rights in a general or philosophical way, they do make a number of assertions which, taken together, form the foundation of Western civilization's understanding of human nature, human law, and human rights.[19]

Equality and Dignity

In the very first chapter of the Book of Genesis, on the sixth day of creation, God makes the first human beings in his image and likeness (v. 27). Through the centuries, much has been written about the meaning of being created in God's image, and there is general agreement that the image and likeness are spiritual rather than physical in nature. That is, human beings are like God in that they have spiritual qualities such as intelligence and free will. But if all human beings have these essential qualities, then all human beings are essentially equal, even if one is born tall and another short, one dark-skinned and another light-skinned, one rich and another poor, one male and another female.

At the beginning, the Israelites did not understand the full implications of this revelation, for in their history they distinguished between the rights of males and those of females, as well as between the rights of Israelites and those of gentiles. But they certainly did appreciate that they had a right to be free even though they were enslaved in Egypt, for they called to God and he heard their plea (Exodus 2: 7–10).[20] And as we have seen, the prophets insisted that the poor had rights when they were being oppressed by the rich. Jesus equated treatment of unimportant people with treatment of himself (Matthew 25:40 and 45), and St. Paul insisted on the fundamental equality of all those who accepted Christ (Galatians 3:28). By the time of the American Revolution, the Founding Fathers understood that men of property were equal, even if they were not Christians. The history of amendments to the Constitution is, in part, the history of Americans implementing more and more fully the biblical teaching that all human beings are created in the image and likeness of God and therefore essentially equal.

Being made in the spiritual image and likeness of God is also the basis of human dignity, for it implies that every human spirit is like God and reflects the divine spirit in some way. The Israelites understood this to some extent, for they knew that God had breathed his spirit into Adam, and they acknowledged that they were supposed to imitate God by being just and compassionate.[21] Jesus went even further and taught that all his listeners—and implicitly all people—had God as their Father.[22] All people are children of God and deserve to be treated as such, with respect and as having dignity.

Treatment of Foreigners

As already noted, the Law of Moses singled out some people for special treatment: widows, orphans, foreigners, and others who had no one to protect them and provide for their welfare.[23] The Law commanded special compassion for foreigners (also called aliens and strangers in different translations), reminding the Israelites that, having been treated harshly in Egypt, they knew what it felt like to be foreigners in a foreign land.[24]

The biblical attitude toward foreigners seeking refuge and a better life is not hostility but hospitality, not suspicion but support, not stinginess but generosity. This spirit is well captured in the inscription on the Statue of Liberty that stands in New York harbor:

>Give me your tired, your poor,
>Your huddled masses yearning to breathe free,

> The wretched refuse of your teeming shore.
> Send these, the homeless, tempest-tossed to me,
> I lift my lamp beside the golden door!²⁵

In Jesus' day, the main foreigners in Israel were Samaritans and Romans. The Samaritans were regarded by the Jews as heretics, and the Romans were regarded by everyone (except themselves) as oppressors. Yet Jesus treated both with dignity and respect, carrying on a conversation with a Samaritan woman and healing the servant of a Roman officer.²⁶ Likewise in the early church, baptism was extended to Africans and Romans, and St. Paul undertook three long missionary journeys to bring the gospel of Christ to gentiles—the Jewish term for non-Jews or foreigners.²⁷ In the New Testament as well as in the Old, the principle to be followed is kindness and generosity to strangers.

Punishment of Crimes

The Law of Moses certainly allowed for punishment, even for the death penalty, but not for imprisonment. This is probably because when the Law was given by God to the Israelites, they were still living in tents and other types of temporary shelters not very suitable for locking people up. Nonetheless, the Old Testament is still remarkable in that it envisages a system of justice that operates without any need for jails and prisons.²⁸

The Law regarding relationships between people* was based on two principles: prohibition of harmful behavior and compensation of victims. Chapters 21 and 22 of Exodus, for example, prescribe the restitution of stolen goods plus compensation of two to five times the value of what was taken. Moreover, the harming or killing of someone else's animal had to be compensated even if it had been done unintentionally. Interestingly, the rape of virgins and the harming of slaves were treated as property crimes (since in those days females and slaves were regarded as chattel), and

---

* Other parts of the Law regarded people's relationship with God, for example, rules about proper worship.

the perpetrator had to compensate the owner for the loss or damage caused to his goods.[29]

The Law prescribed death for a limited number of crimes, primarily murder,* but also for cursing or striking a parent, for blaspheming against God, and for sexual offenses such as adultery, incest, homosexuality, and bestiality.[30] Causing someone's death accidentally was not a punishable offense, and the punishment for unpremeditated murder was exile rather than death.[31] One reason for the imposition of exile was to limit revenge and to prevent a spiral of retaliation that could get out of hand—like the feuding Hatfields and McCoy's in rural Appalachia, or like the Catholics and Protestants in Northern Ireland more recently, or like the Palestinians and Israelis today. Even though the first death in a destructive spiral might have been unintended, the later deaths become increasingly premeditated.

Probably the most quoted moral maxim in the Old Testament is "An eye for an eye and a tooth for a tooth," shortened from "Life for life, eye for eye, tooth for tooth, hand for hand, foot for foot" (Deuteronomy 19:21).[32] This is often taken to mean "Show no mercy and get even," but many Bible scholars believe that it was meant to set a limit on retribution. When people are injured and offended, they often want more than they lost: two eyes for one, a jaw for a tooth, or a life for a wound. God's law for Israel recognized this human tendency toward vengeance and said, in effect, no more than one eye for one eye, one tooth for one tooth, and so on.[33]

---

* The commandment in the Decalogue against killing and parallel passages in the Torah were understood as protecting the lives of free Israelite males. Since females and slaves were regarded as property, they were covered by different laws. Likewise, the punishment for murder did not apply to the killing of non-Israelites in war and other circumstances. Nevertheless, as already noted, the law of hospitality to foreigners was in some ways stronger than the law prohibiting murder.

In the Bible, then, the purpose of punishment is the restoration of social order and, with the exception of capital offenses, the reintegration of transgressors into society. In the Pentateuch, the only one who is said to punish is God, and in the rest of the Bible, punishment is mainly seen as coming from God. The prophets foresaw the destruction of the northern and southern kingdoms as God's punishment for infidelity and injustice. Punishment, in other words, is primarily something that God does, not something that human beings do, although the Bible does occasionally refer to the punishment of subjects by rulers and the punishment of children by parents.[34] Moreover, the purpose of God's punishment, like the ordinances in the Law of Moses, is not revenge but the restoration of justice in society and peace in the world. In fact, the Bible admonishes human beings not to take vengeance: "Do not take revenge, my friends, but leave room for God's wrath, for it is written: 'It is mine to avenge; I will repay,' says the Lord" (Romans 12:19 NIV).

Nowhere in the New Testament does Jesus say anything that commands or condones the punishment of some human beings by others. Both Jesus and St. Paul do, however, refer to a rabbinical practice known as binding and loosing, similar to the Amish practice of shunning. If someone in the community did something wrong and would not repent, the community was to restrict that person from normal social contact with it (the binding). Then, if and when the offender was ready to ask forgiveness and to demonstrate a change in behavior, the community was to relax the restrictions and allow that person back in (the loosing).[35] In a broad sense, this is a form of punishment, but it is nothing like the severe punishments mandated by modern penal codes. And like the Law of Moses, this early Christian practice was aimed at the restoration of social order and the reintegration of individuals into society.

The Golden Rule

Jesus did not say anything specifically about the treatment of people who commit crimes and hurt others, but he did talk about how sinners would be treated by God and about how his followers should treat everyone.

In the parable of the Final Judgment (already discussed in the previous chapter), two types of deeds that merit eternal reward are welcoming strangers and visiting people who are in prison. Conversely, two types of deeds that merit eternal punishment are being inhospitable to strangers and leaving prisoners without the comfort of human contact (Matthew 25:31–46). Jesus nowhere commands that each follower must perform these specific works of mercy, but the story makes it clear that these are the kinds of things that his followers—and indeed all people who are morally upright—should do. Other deeds include feeding the poor, giving drink to the thirsty, and clothing the naked—and Jesus says that all these things, when done to others, are done to him, whether people realize it or not.

If that sounds abstract and a little hard to grasp, Jesus also puts this same principle of morality in a way that everyone can understand: "In everything do to others as you would have them do to you, for this is the whole law and the prophets" (Matthew 7:12).[36] This echoes what Jesus taught elsewhere, to love God above all and to love one's neighbor as oneself, which is another way of summing up what was taught by the Law of Moses and the prophets of Israel.[37]

Conclusions

In both the Old and New Testament, we find that God wants people to be treated with dignity and respect. All human beings, regardless of their circumstances, are made in the image and likeness of God, and are children of God. It may be easy to believe this about relatives and friends, about people of the same religion and country, and about people of the same economic and social class, but the Bible teaches that *all* people have God as their Father and deserve to be honored as children of an almighty parent. One might even say that the Bible goes out of its way to make this point by insisting that the followers of Moses and the followers of Jesus show compassion and respect to people who were looked down upon in biblical times, especially foreigners. Like husbandless women and fatherless children, foreigners in Israel had no family to stand up for them, so God commanded the Chosen People to look out for the welfare of his other children in their midst. Jesus extended this even further, and commanded his followers to care about the welfare of all God's children, near and far.

God's care for people extends even to those who do wrong and who will therefore suffer the consequences, which is God's punishment. Widespread injustice always leads to social chaos, if not sooner then later, and out of the chaos will hopefully emerge a more just and equitable social order—if people learn from their mistakes and the mistakes of others. The purpose of God's punishment is to have people mend their hurtful ways and treat each other the way they are supposed to be treated. The laws of restitution in the Torah were intended both to compensate victims for their losses and to teach offenders how to behave properly. The same can be said of various fines that were imposed for some infractions. The death penalty too was a punishment designed to maintain social order in a culture where blood feuds were common and honor had to be satisfied, lest the killing of one person lead to a downward spiral of violence. The purpose of killing a killer was to stop further killing, not by the killer, but by the victim's relatives. In a world without prisons, it was the only way to prevent further bloodshed.

Human Rights and Civil Rights

The phrase *human rights* does not appear in any of the major speeches of George W. Bush, although, as noted at the beginning of this chapter, the words *life, liberty, equality,* and *freedom* appear rather regularly.[38] It is somewhat ironic, therefore, that these are precisely the rights that are most often violated by the current administration.

In traditional ethics books, a right is defined somewhat tersely as a just due. In other words, it is something due in justice or owed in fairness to a person or group.

Civil rights are those rights that citizens have, and they are granted by law. For many decades, women in the United States did not have the right to vote, but the persistent efforts of the women's suffrage movement succeeded in persuading Congress and the states to pass a constitutional amendment in 1920 granting them the franchise. The civil rights movement of the 1950s and 1960s won for African Americans the rights of assembly, education, and voting that they were supposed to have as American citizens but were denied in many of our southern states. Since civil rights are granted by governments, such rights vary from country to country. Americans have broader rights to own guns, for example, than most Europeans have. On the other hand, all Europeans have a right to free medical care, which Americans do not.

Human rights, unlike civil rights, are those rights that all human beings have, and they are given (as the Declaration of Independence says) by God. Such rights are unalienable, that is, they cannot be taken away, although they can be violated. Human rights are rights to those things that human beings need in order to live a human life. We have a foundational right to life, because being alive is the foundation on which a human life is built. We have fundamental rights to food and water, clothing and shelter, because without these things we cannot live, much less live decently. We have basic rights to safety and security, because when our lives are threatened we live in constant fear, and that is not a human way to live. We have necessary rights to freedom and liberty, because a truly human life entails creativity and development. Since human nature is the same in every human being, we are essentially equal, and we have a right to be treated like other people, without prejudice or discrimination.

Although human rights cannot be lost, they can obviously be violated. They are violated whenever people in positions of power disregard these rights and acts as though they did not exist. Drunk drivers who kill people violate their human rights, as do torturers and terrorists. But human rights are also violated when people are threatened by famine or disease or some other natural danger if others who are not threatened fail to come to their assistance. A child who is drowning in five feet of water when nearby adults could reach over and rescue her is having her right to life violated. People who are dying from easily curable diseases are having their human rights violated when others read about their plight and do nothing about it. Human rights violations can be both active and passive.

In a just society, human rights are enshrined in law and guaranteed as civil rights. Since human rights are not the same as civil rights, however, it is possible to have a human right that is not guaranteed by law as a civil right. Before women in the U.S. acquired the civil right to vote through the passage of the Nineteenth Amendment, part of their human right to freedom and self-determination was not recognized by law. In the famous Dred Scott decision of 1857, the Supreme Court ruled that slaves did not have a civil right to freedom, and so they had to be returned to their masters in the South even if they escaped to the North. Africans never lost their human right to freedom, however, by being legally enslaved in the United States.[39]

It is clear, then, that human rights can be separated from civil rights, and that people can have their human rights violated if a law or a government denies those rights. This seems to be the situation in the United States today with regard to immigrants and refugees and with regard to detainees from the war in Afghanistan. With regard to prisoners in the American penal system, this seems to be a persistent problem that has become more apparent in recent years. In the first two cases, the Bush administration has begun preserving the human rights of U.S. citizens by denying the human rights of foreigners. In the third case, the administration is continuing the policy of protecting the human rights of some of its citizens while denying the rights of other

Americans. The first two cases are active violations of human rights; the third is a passive violation. All three are direct violations of biblical principles.

Immigrants and Refugees

When Attorney General Ashcroft warned terrorists that they would be jailed even if they committed minor violations of the law, he had no way of knowing to whom he was speaking. U.S. intelligence agencies at the time did not know the names of any Al Qaeda operatives in this country, and since then only one name has been publicly disclosed. What he said sounded tough, but in fact he was telling any potential terrorists in America exactly what they needed to do in order to remain concealed: keep your visas up to date and obey all the details of the immigration law. What he said was meant to threaten America's enemies, but in fact it threatened America's friends: people who had come to the United States seeking refuge and opportunity, people who loved to visit the United States, even people who so desperately wanted what America has to offer that they risked arrest and deportation by entering or remaining in the country illegally. Yes, all of them were foreigners, but they were still America's friends.

In the months and years following September 11, 2001, government authorities questioned, photographed and fingerprinted nearly seventy-seven thousand immigrants from Arab and Muslim countries as part of a new special registration program designed to track individuals from countries believed to harbor potential terrorists. Of these people, thirteen thousand are facing deportation for immigration violations, including violations that in the past would have been remedied without arrest and deportation.[40] These were America's friends. They loved America.

During the same time, FBI and INS agents arrested 762 foreigners, mostly Muslim men, and held them in accordance with the terms of the USA PATRIOT Act on suspicion of terrorism without being told the charges against them, without access to a lawyer, without being able to post bond, and without their families being able to find them. Operating under a new "hold until cleared" policy, the U.S. government presumed the detainees guilty until proven innocent instead of presuming them innocent until proven guilty. An investigation by the Justice Department's inspector general revealed that the average length of time that these persons were held in secret was eighty days, and that some of the detainees had been physically abused. Eventually all of them were cleared of links to terrorism.[41] Why? Because these too were America's friends. They too loved America.

The people who were fingerprinted and photographed like criminals talked about their shame with others who were not treated that way. The people who are being deported have relatives who will not be going with them. The people who were detained and denied contact with the outside world have friends and acquaintances who wonder if the same will now happen to them. People who loved America are beginning to have second thoughts about America.

Immigration analysts point out that one key to fighting foreign terrorism is obtaining information from the immigrant community about suspicious persons and potential threats. As soon as noncitizens begin to fear that any contact with the government might lead to their arrest and deportation, however, that source of information dries up. Instead of having more information about potential terrorists, we now have less.[42]

Foreign policy analysts point out that the government's tough new policies against Muslims and Arabs foster anger and resentment in their home countries, and run the risk of undermining friendly relations with the governments whose cooperation is needed most in preventing terrorism. In addition, fewer foreign scientists, academics, and students are coming to this country, some because of long delays in obtaining visas and others because they do not feel comfortable about the current atmosphere of suspicion. In either case, important research is not being performed and schools are not achieving the enrollments they were counting on.[43]

With regard to refugees, the picture is equally dark. As recently as the Reagan administration, the United States was admitting two hundred thousand refugees per year—people fleeing from political oppression, from famine and war, and from threats of torture. In the conservative climate of the 1990s, the annual quota was set at eighty thousand, and the Bush administration was planning to reduce that number to seventy thousand. After September 11, however, the U.S. suspended the immigration of over twenty-two thousand refugees, including almost two thousand already in transit, forcing them to return to refugee camps. As a result of these suspensions, only about twenty-seven thousand refugees were granted asylum in this country in 2002, and recent figures suggest that the total in 2003 was fewer than twenty thousand.[44]

The stranded refugees include men who have been tortured, women who have been raped, and children who have seen members of their family kidnapped, imprisoned, and even killed. A good number of these in 2002 were victims of the Taliban regime in Afghanistan, and today they include victims of oppression and terrorism around the world. Moreover, thousands of asylum seekers in the past few years have been imprisoned and deported rather than being welcomed and offered a fair hearing. In April 2003, Attorney General John Ashcroft raised the barrier even higher when it was ruled that undocumented asylum seekers, primarily from Haiti, could be detained indefinitely without bond and without other legal recourses.[45]

This is a far cry from the biblical principle of kindness and generosity to strangers, not to mention America's long tradition of offering safe haven for immigrants and refugees. It is also a far cry from recognizing the human rights of people who are suffering, especially the right to freedom from unjust detention. These restrictive policies have caused documented cases of depression, anxiety, and post-traumatic stress disorder in people who so loved America that they left everything behind in order to start a new life here.[46]

Immigration has long been recognized as one of America's greatest blessings. Without immigrants, the continent could not have been populated. Without immigrants, the railroads would never have been built. Without immigrants, the United States would never have become an industrial power. Without refugees from Nazi Germany and the Soviet Union, the U.S. would not have become a world leader in science and technology. But the policies of the Bush administration, which punish immigrants and refugees for the sins of the September 11 hijackers, have already reduced this source of blessing to America, and unless changed, they will continue to do so in the future.

Detainees from Afghanistan

Besides the matter of innocent people who were captured and imprisoned after the war in Afghanistan, and besides the matter of detainees being sent to foreign countries for possible torture, there is the matter of the men who did indeed fight in the war on the losing side, and who were sent to the military detention center at Guantánamo Bay. Although they have no civil rights under U.S. law, and although the government has denied that they have any rights under international law, they still have unalienable human rights. For believers in the Bible, this means that they have a right to be treated—as all human beings do—with dignity, for they are created in the image and likeness God. For followers of Jesus, it means that they have a right to be treated the way we would want to be treated.

Government treatment of the Guantánamo detainees has been and continues to be well documented both by news media and by human rights organizations:[47]

- They arrived in hoods and shackles, unable to see and forbidden to speak.

- Originally they were confined to outdoor cages, six feet by eight feet, in which they had to eat and sleep and perform their bodily functions with no partitions for privacy and no shelter against the weather.

- They were allowed out of their cages for only two fifteen-minute exercise breaks per week.
- They were not able to pray in the traditional Muslim way, which requires them to face east and to pray aloud in a number of different postures.
- When taken for interrogation, they were subject to standing, squatting, and kneeling in uncomfortable positions for prolonged periods of time, and they were intentionally deprived of sleep.
- Sometimes they were forced to wear black hoods or spray-painted goggles. Alternatively, they were exposed to prolonged periods of bright light and loud music.
- When they were moved from the cages of Camp X-Ray to the cinder-block cells of Camp Delta, they were still kept in solitary confinement.
- They were and remain completely cut off from the outside world.
- They do not know whether they will ever be released or even whether they will ever be charged with a crime.
- Dozens are being treated with antidepressants because their depression has reached clinical proportions.
- At least twenty-five of them have attempted to commit suicide out of desperation and despair.
- In addition, two prisoners at the Bagram air base in Afghanistan were found dead in December 2002, killed by "blunt force injuries" while in U.S. custody.[48]

If Americans heard that members of their armed forces had been treated this way, they would be outraged, as indeed they were when they learned of GIs in World War II being mistreated and tortured by the Germans and Japanese, and when they later learned of similar atrocities being committed by the Communists in Korea and Vietnam. Instinctively, Americans knew that human rights had been violated, as had God's rule of treating others as one wanted to be treated. Instinctively they understood that what was done to these POWs was wrong and evil, even if they had never read the terms of the Geneva Convention. Even those who had never read the Bible were repulsed by such wanton disregard for the God-given rights of human beings. Because the fundamental laws of moral conduct are written into human nature by God himself, human beings do not need the revelation of the Scriptures to know when they are violated.[49]

Unfortunately for Americans today, this is now true in reverse. Rightly or wrongly, people around the world are looking at America the way we looked at imperial Japan, Nazi Germany, and godless Communism. They instinctively perceive that such mistreatment of prisoners is wrong and evil, and they accuse America of violating the very rights it claims to stand for. Our government officials may deny that the United States practices torture, but all governments consistently deny that they are guilty of illegal practices, so such denials have virtually no credibility. To its credit, the U.S. government has released prisoners who were wrongly detained. To its embarrassment, however, it has not been able to stop the freed prisoners from talking.[50]

Abuse and torture are notoriously unreliable sources of truthful information. People in physical pain and psychological anguish are apt to say anything in order to ease their suffering. This was true in the medieval hunt for witches in Europe, it was true in the Communist brainwashing of American servicemen, and it is true today in the war against terrorism.

More importantly, torture and other violations of human rights invite the very behavior they seek to suppress. Psychological studies and personal accounts report that people who are mistreated experience feelings of revenge, and that people who are tortured are overwhelmed by an intense desire for retaliation.[51]

Moreover, such feelings and desires are not limited to the victims of inhuman treatment. Their families and acquaintances, and especially their companions in their struggle, spontaneously rally against the perpetrators of such wickedness, just as many Americans spontaneously desired vengeance against those responsible for the September 11 crimes against humanity. It is a perfectly natural human reaction, and a perfectly disastrous one, for it feeds and sustains a spiral of violence.

Violations of human rights can also be used to justify violence. When indiscriminate imprisonment is used to promote freedom, it looks like hypocrisy. When abuse and mistreatment are used in the name of justice, they make justice seem to be an empty word. When international law is violated in defense of international law, it reduces international respect for law. This is why, when torture is used to fight terrorism, it increases terrorism.[52]

To Christians, this should come as no surprise. People who violate the law of God inscribed on the human heart can expect to reap the consequences.

Prisoners in the United States

Since imprisonment is nowhere sanctioned in the Bible, it could be argued that all prison systems are unbiblical and contrary to the will of God. Over thirty years ago, noted psychiatrist Karl Menninger wrote *The Crime of Punishment* from a purely secular point of view, arguing that punishment is an antiquated notion that does more harm than good. More than that, he said, the modern penal system is self-defeating, self-destructive, and a form of institutional evil.[53] A similar analysis, cast in Christian terms, would take a book in itself.

Let us assume for the present, however, that prisons are not intrinsically evil, and that the absence of imprisonment from biblical punishments is due to cultural rather than moral reasons. In the context of human rights, we can still compare what the Bible says about punishment with some of the more obvious features of the American penal system.

The biblical purpose of punishment, as we have seen above, is the restoration of social order and the reintegration of individuals into society. By both of these measures, our penal system falls short.

First, instead of restoring society to the order that existed before a crime was committed, the current system has created a new and growing social order of its own, sometimes referred to as the prison industrial complex. In raw statistics, during the past thirty years the U.S. prison population has increased tenfold from two hundred thousand to two million inmates. Moreover, except in the rarest of cases, victims of crime are not compensated for their losses, and they are left to manage on their own. With no provision for real restitution as a means of restoring the balance, citizens who are afraid of being crime victims have demanded harsher and harsher penalties as a symbolic means of getting even. But symbol is not reality, and victims sometimes express dismay that the prison sentences meted out to others are not emotionally satisfying to them. The social order is not really restored.[54]

With regard to the reintegration of offenders into society, the current system is again wanting. Not too long ago, an important goal of the criminal justice system was rehabilitation, but that is no longer the case. In recent decades, the primary goals have become punishment (paying for the crime by doing time) and safety (getting criminals off the streets), as is evidenced by mandatory sentencing laws, lengthier sentences for crimes, and reduced rates of probation and parole. Moreover, the dramatic increase in incarcerations has been accompanied by dramatic reductions in education and training programs in prisons that would enable ex-offenders to succeed in the world without having to resort to criminal activity. As a result, about two-thirds of those released from U.S. prisons are rearrested within three years.[55]

With regard to other human rights issues, a great amount of evidence suggests that people in prison are not respected as human beings, that they are stripped of human dignity, and that they are not treated the way Christians would want to be treated. Prisoners are subjected to overcrowding and lack of privacy in smaller facilities, excessive isolation and arbitrary physical restraint in larger ones. Both men and women are exposed to being raped, and prisoners are liable to strip searches that include inspection of their anal and vaginal openings. Nor are these indignities limited to adults, since in the United States minors can be tried and sentenced as adults.[56] Also in the United States, unlike in other developed countries, both minors and the mentally handicapped can be sentenced to death.[57]

Finally, an issue of distributive justice needs to be raised. The increasing number of incarcerations, combined with regular increases in the cost of living, has pushed the annual cost of incarceration to between $20 thousand and $25 thousand per bed. This is two to four times the annual tuition at a state college or university, and more than the annual cost per student at most private institutions. During the past fifteen years, moreover, state prison budgets have increased six times faster than the rate of state spending on higher education. At the same time, states have continually raised the amount that students have to pay for tuition, increasing the financial strain on poor families and forcing some students out of college. When studies have shown that education is one of the surest and most cost-effective ways of keeping people out of the criminal justice system (and of enabling them to stay out of trouble after being released from prison), the conservative agenda of being "tough on crime" seems to be distributing tax dollars in ways that are unwise as well as unfair to the American public.[58]

Christian Reflections

A common feature of gospel parables is that they turn perceptions upside down and inside out. Jesus told the story of the good Samaritan (Luke 10:29–37) to a crowd that believed there was no such thing as a good Samaritan. He told the story of the one lost sheep (Luke 15:4–7) to shepherds who had enough common sense to stay with the flock rather than chase after a stupid stray. (His listeners also probably believed that God was more pleased with ninety-nine good people than with one repentant sinner.) He told the story of the weeds and the wheat (Matthew 13:24–30, 36–43) to people who thought that the wicked are supposed to be punished by God in this life (because many Jews did not believe in an afterlife).[59]

New Testament scholars tell us that Jesus told such stories to startle his listeners into realizing that his message was radically different from what they were used to hearing and thinking.[60] Just as the prophet Isaiah had proclaimed that God's ways are not man's ways and God's thoughts are not man's thoughts (55:8–9), Jesus was now proclaiming that his way is not the way people usually live, and his teaching is not what most people think. The good news he was announcing was both good and news—something wonderful that had not been heard before.

It certainly would be radical to suggest that Christians ought to do nothing about people who might be terrorists, about their country's enemies, and about convicted criminals. But it would also be unbiblical. There is nothing in the scriptures to suggest that the followers of Jesus should naïvely allow malicious individuals or groups to have their way, even though (as we shall see in the next chapter) a strong biblical case can be made for nonviolent responses to violence. The biblical principles that we have uncovered in this chapter are not that extreme. Indeed, they are almost intuitive when we apply them to ourselves instead of people whom we mistakenly assume are not like us—foreigners, militants, and criminals.

Suppose we were immigrants or refugees. How would we want to be treated? Certainly we could understand our adopted country's need to protect itself. Certainly we would not expect to have all the civil rights that citizens enjoy. But would we not want our human rights to be respected? Would we not want to be treated courteously as people who could help find threats to the peace and safety of our new homeland? Would we not want to be treated as future citizens rather than as potential enemies?

Suppose we were captured in a war. How would we want to be treated? Certainly we could understand our captors' need to detain us from further fighting. Certainly we could understand their desire to obtain information from us. But would we not want to be treated as human beings and not as animals? Certainly we would not want to be physically or emotionally abused. Certainly we would not want to be tortured. Would we not want our loved ones to know that we have been captured? And after the war is over, would we not want due process—either release or a fair trial?

Suppose we were in prison for a crime we had committed. How would we want to be treated? Certainly we could understand society's need for our incarceration, if we were honest with ourselves. But would we not want to be treated with respect—as the person we might become, rather than as the person we used to be? Once we understood the harm that we had done, would we not want a chance to express our remorse, to be forgiven by our victims, and to make whatever reparation we could? Would we not want to be able to love ourselves, to accept our situation, and to forgive ourselves for what we had done? Would we not want to learn how to get along with others, how to be a contributing member of society, and how to succeed in the world after we have served our time?

Asking questions such as these puts us in direct contact with the Golden Rule: "Do to others as you would have them do to you" (Luke 6:31). Remember that, according to Jesus, behaving this way is the same as fulfilling the commandments of the Law and the teachings of the prophets (Matthew 7:12). Behaving this way is doing everything that God wants of us in our dealings with other human beings.

Such an idea, so basic and obvious, can certainly turn our world upside down when we apply it not just to the people in our family, not just to our friends and relatives, not just to the people we meet at school and at work, but to everyone, to all human beings, even to those we think we have a right to fear and hate and despise. God did not teach the Israelites to love their countrymen but fear strangers. Jesus did not tell his followers to love their friends but hate their enemies. Neither the Old Testament nor the New Testament proposes that people who do wrong should be despised; rather, they teach the need for repentance and forgiveness.

Nor should we think that such a revolution in human thinking is merely a suggestion on God's part. If it were merely a nice idea, we would have to think that God went through a lot of effort to communicate something that we did not need to know. He freed the Israelites from slavery and gave them the Law of Moses as their guide for living. He sent them the prophets when they strayed from the Law. He destroyed their kingdoms when they ignored the prophets' call for justice and compassion. Finally, he sent his Son and allowed him to be crucified for perfectly fulfilling the Law and the prophets. In more traditional theological language, Jesus died because of our sins—including the sins of fearing and hating and despising others. And Jesus also died *for* our sins, accepting the punishment that should have been ours.

For sin does have consequences—divine punishment, if you will. Unfortunately, however, it is not always the guilty who suffer, especially in the case of social sins.

Considering just the violations of God's law discussed in this chapter, the first wave of victims are those who suffer from the self-righteousness of the perpetrators—immigrants and refugees, prisoners of war, and people who are incarcerated. The second wave of victims are those who know and care about the first victims, who resent how they are being treated, and who lose respect for the system that violates human rights in the name of defending human rights. The third wave of victims are those who, some time later, suffer from the pent-up anger and resentment of the first and second groups. In the words of the old Jewish proverb, "The parents have eaten sour grapes, and the children's teeth are set on edge" (Ezekiel 18:2).[61]

Injustice breeds anger, mistreatment breeds resentment, and violence breeds revenge. Aware of this, God limited the Israelites to taking no more than an eye for an eye, and no more than a tooth for a tooth. But God's Son went further and said, in effect, do not even take the eye or tooth to which you feel entitled. Let the doing of evil stop with you, so that others cannot use your behavior as an excuse for doing harm to others.[62]

Conclusion

It is easy to look at other people and see them as different from us. We do it all the time. And we all do it, ironically, because we are just like everybody else who does it. In other words, we are all fundamentally alike in having the ability to think of others as fundamentally different.

Psychologists tell us that in order to hate and harm other human beings, we have to mentally dehumanize them first. We need to make them less than human, other than human, different than human. We need to demonize them, call them demons, devils, evil, wicked, or bad guys. By doing that, we give ourselves psychological permission to think of them as targets of our righteous anger rather than as human beings who feel as we do, who have loved ones as we do, who have human rights as we do.[63] It should come as no surprise that this attitude is not approved by God.

Although the words *wicked* and *evil* are found in the Bible, they are used in a variety of ways. In the Old Testament, God calls the Israelites and other people wicked and evil because of their sinful ways, people call themselves wicked and evil when confessing their shortcomings to God, and the Israelites call their enemies and the enemies of God wicked and evil. Very often these words are used to describe people who are malicious and actions that are hurtful. Likewise in the New Testament, Jesus calls people and spirits wicked and evil because of the way they behave, and St. Paul uses these words to refer to immoral and unethical behavior.[64] Quite revealingly, however, the Bible never exhorts people to hurt or kill people who are called wicked or evil. The Bible never even encourages the dehumanizing or demonizing of others. All human beings are created in the image and likeness of God.

In the Bible, moreover, the punishment and destruction of evil are always left to God. Even though the Psalms sometimes hope for bloody revenge against Israel's enemies,[65] the prayer and expectation is that God will be the one to wreak havoc on both people and property. Nowhere is there an invitation or permission for people to take the matter into their own hands (although presumably, given the way men think, there would have been Jews who wanted to be God's instruments of slaughter). Since God alone is just, only God can justifiably kill the wicked.

Presumably, if God got rid of all the evildoers in the world, then the whole world would be ruled by God, and God's kingdom would be established on the earth as well as in heaven. For one definition of the kingdom of God is that it is the place where God's rule is obeyed, where God's will is done.[66] This in fact is the vision Jesus communicated to his followers when he taught them the Lord's Prayer:

> Our Father which art in heaven,
> Hallowed be thy name.
> Thy kingdom come,
> Thy will be done in earth, as it is in heaven.
> Give us this day our daily bread.
> And forgive us our debts, as we forgive our debtors.
> And lead us not into temptation, but deliver us from evil:
> For thine is the kingdom, and the power,
> and the glory, for ever. Amen. (Matthew 6:9-13 KJV)

This prayer is probably said millions of times around the world everyday by millions of Christians. Yet most Christians do not realize how revolutionary this prayer was at the time when Jesus first spoke it, and how revolutionary it still is.[67] It asks that "Thy will be done in earth, as it is in heaven." But we have already seen that what God wants done on the earth is justice and compassion, for all people are essentially equal and are deserving of respect and dignity. So if Christians call themselves followers of Christ, by praying this prayer they are saying that they themselves want to be doers of God's will on earth, that is, to practice justice and compassion. It follows that every time that people do not follow the principles of justice, and every time that they are not compassionate to those in need, they are acting contrary to the Lord's Prayer. For whenever human rights are not respected, whenever human beings are not treated with respect, God's will is not being done.

But this is not all. Although it is not generally recognized as such, the prayer also contains a potential curse. For the prayer goes on to say, "Forgive us our debts, as we forgive our debtors," but the word *debts* (sometimes translated as *trespasses*) does not mean merely monetary debts. It is much broader than that. It means whatever we owe to God, or rather in this context, whatever we should have done and have not done. Perhaps *failures* would be a better, more general word, or, as Luke's version of the Lord's Prayer calls them, *sins* (11:2-4).

So in the Lord's Prayer we ask God to forgive our sins as we forgive the sins of others, or, even more broadly, to forgive us as we forgive others.[68]

But what are we asking God to do, then, if we do not forgive others?

Notes

[1] A CNN transcript of President Bush's speech on Goree Island, Senegal, on July 8, 2003, is available from Global Black News at www.globalblacknews.com.

[2] For an early review of this policy, see Ann Harrison, "Detained for Terror" (November 7, 2001), available at www.alternet.org by typing the title of the article in the Search box on the AlterNet home page.

³ Provisions and analysis of this legislation are available at a number of websites that can be accessed by typing "USA PATRIOT Act" into an Internet search engine.

⁴ For more information, go to the Department of Homeland Security home page at www.whitehouse.gov/homeland. Also "U.S. Immigration Policy Post September 11th," a Foreign Policy Association report, available at www.fpa.org; click on Your Guides in the left margin of the home page, then scroll down to Refugees and click on that to find the story.

⁵ See Dave Eberhart, "Inspector General Blasts Handling of 9/11 Detainees," (June 4, 2003), available at www.newsmax.com; click on Archives, then scroll down to find title by date. Also Seth Stern, "Detainees get boost from Justice review," *Christian Science Monitor* (June 4, 2003), available at www.csmonitor.com; click on Archive, then type the first few words of the title in Fast Search line.

⁶ For background on Osama bin Laden, including a 1998 interview about his beliefs and motives, go to the Frontline website at www.pbs.org/wgbh/pages/ frontline/shows/binladen.

⁷ For a thorough review of the U.S. treatment of prisoners shortly after the war, see Dana Priest and Barton Gellman, "U.S. Decries Abuse but Defends Interrogations," *Washington Post* (December 26, 2002), p. A1, and also available in the archives at www.washingtonpost.com.

⁸ Priest and Gellman quote the head of the CIA Counterterrorist Center, speaking before a joint hearing of the House and Senate intelligence committees on September 26, 2002: "This is a very highly classified area, but I have to say that all you need to know: There was a before 9/11, and there was an after 9/11. After 9/11 the gloves came off."

⁹ Priest and Gellman report an unnamed U.S. intelligence official saying in an interview, "If you don't violate someone's human rights some of the time, you probably aren't doing your job." Although the U.S. government has never publicly investigated allegations of prisoner mistreatment, the president has affirmed his opposition to torture anywhere in the world. The president's most forceful statement is available at www.whitehouse.gov; under News by Date, click on June

2003, then on Statement of the President [on the United Nations International Day in Support of Victims of Torture].

[10] Priest and Gellman quote another official who was involved with turning captives over to foreign governments as saying, "We don't kick the [expletive] out of them. We send them to other countries so *they* can kick the [expletive] out of them." Although the Department of Defense admits that it has sent captives to other countries, it denies that the purpose is to extract information through torture. See "Letter from Department of Defense General Counsel William Haynes to U.S. Senator Patrick Leahy," available at http://hrw.org/press/2003/06/tortureday.htm, or by typing "Bush Administration Rules Out Using Cruel Treatment to Fight Terrorism" in a search engine.

[11] As of March 2004, over 100 detainees had been released after being held for over a year. Some were Afghans and Pakistanis who were "in the wrong place at the wrong time," some were over seventy years old, and most complained of being physically abused. The numbers are hard to verify because stories of the releases are seldom covered by mainstream media companies, and because empty cells are continually refilled with new detainees brought from overseas. To find these stories, use any Internet search engine and type in the keywords Guantánamo, detainees, and released. (Do not put quotation marks around the string of words.) To find stories about children being detained, type in the keywords Guantánamo, detainees, and children. The number of children under the age of sixteen has never been disclosed, although three were released in January 2004. See "U.S.: Despite Releases, Children Still Held at Guantánamo," a press release from Human Rights Watch, available at www.hrw.org; click on News Releases, then scroll to January 29, 2004, or type the title into the Search line.

[12] Statistically, about 14 percent of the individuals convicted of murder and sentenced to death since 1976 have been found to be innocent. According to the Innocence Project Northwest, "As many as 10 percent of inmates in the United States may be factually innocent of the crimes of which they were convicted. . . . That's as many as 200,000 innocent people languishing in American prisons. This is a national problem." See Askia Muhammad, "100th Death Row Inmate Freed," *The Final Call* (April 25, 2002), available at the NCM Online Archives, but more quickly

reachable by typing the name of the article into a search engine. See also the Innocence Project Northwest at www.law.washington.edu/ipnw for more information and links to related websites.

[13] Scott Shane, "Locked up in the land of the free," *Baltimore Sun* (June 1, 2003), p. 2A, available through the *Sun* archives at www.sunspot.net or by typing "U.S. prison population largest in the world" into a search engine. See also "New Inmate Population Figures Demonstrate Need for Policy Reform," a press release of The Sentencing Project, a non-profit research and advocacy organization, available at www.sentencing project.org; click on In the News, then on the title of the press release.

[14] The averages have not changed much since 2000. See *Human Rights Watch World Report 2002*, available at www.hrw.org/wr2k2/us.html; click on "Overincarceration, Drugs, and Race." Also Patricia Lefevere, "Locked Up," *National Catholic Reporter* (May 2, 2003), p. 10, and available at www.natcath.org under either Back Issues or Archives.

[15] Eric Schlosser, "The Prison-Industrial Complex," *The Atlantic Monthly* (December 1998), p. 51–77; also available on line at www.theatlantic.com; click on The Archive, then type in the name of the article.

[16] Schlosser, p. 54. The figures are from 1998 or earlier. The numbers have gone up since then. See the statistics and reports available from the Sentencing Project, a non-profit research and advocacy organization, at www.sentencingproject.org > Issues > Incarceration.

[17] See Schlosser, pp. 51–52. Also Marc Mauer, *The Race to Incarcerate* (The New Press, 1999).

[18] See "Recidivism of State Prisoners," available at www.sentencing project.org > Issues > Incarceration. The latest publicly available figures can be obtained from the Bureau of Justice Statistics in the Office of Justice Programs, available at www.ojp.usdoj.gov.

[19] According to Huston Smith, "one third of our Western civilization bears the marks of its Jewish ancestry," including Western notions of morality and justice. See chapter 7 in Smith's influential book, *The Religions of Man* (Harper and Brothers, 1958), revised and published as *The World's Religions* (HarperSanFrancisco, 1991).

[20] See also Exodus 13:3; 13:14; 20:2; Leviticus 26:13; Deuteronomy 5:6–7; 5:15; 6:12; 6:21; 7:8.

[21] See Genesis 2:7; Deuteronomy 16:20; 1 Kings 10:9; Psalm 72:1; Isaiah 1:21; Jeremiah 21:12; Hosea 12:6; Amos 5:15; Zechariah 7:9.

[22] Besides teaching his followers to address God as "Our Father" when they pray (Matthew 6:9; Luke 11:2), Jesus refers to God as "your Father" many times in the Sermon on the Mount (Matthew 5–7) and regularly throughout the synoptic gospels. In the fourth gospel, Jesus often speaks of God as his Father, and once as "my Father and your Father" (John 20:17).

[23] See Exodus 22:21–22; Leviticus 19:9–10; Deuteronomy 10:17–19; 24:17–21; 26:12–13; 27:19.

[24] See Exodus 22:21; Leviticus 19:33-34; Deuteronomy 10:19; 15:15; 16:12.

[25] The words are taken from "The New Colossus" by Emma Lazarus. The full poem expresses more completely the welcoming spirit that was felt by millions of immigrants who came to America through New York harbor.

> Not like the brazen giant of Greek fame,
> With conquering limbs astride from land to land;
> Here at our sea-washed, sunset gates shall stand
> A mighty woman with a torch, whose flame
> Is the imprisoned lightning, and her name
> Mother of Exiles. From her beacon-hand
> Glows world-wide welcome; her mild eyes command
> The air-bridged harbor that twin cities frame.
> "Keep, ancient lands, your storied pomp!" cries she
> With silent lips. "Give me your tired, your poor,
> Your huddled masses yearning to breathe free,
> The wretched refuse of your teeming shore.
> Send these, the homeless, tempest-tost [sic] to me,
> I lift my lamp beside the golden door!"

[26] See John 4:5–30 and Matthew 8:5–13.

[27] See Acts 8:26–40; 10:1–48; 13–21.

[28] In the Bible, most of the people who get imprisoned are good people such as Joseph in Egypt, Samson, Jeremiah, John the Baptist, St. Peter, and St. Paul. Prisons were used by the rulers of cities and kingdoms for political enemies (not always justly) and to hold captured soldiers. The Bible nowhere commands or even suggests imprisonment as a punishment for crime.

[29] See Exodus 21:12–22:17. At the same time, however, slaves and females did have rights; see Exodus 21:1–4, 8–11, 26–27.

[30] See Exodus 21:12–17 and 22:9. Also Leviticus 20:9–16 and 24:17 and 23.

[31] See Exodus 21:13; also Deuteronomy 19:1–13.

[32] See also Exodus 18:25; Leviticus 24:17–22.

[33] For example, *Peake's Commentary on the Bible* (Thomas Nelson and Sons, 1963) calls this "a principle of justice widespread in early societies, effecting fit punishment and at the same time imposing limits upon vengeance (p. 230). *The Jerome Biblical Commentary* (Prentice-Hall, 1968) agrees, saying that it "was intended to limit revenge" and impose "proportionate compensation" (p. 59).

[34] You can verify this by looking up the word *punish* in any standard Bible concordance, or by using the electronic concordance provided by Bible Gateway at www.biblegateway.com. Except for a half dozen passages that speak of punishment by human beings, the 188 passages in the New International Version that contain the words *punish*, *punished*, *punishment*, etc. refer to punishment by God.

[35] See Matthew 18:15–18; 1 Corinthians 5:1–2; 2 Corinthians 2:5–11.

[36] See also Luke 6:31.

[37] See Matthew 22:34–40.

[38] President Bush occasionally uses the terms *human rights* and *civil rights* in some of his minor speeches, however, as in an address to the U.S. Chamber of Commerce on November 6, 2003, and at a state dinner in England on November 19, 2003. Both of these speeches are available at www.georgewbush.com > News Room > Speeches > search by date.

[39] The Court went even further and declared that because the U.S. Constitution gave Americans a civil right to own slaves, laws prohibiting slavery in so-called free states were unconstitutional. According to Chief Justice Roger B. Taney, since according to the Constitution slaves were property, slave owners could take their slaves into any part of the country, and state laws could not prohibit them from doing so. This is why a constitutional amendment was needed to abolish slavery at the national level. For a summary of the history, go to www.nps.gov/jeff/ocv-dscottd.htm.

[40] See Christian Bourge, "Analysis: Immigration policy spurs debate," *The Washington Times* (July 11, 2003). Available at www.washtimes.com but most easily accessed by typing the name of the article into a search engine.

[41] See Bourge, above. Also Kellie Lunney, "Justice inspector raps FBI, INS over post-Sept. 11 detentions," *Government Executive Magazine* (June 2, 2003). Available at www.govexec.com by typing in the first words of the title in the Search line of the magazine's home page.

[42] See "Immigrants in the Crosshairs: The Quiet Backlash Against America's Immigrants and Refugees," an American Immigration Forum Backgrounder dated December 16, 2002, available at www.immigrationforum.org but more easily retrievable by typing "Immigrants in the Crosshairs" into a search engine. (Be sure to click on the December 2002 report and not on the July 2003 report with the same title but different subtitle.)

[43] See "Foreign Policy Fallout: Assessing the Risks of Post-Sept. 11 Immigration Policies," a report of the American Immigration Law Foundation dated May 2003, available at www.ailf.org by typing the three words of the title into the Search line on the AILF home page. See also "U.S. Immigration Policy Post September 11th," an *In Focus* report of the Foreign Policy Association, available at www.fpa.org. In the left margin, click on Your Guides for a drop-down menu, then click on the topic of Refugees for this and other articles and reports.

[44] See Magin McKenna, "Why the door closed on those huddled masses," *The Sunday Herald*, Scotland (September 28, 2003), available at www.sunday herald.com; click on Archive, then on Back Issue, then type the title

in the Search line. Rather extensive documentation of the refugee situation since September 2001 is provided by the Lawyers Committee for Human Rights in their on-line issues of *Asylum Protection News* beginning October 31, 2001. Go to www.lchr.org and in the Search line type "Asylum Protection News." Clicking on any of the issues of the newsletter will bring up a copy of that issue with links to other issues in the left margin.

[45] See "Attorney General Ashcroft Calls for Blanket Detentions of Haitian Asylum Seekers," *Asylum Protection News, No. 13* at the above-mentioned website.

[46] See "From Persecution to Prison: The Health Consequences of Detention for Asylum Seekers," a report by Physicians for Human Rights and the Belleview/NYU Program for Survivors of Torture (June 2003), available at www.phrusa.org by entering the title in the Search line on the home page, or by entering the title in an Internet search engine.

[47] A number of relevant stories are available online from BBC News, including "US bides its time in Guantánamo" (August 24, 2002); "Afghans tell of Guantánamo ordeal" (October 29, 2002); "Campaigners demand US 'torture' probe" (December 27, 2002); "No fast track at Guantánamo Bay" (January 11, 2003); and "Amnesty plea for Cuba detainees (January 11, 2003). They are most easily accessed by title, using a search engine. See also multiple reports and analyses available from Amnesty International at www.amnesty.org, including "Guantánamo detainees – the legal black hole deepens," and "United States of America: The threat of a bad example." The AI online library also has information about similar treatment of detainees in Iraq.

[48] See Duncan Campbell, "Afghan prisoners beaten to death at US military interrogation base," *The Guardian* (March 7, 2003); available at www.guardian.co.uk by typing "blunt force injuries" in the search line of the newspaper's home page.

[49] This is St. Paul's clear argument in the Epistle to the Romans (1:18–2:29), that the Law of Moses reveals what can also be known by human reason unassisted by God's revelation.

50 See Carlotta Gall, "Afghans freed from Guantánamo say they are angry and stunned," *International Herald Tribune* (March 26, 2003), p. 4; also Carlotta Gall and Neil A. Lewis, "Freed Guantánamo captives tell of suicidal despair," *International Herald Tribune* (June 18, 2003), p. 1.

51 See Elaine Scarry, *The Body in Pain: The Making and Unmaking of the World* (Oxford University Press, 1987), especially chapter 1. Also Jean Améry, *At the Mind's Limits: Contemplations by a Survivor on Auschwitz and Its Realities* (Indiana University Press, 1998).

52 See Eyal Press, "Tortured Logic: Thumbscrewing International Law," *Amnesty Now* (Summer 2003), pp. 20–28, especially p. 23.

53 Karl Menninger, M.D., *The Crime of Punishment* (Viking Press, 1966).

54 See Ted Grimsrud and Howard Zehr, "Rethinking God, justice, and treatment of offenders," *Journal of Offender Rehabilitation* (Vol. 35, 2002), pp. 259–285; Marla L. Domino and Marcus T. Boccaccini, "Doubting Thomas: Should family members of victims watch executions?" *Law and Psychology Review* (Spring 2000), pp. 59–75.

55 Various reports and charts are available from the U.S. Bureau of Justice Statistics, www.ojp.usdoj.gov/bjs/. On the Search line of the home page, enter "recidivism."

56 For a quick overview, see the following Human Rights Watch reports available at www.hrw.org: "Incarcerated America" (April 2003); "No Escape: Male Rape in U.S. Prisons" (April 2001); "Out of Sight: Super-Maximum Security Confinement in the United States" (February 2000); "All Too Familiar: Sexual Abuse of Women in U.S. State Prisons" (December 1996). The 1998 report, "Prisons in the United States of America," contains references and links to many other HRW reports as well as stories from other sources. For more thorough treatment, see Paul Wright and Tara Herivel (eds.), *Prison Nation: The Warehousing of America's Poor* (Routledge, 2003); Elihu Rosenblatt (ed.), *Criminal Injustice: Confronting the Prison Crisis* (South End Press, 1996); Robert Johnson, *Hard Time: Understanding and Reforming the Prison* (Second Edition, Wadsworth, 1995).

57 For a synopsis of stories related to the death penalty, including juvenile and mentally handicapped offenders, go to the Amnesty

International Program to Abolish the Death Penalty at www.amnesty usa.org/abolish. See also Amnesty International's piece on "Torture and abuse of prisoners," and the Reuters News Service analysis by Alan Eisner, "Huge U.S. Prison Population Social Cost," both of which are most easily available by typing the title in a search engine.

[58] See the Justice Policy Institute report, "Cellblocks or Classrooms?" (August 2002), available at www.justicepolicy.org, which also carries other informative reports and analyses. Also, David Phinny, "Prison Funding Explodes in Growth" (July 9, 1999), available at www.abc news.com. Also, Dan Usher, "Education as a Deterrent to Crime," *Canadian Journal of Economics* (May 1997), pp. 367–384. All three pieces are accessible by typing the title in a search engine.

[59] Luke's gospel is the richest in parables of this sort. See also the guests invited to the banquet (14:15–24), the prodigal son (15:11–32), the rich man and Lazarus (16:19–31), and the Pharisee and the tax collector (18:10–14).

[60] See John Dominic Crossan, *In Parables: The Challenge of the Historical Jesus* (Harper and Row, 1973), especially chapter 3; also Richard N. Longenecker (ed.), *The Challenge of Jesus' Parables* (William B. Eerdmans, 2000).

[61] See also Jeremiah 31:29–30.

[62] See Matthew 5:38–42.

[63] See William Brennan, *Dehumanizing the Vulnerable: When Word Games Take Lives* (Loyola University Press, 1995); John H. Ellard et al., "Just World Processes in Demonizing," in Michael Ross and Dale T. Miller, *The Justice Motive in Everyday Life*, (Cambridge University Press, 2002); Robert S. Wistrich, *Demonizing the Other: Antisemitism, Racism and Xenophobia* (Routledge, 1999); Jodie Kliman and Roxana Llerena-Quinn, "Dehumanizing and Rehumanizing Responses to September 11," *Journal of Systemic Therapies* (October 2002), pp. 8–18.

[64] There are literally too many scripture references to list them all. The electronic concordance available at www.biblegateway.com counts 466 instances of *wicked* and *wickedness*, and 442 times that the word *evil* appears in the New International Version (NIV).

[65] See, for example, Psalm 68:20-23 and Psalm 137:8–9.

[66] For an introduction to the scriptural notion of the kingdom (or reign) of God, see Glen H. Stassen and David P. Gushee, *Kingdom Ethics: Following Jesus in Contemporary Context* (InterVarsity Press, 2003), especially Chapter 1, "The Reign of God."

[67] See, for example, Michael Crosby, *Thy Will Be Done: Praying the Our Father as a Subversive Activity* (Orbis Books, 1977).

[68] Jesus himself understood the implications of this prayer. He goes on to say, "For if you forgive others their trespasses, your heavenly Father will also forgive you; but if you do not forgive others, neither will your Father forgive your trespasses" (Matthew 6:14). See also Jesus' parable of the unforgiving debtor in Matthew 18:23–35.

5

War and Peace

"Love your enemies; do good to those who hate you."
(Luke 6: 27)

George W. Bush is the only president in U.S. history to have led the country into two wars in two years. In his own mind, the necessity for war each time was a clear and present danger, and the link between the first conflict and the second was undeniable.

Just nine days after September 11, 2001, when it was certain that the attacks on the World Trade Center and the Pentagon (as well as another disastrous hijacking) had been perpetrated by agents of the Al Qaeda network, President Bush declared a war on terrorism, starting with Osama bin Laden and his bases in Afghanistan. "Whether we bring our enemies to justice, or bring justice to our enemies," the president said solemnly, "justice will be done."

Virtually overnight, Americans found themselves faced with a new enemy. A decade before, they had been celebrating the disappearance of world communism; now they were confronting the specter of world terrorism. Moreover, just as during the Cold War, now there could be no middle ground: "Every nation, in every region, now has a decision to make. Either you are with us, or you are with the terrorists."

When the government of Afghanistan refused to hand over the leaders of Al Qaeda, the United States took military action with the support of the United Nations. On October 7, the president announced to the nation that coalition forces had begun striking terrorist training camps and military installations of the Taliban regime. Even though the war in that country was swift and successful, Mr. Bush understood that the conclusion of fighting gave little cause for celebration. As he explained to the American people in the State of the Union message the following January, "Our war on terrorism is well begun, but it is only begun. This campaign may not be finished on our watch—yet it must be and it will be waged on our watch."

One day after the first anniversary of the Al Qaeda attacks, President Bush turned his attention to the situation in Iraq. Twelve years before, that country had invaded neighboring Kuwait and had put itself in a position to threaten other countries in the Persian Gulf region. After being defeated but not dislodged from power, Iraq's military dictator deceived U.N. weapons inspectors and defied U.S. calls for his overthrow while his people suffered under global economic sanctions. Speaking before the United Nations on September 12, 2002, Mr. Bush reviewed the facts and concluded, "Saddam Hussein's regime is a grave and gathering danger."

During the next few months, the president sought to secure international support for a military response to the threats he clearly perceived. Despite his best efforts, however, as well as those of Secretary of State Colin Powell, the world did not respond with the same willing unity it had shown a year before. In his 2003 State of the Union address, Mr. Bush had anticipated that "some governments will be timid in the face of terror. And make no mistake about it: If they do not act, America will."

On March 20, 2003, with a small but solid coalition of countries, America took the predicted action.

The Public Record

From his speeches and spontaneous remarks, it is clear that George W. Bush believes in the rightness of the military policies he has pursued. Speaking to Congress and the American people on September 20, 2001, he made this appeal:

> Fellow citizens, we'll meet violence with patient justice—assured of the rightness of our cause, and confident of the victories to come. In all that lies before us, may God grant us wisdom, and may He watch over the United States of America.

Likewise on September 11, 2002, Mr. Bush affirmed:

> America strives to be tolerant and just. . . . We do not fight to impose our will, but to defend ourselves and extend the blessings of freedom.

For centuries, Christians have fought in their own self-defense and in defense of others whose freedom was denied or threatened. Christian moralists in the Middle Ages developed the just war theory to explain when and how the followers of the Prince of Peace could justifiably resort to the brutality of military violence. At the same time, other Christian thinkers have proposed that nonviolence is the only Christ-like response to the threat of force, even lethal force. The military actions of a Christian president should be examined in the light of both of these traditions.

The War in the Persian Gulf (1991)

The recent war in Iraq cannot be fully understood without an appreciation for the major facts surrounding the U.S.-led war against Iraq over a decade ago.

In 1963, the Ba'ath party seized control of Iraq by means of a bloody coup against Abdul Karim Kassim, who had overthrown that country's monarchy in 1958. Saddam Hussein rose through government ranks through his affiliation with the party, becoming vice president in 1968 and general of the armed forces in 1973. Using these positions to increase and consolidate his power, Saddam slowly became the de facto ruler of Iraq, and in 1979 he forced the elderly president to resign and assumed the presidency himself.[1]

One of Saddam's first acts as president was to arrest and execute those members of the Ba'ath party who might oppose his leadership. He went on to suppress all political opposition, imprisoning and torturing suspected enemies, including the leaders of ethnic and religious minorities in Iraq such as the Kurds in the north and the Shiite (or Shi'a) Muslims in the south. In 1980 he invaded neighboring Iran, which had recently been taken over by Shiite fundamentalists under the religious leadership of Ayatollah Khomeini, but the war ended in a stalemate in 1988, by which time it had cost a total of almost two million lives. Iraq used chemical weapons, which are illegal according to international law, both against the Iranian army and against Iraqi Kurds who opposed the government of Saddam Hussein.

In 1990, Iraq invaded and occupied neighboring Kuwait, perhaps expecting that this move would be regarded with the same indifference that the international community had given to Saddam's other military exploits. Instead, U.S. president George Bush denounced the invasion as a violation of national sovereignty, and in 1991 the United States led an international coalition of forces to expel the Iraqi army from Kuwait. Having succeeded in doing so, the president and the country's top military officer, General Colin Powell, called an end to the fighting, leaving Saddam Hussein in political control of the country but with a greatly weakened military.

After the war, Iraq agreed to destroy any and all weapons that could be used to threaten its neighbors, especially long-range missiles and chemical weapons. International inspectors constantly encountered obstacles to thorough and unfettered access, however, leading to suspicions that Iraq was concealing old stockpiles of weapons and was developing new ones. A series of United Nations resolutions called for Iraq to return all prisoners of war and to cease the repression of its own people. Instead, Saddam ordered the brutal suppression of uprisings in both the north and south, in response to which the United States and United Kingdom established "no fly" zones in order to, at the very least, protect these populations from attacks by Iraqi aircraft.

In response to these violations of international standards of behavior, the U.S. urged the United Nations to impose severe trade sanctions in the hope that internal dissatisfaction and dissent would lead to a change in the country's political regime. The sanctions were also designed to deprive Saddam of the materials and technology needed for weapons of mass destruction. Even with the sanctions in place, however, by 2002 the U.S. and U.K. had accumulated sufficient intelligence[*] to conclude that Iraq had again become a threat to its neighbors. Disturbed by these new developments, President George W. Bush felt compelled to go before the United Nations and present the case for further international action against Iraq, perhaps even military action.[2]

The War in Afghanistan (2002)

It is conceivable that if the events of September 2001 had never taken place, the situation in Iraq would not have been perceived to be so menacing. But the attacks by Al Qaeda on U.S. soil heightened American awareness of global terrorist organizations and its own vulnerability to them. No longer was terrorism something that happened in other countries, even if it sometimes happened to U.S. citizens. No longer was terrorism something that the FBI could ignore because monitoring foreign threats was the job of the CIA. No longer was terrorism something that could be lumped together with regional conflicts, civil wars, natural disasters, poverty, and disease as threats to global peace and security. Now terrorism was Public Enemy Number One.

Energized with this new sensitivity, American and European intelligence agencies began paying more careful attention to the countries (mostly Muslim and Arabic) and organizations (mostly militant and fundamentalist) that regarded the United States and its NATO allies as their enemies. Not surprisingly, they looked

---

[*] Intelligence differs from information, or the raw data gathered by surveillance and espionage, in that the data have been drawn together and analyzed for their meaning and implications. Intelligence, then, is information that has been interpreted by specialists who try to see how the pieces of data fit into a larger picture.

very closely for what Iraq might be hiding and for possible links between Saddam Hussein and Osama bin Laden. Especially after the conclusion of the war in Afghanistan, by interrogating prisoners and by tracing the escape routes of enemy combatants, they found the links they had been looking for. They also found information that suggested that Iraq had been hiding much more than previously suspected.

The war in Afghanistan, triggered by the September 11 attacks, is the bridge by which the Bush administration crossed from being patient with Saddam to insisting on regime change.

The war itself enjoyed enormous international support with few exceptions. Even Arab governments not normally friendly to the U.S. agreed that the crimes committed by Al Qaeda were egregious enough to warrant retaliation. Even Muslim governments and organizations not normally sympathetic to Western values agreed that the brand of Islam practiced by the Taliban was an aberration that deviated from all other Muslim traditions. In addition to being harshly repressive toward its enemies, the Taliban government of Afghanistan imposed its fundamentalism on the whole country, forcing men to wear long beards and women to wear burkhas covering them from head to toe, forbidding girls to attend school, and prohibiting women from working outside the home. The economy was in a shambles after years of civil war, and the country's principal cash crop was opium, which got converted into 70 percent of the world's heroin. Not many months before, the government had ordered the dynamiting of two giant Buddha statues carved into the face of a stone cliff, artifacts of an older Buddhist culture in that region, but viewed by the Taliban as sacrilegious graven images. The world had little sympathy for the Taliban.[3]

Code named Operation Enduring Freedom, the war began on October 7, 2001, and wound down later that year with coalition control of the capital, Kabul, and the installation of the Afghan Interim Authority with Hamid Karzai as chairman, whose position was reaffirmed by a Loya Jirga (Grand Assembly) of Afghan leaders in June 2002. Nevertheless, sporadic fighting continued in remote parts of the country as coalition forces searched for remnants of the Taliban government and military, as well as for Al Qaeda fighters and Osama bin Laden.[4]

Two years later, the country is still in the process of reconstruction, slowly overcoming the legacy of two decades of civil war.

The War in Iraq (2003)

At the United Nations on September 12, 2002, President Bush argued that the world could not afford to remain complacent about Iraq. Saddam Hussein had agreed to U.N. inspections for weapons of mass destruction, but the inspection program had terminated in 1998 without conclusive proof that Iraq had no more chemical or biological weapons. The United Nations had passed resolutions that Iraq cease the repression of its own people, but Saddam Hussein was continuing to repress minorities and persecute individuals. Recent intelligence strongly suggested that Iraq had built facilities to produce banned weapons, that it was seeking to develop nuclear weapons, and that it was harboring terrorists from other countries. The president therefore urged the U.N. to demand that Iraq honor its obligations or face action by the members of that world body.

On November 8, the U.N. Security Council indeed declared that Iraq was in "material breach" of its obligations, and it warned of "serious consequences" if violations continued. In the months that followed, weapons inspections were resumed, but they did not account for stockpiles that had existed in 1991 and were never proven to be destroyed. To increase national and international support for the possibility of military action in Iraq, the president authorized the use of classified information gathered by U.S. and other intelligence agencies to show what Saddam Hussein was trying to hide. On December 19, Secretary of State Colin Powell presented the evidence for the United States' position before the United Nations.

Notwithstanding these efforts, President Bush was not able to convince the heads of many governments that regime change in Iraq was not merely desirable but imperative. In Europe, Tony Blair of Great Britain, Jose Maria Aznar of Spain, and Silvio Berlusconi of Italy fully supported the American position, but only Blair's government agreed to contribute troops to the effort. Junichiro Koizumi of Japan and John Howard of Australia likewise supported Mr. Bush, but Japan was constitutionally prevented from sending its military overseas, so only Australia could send troops to the Middle East. In the end, the United States did receive official approval from about fifty nations around the world for taking military action against Iraq if Saddam Hussein did not fully comply with the demands of the Security Council.

World opinion was still divided in early 2003 as the United States, Britain and Australia began deploying a force of more than three hundred thousand in the Middle East, preparing for the eventuality of war. Then, at a press conference in March, Mr. Bush reiterated his convictions about the imminent danger faced by the nation and the world:

> Saddam Hussein is a threat to our nation. September the 11th changed the strategic thinking, at least, as far as I was concerned, for how to protect our country. My job is to protect the American people. It used to be that we could think that you could contain a person like Saddam Hussein, that oceans would protect us from his type of terror. September the 11th should say to the American people that we're now a battlefield, that weapons of mass destruction in the hands of a terrorist organization could be deployed here at home.[5]

Mr. Bush was considering the possibility that Saddam Hussein could provide biological and chemical weapons to terrorists who would use them in America.

On March 17, when coalition forces surrounding Iraq were prepared to commence Operation Iraqi Freedom, the president issued a forty-eight-hour ultimatum to Saddam Hussein to willingly leave the country or face the consequences. Receiving no reply, two days later the invasion began.[6]

By April 15, major fighting was over and Iraq was liberated. Saddam's two sons and many other high-ranking military and Ba'ath party members were either captured or killed, and Saddam himself was taken into custody eight months later. President Bush repeatedly insisted that the United States had no desire to occupy the country for a long period of time, and that its primary interest was the political freedom of the Iraqi people from a brutal dictatorship and their economic recovery after years of terrible living conditions.

Disappointingly, no weapons of mass destruction were found among the ruins of war, and members of the Bush administration speculated that they might have been destroyed prior to the start of the invasion. But Mr. Bush was satisfied that the world was now a safer place, and this fact in itself had made the effort worthwhile.

The Just War Theory

War is an arduous undertaking, and as such it requires justification. The first Christian thinker to attempt to do so was Augustine of Hippo (354–430 AD), who wrote at a time when barbarian invasions were threatening the Roman Empire, which by that time was largely Christian. Augustine recognized that war is always evil, in that it causes suffering and death, not to mention destruction of property and disruption of society. At the same time, however, doing nothing about unjust aggression could cause even greater evil.

Christ had told his followers to love their enemies (Luke 6:27), but Augustine believed that a truly Christian soldier could fight to defend the innocent without holding hatred in his heart toward the aggressor. Indeed, a Christian who risked personal harm to defend the defenseless was laying down his life on behalf of others—the greatest act of love (John 15:13). The violence of war could be justified, therefore, if it were done with the proper spiritual disposition for the benefit of people who were being threatened with harm. In Augustine's mind, however, an individual Christian could not fight in personal self-defense without violating Jesus' precept to offer the wicked no resistance and turn the other cheek (Matthew 5:39).[7]

During the Middle Ages, Augustine's thoughts justifying war in certain circumstances were expanded into what has become known as the just war theory. Although different theologians offered differing criteria for when and how war might be justified, the following list is representative of that era.

First, the military action has to be instigated and conducted by a *legitimate authority*, such as a sovereign ruler. The purpose of this criterion was to prevent knights and vassals from fighting among themselves. Such behavior would undermine the peace within a country's borders, and unauthorized aggression would disturb the peace with a neighboring realm.

Second, there must be a *just reason* for undertaking military action. This could be the protection of innocent lives, but it could also be the recovery of seized territory or stolen property. A just cause had to be either self-defense or to redress some harm.

Third, war has to be initiated only as a *last resort*. Before declaring a war, all nonviolent means of settling the dispute would have to be tried first. The purpose of this criterion was to slow down the rush to war and to avoid the unavoidable evils of war if at all possible.

Fourth, once hostilities begin, a war must be fought with the *right intention*, that is, to redress wrongs and establish a just peace. Fighting for personal glory, to obtain the spoils of war, to humiliate the enemy, or to vent one's anger were not considered worthy Christian motives for going into battle. One indicator of whether or not a war was waged with right intentions was whether the defeated enemy was treated fairly or not.

Fifth, there must be some *proportionality* between the harm caused and the good accomplished by the war. Proportionality must be assessed before undertaking military action, and it needs be reviewed again after hostilities have ceased. A war that does more harm than good cannot be morally justified.

Sixth, there must be *discrimination* between combatants and noncombatants in the waging of hostilities. Only combatants may be deliberately attacked, and injury to noncombatants must be avoided. This principle was easier to observe when wars were fought by armies on fields of combat, but it was easily broken during sieges of cities and during cross-country campaigns.[8]

Christian moralists through the centuries have agreed that these principles are easier to state in theory than to apply in practice. If two countries each have something of a just cause against the other, rooted perhaps in long-standing grievances, would either one be morally justified in attacking the other? Who decides when diplomacy has been exhausted and war is a last resort? How far can bad motives vitiate good intentions before a war becomes immoral? How does one realistically measure the good versus the harm caused by war? Especially in modern warfare, how does one avoid killing and injuring innocent civilians? Some moralists would argue that few wars have been morally justifiable in retrospect, even those that were initially undertaken for a just cause and with the right intentions.[9] War has a way of bringing out the worst in people.

Almost all just war theorists contend that, for a military action to be morally just, all six criteria* must be met. A war that fails to meet even one of the criteria is not morally just. At the very least, such a war would be morally unjust in certain respects.

Christian Nonviolence

Although the just war tradition has an ancient pedigree, it is not as old as the Christian tradition of pacifism or nonviolence. Before the fourth century, when Christianity was first tolerated,

---

* Some versions of the theory add other criteria, such as a reasonable chance of success, avoiding banned weapons, and observing international conventions regarding conduct in warfare.

then approved, and finally made the state religion of the Roman Empire (in Augustine's day), Christians had a very different attitude toward fighting and killing in wars.[10]

Jesus did not teach anything specifically about war, or about serving in or fighting in the military, perhaps because for his listeners it was not an option. Judea, Galilee, and Samaria were occupied territories, and their inhabitants were not eligible to serve in the Roman army. Even if they were, Jews would never burn incense to the image of the emperor, which all soldiers had to do when they swore allegiance to the empire. John the Baptist's only advice to soldiers was that they be content with their pay (Luke 3:14). Jesus himself did not object to paying taxes to support the Roman Empire, and on one occasion he cured the servant of a Roman soldier (Matthew 22:15–22; Luke 17:1–10). Neither the New Testament epistles nor the Acts of the Apostles gives any hint of opposition to the Roman Empire and its imposition of colonial rule by military force.

The historical record is quite clear, however, that during the first three centuries, Christians considered military service as incompatible with their faith. Jesus had preached personal nonviolence, and his followers for centuries took this to mean that they could not engage in any profession in which they might endanger human life. Christians could not be pharmacists, for example, since pharmacists dispensed poisons as well as medicines. Nor could they be soldiers. They might remain in the army after having accepted Christ, but they had to quit the service before being baptized.[11]

By the time of Augustine, toward the end of the fourth century, the situation had changed. Christianity had become the religion of the state, and probably the majority of soldiers in the Roman army were baptized. At that point, it seemed irresponsible to leaders in the church to promote the Christian tradition of nonviolence if it resulted in innocent people being slain by invading barbarians. All the same, Augustine continued to hold to the tradition of personal nonviolence.

Jesus and Nonviolence

In his teaching and in his miracles, Jesus demonstrated that he wanted people to experience peace and joy in this life as well as in the next. When they did not understand how to live in right relationship with one another, he taught them. When they were experiencing physical or spiritual distress, he healed them. He lived and preached a message of inner and outer peace. His proclamation that "the kingdom of God is within you" can also be translated, "the kingdom of God is among you" (Luke 17:21).

Although on one occasion he took after merchants and money changers in the temple with a whip, none of the gospels say he hit anyone. In fact, three of the four gospels say nothing about a whip at all.[12] In itself, the story does not seem to condone violence; rather, it reveals Jesus' anger with the desecration of religion by commerce. Also, taken in its context, the story illustrates how even mildly violent behavior can produce an even more violent backlash—in this case, the arrest and crucifixion of Jesus at the instigation of the temple authorities.

Most of what Jesus said about violent behavior can be found in the Sermon on the Mount (Matthew 5:1–7:39) and in what is sometimes called the Sermon on the Plain (Luke 6:17–49). The words are so familiar to Christians that their revolutionary impact often goes unnoticed.

Here is Matthew's wording of Jesus' teaching:

> You have heard that it was said to those of ancient times, "You shall not murder"; and "whoever murders shall be liable to judgment." But I say to you that if you are angry with a brother or sister, you will be liable to judgment....
>
> You have heard that it was said, "An eye for an eye and a tooth for a tooth." But I say to you, do not resist an evildoer. But if anyone strikes you on the right cheek, turn the other also....
>
> You have heard that it was said, "You shall love your neighbor and hate your enemy." But I say to you, Love you enemies and pray for those who persecute you, so that you

may be children of your Father in heaven; for he makes his sun to rise on the evil and on the good, and sends rain on the righteous and on the unrighteous.

(Matthew 5:21–22; 38–39; 43–45)

Luke's wording seems to intensify the meaning of this teaching and focus it even more clearly:

> But I say to you that listen, Love your enemies, do good to those who hate you, bless those who curse you, pray for those who abuse you. If anyone strikes you on the cheek, offer the other also. . . .
>
> Do to others as you would have them do to you. If you love those who love you, what credit is that to you? For even sinners love those who love them. If you do good to those who do good to you, what credit is that to you? For even sinners do the same. If you lend to those from whom you hope to receive, what credit is that to you? Even sinners lend to sinners, to receive as much again. But love your enemies, do good, and lend, expecting nothing in return. Your reward will be great, and you will be children of the Most High; for he is kind to the ungrateful and the wicked. Be merciful, just as your Father is merciful.
>
> Do not judge, and you will not be judged; do not condemn, and you will not be condemned. Forgive, and you will be forgiven; give, and it will be given to you. A good measure, pressed down, shaken together, running over, will be put into your lap; for the measure you give will be the measure you get back.

(Luke 6:27–29; 31–36; 37–38)

It is important to remember that Jesus was not offering his disciples instructions on how to conduct themselves during a war. Rather, he was telling them how to treat those they regarded as enemies (or who regarded them as enemies) *before* they might be attacked. Even the admonition to turn the other cheek is not about being attacked but about being insulted. This is clearer in Matthew's gospel than in Luke's, since Matthew includes the detail of being hit on the *right* cheek—in other words, receiving a backhanded slap from someone who is angry and perhaps trying to provoke a fight.

The theme that runs through all of these gospel passages is not so much nonviolence as benevolence, a word that means good will. Willing the good of the other person short-circuits the temptation to anger. Willing the good of the other person makes it possible to stand up to insults without fighting back. Willing the good of the other person (even if that person is an enemy) enables ordinary people to act like children of God, to treat people evenhandedly just as God is evenhanded in distributing his gifts, and to be merciful in the same way that God is merciful.

Willing the good of the other person can disarm that person, defusing the impulse to violence. Refusing to be judgmental and condemnatory can open up a space in which the other can refrain from condemnatory judgments. Offering forgiveness enables the other to consider the possibility of offering forgiveness. This is what is meant by receiving back in good measure that which is given. And the opposite is also true, for not behaving in this way is sure to bring retaliation and violence.

Willing the good of the other is the beginning of *agâpé* love, and *agâpé* turned into action is what caring is all about. Caring about the well-being of enemies is what the love of enemies is about. It is not about liking them, but it is about regarding them as human beings, as God's children, and not demonizing them. It is about seeing them as sons and daughters, as fathers and mothers, with families and hopes and fears very much like our own. In the end, it is about treating other people, even enemies, the way we ourselves want to be treated. It is about caring for others and their well-being in such a way that war becomes the furthest thing from their minds.[13]

If we wait until the war begins, however, it is too late. Violence once started tends to escalate. Violence breeds violence, and once the murderous violence of war gets rolling, it does not stop until one side is vanquished or both sides are exhausted. But Jesus was not talking about war; he was talking about peace, and about what to do in order to prevent violence from starting and then escalating.

Still, there are no personal guarantees. Peter and Paul were killed for preaching the gospel. Abraham Lincoln was killed for emancipating slaves. Franz Jägerstetter was killed for refusing to fight in Hitler's army. Martin Luther King was killed for dreaming of an America without racial hatred. Robert Kennedy was killed for championing human rights. Oscar Romero was killed for protesting against the oppression of the poor. Jesus did not promise that those who follow his way would succeed. Jesus said only that those who lay down their lives for others would be doing God's will:

> Blessed are the peacemakers, for they will be called children of God. Blessed are those who are persecuted for righteousness' sake, for theirs is the kingdom of heaven.
> (Matthew 5:9–10)

Toward the end of his ministry, Jesus was beginning to be recognized by many as a prophet, and perhaps even as the messiah promised by God. As he was about to ride into Jerusalem on a donkey, crowds cheered him on, honored him by spreading their cloaks on the road before him, and shouted "Hosanna," which means "Save us please" or "Save us now" (Mark 11:9 and parallels). Matthew's version of the story notes that this event in the life of Jesus fulfilled the words of one of the Jewish prophets:

> Rejoice greatly, O Daughter of Zion!
> Shout, Daughter of Jerusalem!
> See, your king comes to you;
> righteous and having salvation,
> gentle and riding on a donkey,
> on a colt, the foal of a donkey.
> (Zechariah 9:9 NIV)[14]

What kind of king was this? What kind of salvation did he bring? The next verse of Zechariah's prophecy makes it clear:

> He will take away the chariots from Ephraim
> and the war-horses from Jerusalem,

> and the battle bow will be broken.
> He will proclaim peace to the nations.
> His rule will extend from sea to sea
> And from the River to the ends of the earth.
> (9:10 NIV)[15]

If the generation of Christians in which the gospels were written understood that Jesus Christ was—and is—the prince of peace, then it stood to reason that they would be committed to nonviolence as a way of life.

War and Nonviolence in the Old Testament

People who regard war as a divinely approved activity generally appeal to images of God in the Old Testament fighting for the Israelites against their enemies. With such images in mind, it is easy to believe that God will be on our side when we go into battle.

Taking the Old Testament as a whole, however, we discover that God supported war mainly at the beginning of Israel's history. God promised the land of Canaan to the sons of Israel, and so he fought to give these former slaves a homeland. In one sense, the underlying message here is that God supports the weak and favors the underprivileged. Moreover, the moral perspective of these stories is rather simple: the Israelites are the good guys and all their opponents are the bad guys. Still, if the stories recount actual events, there is no denying that the devastation was systematic and the slaughter was sometimes grisly.[16]

As biblical history moves from the era of conquest and settlement to the era of the united monarchy (under Saul, David and Solomon), the picture changes and becomes somewhat more complex. Remember that God was not pleased with the Israelites' request for a human king because in the previous era the people had recognized God alone as their ruler. In the First Book of Samuel, Saul fights his battles, which God sometimes blesses and sometimes does not. The young David has God on his side when he fights Goliath, and David prays to God before going into battle, but God is not presented as participating in these military campaigns the way he was in the Exodus from Egypt.[17]

The Second Book of Samuel opens with some factional fighting between David's supporters and those loyal to the sons of Saul, and God is not mentioned in these descriptions of skirmishes and intrigues. In Chapter 5, God's appearance is limited to some advice he gives to David before a crucial battle. Chapter 8 lists some of David's wars and notes that in each of them, God gave him victory. Chapters 10 through 12 recount David's successful campaigns against the Ammonites, but God is not mentioned in connection with them.

The books of 1 and 2 Kings move into the period of the divided monarchy and the eventual downfall of both the northern and southern kingdoms. In this part of the Bible, God is mentioned less and less in connection with war. Prophets speaking for God occasionally give military advice, but God's assistance does not go beyond that. God favors various kings on both sides when they are good, and he punishes them with defeat when they are bad. Eventually, both Israel and Judah do what is displeasing to God, and God's judgment against them is carried out by the Assyrians and Babylonians.[18]

The two books of Chronicles recount the history of Israel and Judah from a somewhat different perspective, having been written after the return from the Babylonian exile. Much of the history in the books of Samuel and Kings is recapitulated, and in the brief sections devoted to wars God is described as giving victory to those who had faith in him.[19] After this, war is treated in the prophetic books rather negatively, as a scourge of God punishing Israel and Judah for their sins. The prophets occasionally assert the futility of military defense against enemies that are the unwitting instruments of God's justice.[20]

The Old Testament's attitude toward war is therefore not uniform but mixed. God is portrayed as using war first to establish Israel, then to protect it, and finally to destroy it. War is sometimes described almost mythically as something instigated and fought by God, while at other times it is described in rather secular terms, with human beings praying for God's assistance before the battle and thanking him for victory afterwards, much as they do today. Human beings do not know which side God is on, however, until the battle is over. Moreover, belief in God's approval is no guarantee of God's protection, for in the Bible God supports the side of justice, not the side of strength.

Being as realistic as it is, the Bible shows both the gory and the glory sides of war. If nothing else, the Old Testament's treatment of war is a tribute to biblical faith in the omnipotence of God: no matter what happens, God has a hand in it. But the Old Testament also contains the seeds of a much less violent approach to dealing with enemies.[21]

Toward the end of the story of Joseph and his brothers, they are afraid that he will exact revenge on them for having sold him into bondage years before, so they throw themselves at his mercy and offer to be his slaves if he will let them live. Joseph, however, reassures them that that he has no desire for retribution. "Even though you intended to do harm to me, God intended it for good" (Genesis 50:20). By reframing the crime they committed against him in terms of God's providence, Joseph is able to act benevolently toward his kidnappers and preserve the family that once turned against him, instead of acting in strict justice and ruining that family—which is his own extended family.

In the story of Saul and David, the aging king attempts to kill his future replacement more than once. Then David has an opportunity to kill Saul while he is sleeping, but he refrains from doing so not once but twice, and Saul is persuaded to have a change of heart. By demonstrating mercy, David is able to inspire restraint in his enemy.[22]

In a somewhat magical story, the prophet Elisha, with God's help, leads an enemy army into a trap. When the Aramaeans are surrounded by Israelites, the king asks the prophet whether he should have the invaders killed. On the contrary, Elisha says that they should be treated decently and given something to eat. So the king orders a feast for the captives, and then sends them back across the border. "And the Aramaeans no longer came raiding into the land of Israel" (2 Kings 6:23). One act of benevolence provoked another.

In the book of Proverbs, we catch another glimpse of this very different ethic for the treatment of enemies:

> Do not say, "I will do to others as they have done to me; I will pay them back for what they have done...."
>
> If your enemies are hungry, give them bread to eat; and if they are thirsty, give them water to drink; for you will heap coals of fire on their heads, and the Lord will reward you.
> (Proverbs 24:29; 25:21–22)

After his conversion to Christianity, Paul the former Pharisee reached into his Jewish heritage and pulled out this piece of wisdom when writing his letter to the Romans. Apparently he thought it was very consonant with the gospel of Christ:

> Bless those who persecute you; bless and do not curse them. ... Do not repay anyone evil for evil, but take thought for what is noble in the sight of all. If it is possible, so far as it depends on you, live peaceably with all. Beloved, never avenge yourselves, but leave room for the wrath of God, for it is written, "Vengeance is mine, I will repay, says the Lord." No, "if your enemies are hungry, feed them; if they are thirsty, give them something to drink; for by doing this you will heap burning coals on their heads." Do not be overcome by evil, but overcome evil with good.
> (Romans 12:14–21)

The Biblical Concept of Peace

Americans and Westerners in general tend to think of peace as tranquility, as the opposite of war and the absence of war. There are very few places in the Bible, however, where the Hebrew word *shalom* has this rather restricted meaning. One of the more famous is in the book of Ecclesiastes, which begins, "For everything there is a season, and a time for every matter under heaven," and which concludes, "a time to love, and a time to hate; a time for war and a time for peace" (3:1–8).[23]

The root meaning of *shalom*, which occurs more than 350 times in the Hebrew Bible, is wholeness or completeness in something that has various components, such as a community or society. In this respect, *shalom* is less a matter of public tranquility than it is a matter of public harmony or cooperation, with the various segments of society making their contributions to the common good. *Shalom* of the body, or health, is a matter of wholeness or wellness in which the parts and functions of the body are all working together to produce a state of energetic well-being. *Shalom* of the soul is not so much peace of mind as a balance among the needs and satisfactions, freedoms, and responsibilities of everyday life.[24]

If this is the case, then a nation may not be at war, yet not experiencing *shalom*, either. Where the young do not respect the old, there is no *shalom*. Where the powerful do not protect the weak, there is no *shalom*. Where the wealthy do not help the poor, there is no *shalom*. Where the merchants are not honest, there is no *shalom*. Where the judges are not fair, there is no *shalom*. Where the rulers do not practice justice, there is no *shalom*.

The absence of peace in this sense is why the prophet could cry, "*Shalom, shalom*, there is no *shalom*," even though the country was not at war.[25] When people are oppressed, when they suffer from injustice, when their needs are neglected by those in power, there may be peace but not *shalom*.[26]

Peace in the biblical sense is the purpose of the Torah, the Law of Moses. The Law was God's great gift to the Israelites because it taught them how to live in right relationship with God and with one another. Indeed, the Hebrew word *Torah*, although usually translated as Law, means something more like a guide for living or a way of life. Without a guide for living, life can be chaotic and uncertain. Without a way of life, living can be aimless and meaningless.

Even the Ten Commandments, a rather thin slice of the entire Law, were aimed at creating and maintaining right relationships between God and people on the one hand, and between people and their neighbors on the other. At the very minimum, people could not kill or steal or lie or covet if they were going to live in harmony and experience *shalom*. Truth, justice, and respect for other people's dignity and property are the necessary foundations for a satisfying life.

This is why Jesus said that the whole Law could be summed up in but two commandments, to love God completely and to love one's neighbor as oneself. And since love in this case is *agâpé*, the commandment to love one's neighbor means to care about and take care of others. In other words, treat others the way you want to be treated. It is that simple—and that difficult—to achieve *shalom*.

Jesus in John's Gospel speaks of peace in his final discourse to his disciples: "Peace I leave with you; my peace I give to you" (14:27). And how are his disciples to experience this *shalom*? "I give you a new commandment, that you love one another. Just as I have loved you, you also should love one another" (13:34). In other words, caring about and caring for others, following the Golden Rule, results in *shalom*.

The peace proclaimed by the prophet Zechariah, then, and the peace proclaimed by the messiah, is not the absence of war but *shalom*, the fulfilling life that is found in a caring community, in a harmonious and well-ordered society. Jesus as the prince of peace is not the ruler of placidness, of tranquility, of nothing bad happening. Jesus as the prince of *shalom* is the Lord of love, of caring, of giving one's life in service to others. To accept Jesus as Lord is to accept his rule of loving others the way he did.

The question Christians must ask today is therefore this: Is war the way to *shalom* in our world after the events of September 11, 2001?

The War on Terrorism

George W. Bush interpreted the events of September 11 as attacks on the United States and therefore as acts of war. In response, the president declared a war on terrorism and Congress concurred, authorizing military action in Afghanistan and in Iraq.

Such a response is understandable. It is a natural human response to treat others the way they have treated us. It is the way that nations have always responded when attacked. It is the historical reason for and the philosophical basis of the just war theory. It is the way that Christian countries have always responded when they felt threatened.

But is it the way that Jesus would have responded? And is it the way that Jesus would have wanted his followers to respond? More pragmatically, is it a way that will lead to peace in the sense of *shalom*?

The attacks on New York City and Washington on September 11 were blamed on terrorists, on evil men, on bad guys. When Mr. Bush asked rhetorically, "Why do they hate us?" he answered his own question by stating,

> They hate our freedoms—our freedom of religion, our freedom of speech, our freedom to vote and assemble and disagree with each other.[27]

But if they hate our freedoms, why did they not target the Statue of Liberty instead of the World Trade Center? And if they hate our form of government, why did they not crash into the U.S. Capitol instead of the Pentagon? Perhaps there were other motives—motives rooted in the recent history of the Middle East.

The War in the Persian Gulf (1991)

When the Bush administration was making its case to go to war against Iraq in 2003, it repeated and repeated a series of accusations against the regime of Saddam Hussein. Some of these go back to before September 2001, and even to before 1990:

- It is a brutal dictatorship.
- It suppresses human rights, forbids freedom of speech, and tortures prisoners.

- It has used chemical weapons against its own people and against neighboring countries.
- It does not provide the Iraqi people with basic human services.

All of these accusations were true. But they did not give the whole picture. Here are some of the missing pieces:

- The 1963 coup that enabled Saddam Hussein to rise to power was supported by and possibly even planned by the U.S. Central Intelligence Agency. During the Cold War, the CIA engineered the overthrow of many governments that were perceived as not being sufficiently anti-communist, and Iraq's was one of them.[28]
- The suppression of human rights under the Iraqi regime of Saddam Hussein from 1979 to 1990 was well known to the United States government, which quietly ignored what was being done to the Iraqi people because the dictatorship provided a stable government that guaranteed the flow of Iraqi oil to the West.[29]
- During the Iran-Iraq war of 1980–1988, the United States clandestinely supported Saddam's regime, especially after 1982, when it appeared that Iran might win the war and establish an Islamic government in Iraq. Vice President George H. W. Bush, a former director of the CIA, was involved in providing this support, as was Donald Rumsfeld.[30]
- The support included conventional weapons, ingredients for chemical and biological weapons, dual-use (civilian and military) equipment, and military intelligence that would be of use to Iraqi commanders in the war against Iran. No money or arms were supplied directly by the United States. Everything was provided by third parties, paid for with loans to Iraq from other

countries that were guaranteed by the U.S. government.[31]

- After the war was over, Saddam turned his chemical and biological weapons against the Kurds in northern Iraq, who had long been agitating for independence. Most of the Kurdish massacres occurred when Iraq was still an ally of the United States, which only mildly protested the atrocities.[32]

Having been so strongly supported by the U.S. and Europe through over a decade of aggression and oppression, it is quite possible the Saddam Hussein felt that the West would not object if he invaded Kuwait to settle some long-standing grievances with that country.[33] As it turned out, he was mistaken, despite what Saddam took to be assurances from U.S. Ambassador April Glaspie that the United States considered the dispute between the two countries to be an Arab-to-Arab matter that would not arouse American concern.[34] On August 2, 1990, Iraqi forces invaded Kuwait, quickly overcoming that country's relatively light defenses.

An international backlash ensued, led by President George H.W. Bush and Prime Minister Margaret Thatcher. The United Nations passed a series of resolutions condemning the invasion, imposing economic and trade sanctions on Iraq, and ordering Saddam to withdraw his troops by January 15, 1991. In an effort to secure Saudi Arabia's support for an attack to be launched from its territory, U.S. officials met with members of the royal family and displayed satellite photographs ostensibly showing Iraqi troops massed along the Saudi border and ready to continue the invasion into that country. These classified photographs were never made public, and other satellite photographs of the same area taken at the same time revealed no military activity at all along the Iraq-Saudi border.[35]

Reportedly, these classified photographs were the reason why the Saudi royal family admitted non-Muslim troops to use its country as a staging area from which to launch an attack against

Iraqi forces in Kuwait. One of the religious extremists who objected strongly to the presence of "infidels" so close to Muslim holy places was Osama bin Laden.[36]

The United States launched an air war against Iraq one day after the U.N. deadline, and on February 24 the ground assault began. U.S.-led coalition forces crashed through the Iraqi line of defense, and on February 26 Iraqi troops began pulling out of Kuwait. The highway from Kuwait to Basra, Iraq, was bombed, leaving a long convoy of over two thousand vehicles unable to move. Over the course of a few hours, U.S. warplanes shot at and dropped incendiary bombs on the immobilized troops, burning to death tens of thousands of soldiers as well as Iraqi civilians attempting to flee from Kuwait.[37] The next day, the United States declared that Kuwait had been liberated, and Saddam Hussein was left in power.

The bombardment of Iraq reduced most of Iraq's infrastructure to rubble. Not only were military sites targeted, but also roads, railways, bridges, factories, oil refineries, power-generating plants, electric power lines, water pumping stations, and sewage-treatment plants. While some of these targets had military value, many were far from Kuwait or Baghdad and would not have been able to help the Iraqi army in what was expected to be a short war. Some theories suggest that the extensive destruction was designed to force Saddam Hussein to appeal for foreign aid after the war; others suggest that the purpose was to weaken Saddam and encourage his overthrow by the Iraqi people.[38]

Much of this infrastructure was not fully restored in the years following the Gulf War, partly because the U.N. sanctions imposed before the war were never lifted. Although other countries favored relaxing the ban on imports, the United States and Great Britain insisted that Saddam Hussein should not be allowed to rebuild his army or produce weapons of mass destruction. Lack of food and clean drinking water, poor sanitation, and virtually no medicine led to a sharp increase in civilian deaths in the years following the war—an estimated 750 thousand people, half of whom were children who died of easily curable diseases such as malnutrition and diarrhea.[39] When Madeleine Albright, Secretary of State during the Clinton administration, was asked about this high cost of continuing the sanctions against Iraq, she said, "I think this is a very hard choice, but the price—we think the price is worth it."[40]

In retrospect, it has been estimated that the human cost of sanctions in Iraq was approximately a World Trade Center's worth of lives every month for twelve years prior to September 2001.[41] The human cost of the war and the sanctions was one of the reasons why many professional theologians judged the Persian Gulf War to have been unjust.[42] In addition, the suffering caused to the people of Iraq, as well as the suffering caused by decades of American support for repressive regimes in the Middle East despite their violations of human rights, may be some of the reasons "why they hate us."

The War in Afghanistan (2002)

Given the atrocities that provoked the U.S. military response against Al Qaeda, and given the way that the war was conducted, it is possible that the coalition operation in Afghanistan could be considered a just war. The war had a just cause, which was self-defense against a terrorist organization that had hijacked planes and crashed them into American buildings (not to mention earlier terrorist attacks attributed to Al Qaeda in other countries) and that was currently based in Afghanistan.[43] The military action was conducted by a legitimate authority, namely, the United States and a large coalition of countries backed with resolutions passed by the United Nations. Diplomatic attempts to get the Taliban government to hand over the Al Qaeda leadership and destroy its training camps had proven to be futile. The war was fought with the right intention of bringing terrorists to justice, although moral questions can be raised about the inhumane treatment of war prisoners. Coalition forces made a good effort to avoid civilian casualties, thus fulfilling the criterion of discrimination, although it is estimated that the bombing campaign nonetheless took the lives of 1,000–1,300 noncombatants.⁴⁴ With the war having been relatively brief, and with the United States contributing to repairing the economic and political structure of Afghanistan after the war, it appears that the cost of the war could be justified.

Nonetheless, disturbing questions can be asked.

One purpose of the war was to bring to justice Osama bin Laden and other Al Qaeda leaders, but bin Laden was never captured, and recordings purportedly made by him are still broadcast periodically by Muslim media. Since this terrorist organization is very decentralized (none of the September 11 hijackers came from Afghanistan, for example), is it possible that the military victory in Afghanistan has aroused Al Qaeda's passion for revenge and increased the likelihood of future terrorist attacks in the United States and against Americans overseas? Those opposed to U.S. dominance of the Middle East can now point to martyred comrades, tortured prisoners of war, dead and maimed civilians, and unfulfilled promises of economic assistance when they seek to recruit new suicide bombers to their cause.⁴⁵

President Bush cited the Taliban's repression of religious freedom and its oppression of women as part of the justification for going to war, but the U.S. government was silent for years about these issues when it was lobbying for an oil pipeline to be built from Central Asia through Afghanistan rather than through Iran. Moreover, when Afghanistan had been under Soviet influence, the CIA had taken advantage of the religious zeal of Muslim fundamentalists, training not only the Taliban but also foreign *mujahideen* (holy warriors) such as Osama bin Laden in the use of terrorist tactics against the Soviet army. After the collapse of the Soviet Union and the departure of its troops in 1989, however, the Afghan people were left at the mercy of competing factions, of which the Taliban eventually emerged as the strongest. How might things have turned out differently if the United States had pursued humanitarian objectives instead of military and economic objectives in Afghanistan during the decades prior to September 2001?⁴⁶

Following the day of four terrorist attacks on American soil, the world poured out its sympathy for the victims and their families, and also for all citizens of the United States who were experiencing grief and shock over the horrific disaster. When President Bush declared his war on terrorism, that sympathy turned into support for military action in Afghanistan in most countries but not all, particularly not in all Muslim countries. Then, when the war on terrorism led to the terrorizing of Muslims and Arabs in the United States, to the detention of immigrants and the rejection of refugees from around the world, and to threats against countries that did not support America's new call for war against Iraq, the world's sympathy dissipated into sadness. Why did the United States insist on responding to violence with violence? Why did the American government refuse to consider other courses of action that would lead to fewer deaths? Why was the U.S. president so adamant that the war on terrorism had to be pursued on the same level on which it had started?[47]

What if the events of September 11, 2001, had been viewed not as acts of war but as crimes against humanity? What if they had been interpreted not as vicious acts of evil but as deranged acts of distorted thinking? What if they had been responded to not with calls for war but a call for a summit meeting on the causes of terrorism around the world?

Such a reframing of the picture would not eliminate the need for police action against the perpetrators of such crimes. Nor would it deny the need for greater security measures in a world in which a few can cause great harm to many. But it would suggest that the way to global peace is through some other route than perpetual war.

President Bush's advisors, however, do not see it that way. They see America today as analogous to Rome in the ancient world—a superpower with no rival, able to maintain peace by force wherever it wants to impose its will. They believe that world peace can be achieved by "a military that is strong and able to meet both present and future challenges; a foreign policy that boldly and purposefully promotes American principles abroad; and national leadership that accepts the United States' global responsibilities."[48] They regard the Empire's *Pax Romana* (Roman peace) as the model for a future *Pax Americana* maintained by military strength.[49]

The Project for the New American Century, a conservative policy institute, envisages the twenty-first century as one dominated by U.S. military strength, much as the ancient Mediterranean world was dominated by Roman military strength. The Rome that they hold up as their model, however, is not the Christian Rome of Constantine and Augustine, fending off hostile attacks from barbarian invaders. Rather it is pagan Rome that they have in mind, Rome in its expansive and military phase, able to "fight and decisively win multiple, simultaneous major theater wars," and able to "perform the 'constabulary' duties associated with shaping the security environment in critical regions."[50] In the first century, the Roman army was able to fight multiple wars and win decisive battles. The Roman army also served as police or constables in the countries that they kept at peace by force of arms, as they did in ancient Galilee and Judea.

Such is the thinking that led to the appointments of Herod and Pilate as proxy rulers in Palestine, to the support of Sadducees and Pharisees as pliant leaders of the Jews, and ultimately to the crucifixion of Jesus on a Roman cross.

To impose peace on the ancient world, the Roman Empire was proactive, stamping out resistance wherever it appeared, and before it could get too strong. In the same way today, according to these global strategists, the United States must recognize "that it is important to shape circumstances before crises emerge, and to meet threats before they become dire."[51]

Such is the thinking that led the United States into a second war against Iraq.

The War in Iraq (2003)

Although the Bush administration attempted to portray its proposed new offensive against Saddam Hussein as a defensive action, in the end it had to admit that such a strategy was preventative or preemptive in nature. American and British intelligence agencies reported that Iraq still had stockpiles of chemical and biological weapons that had escaped detection by U.N. inspectors, that it had developed clever means of producing and concealing new weapons of mass destruction, that it was trying to restart its nuclear weapons programs, and that it had close contacts with terrorist organizations such as Al Qaeda. As a result, both governments were convinced that Iraq posed an imminent threat to its neighbors in the Middle East and an ultimate threat to Europe and the United States.[52]

Looking first at the moral argument for war, there is unfortunately no place for a preemptive war among the criteria of the just war theory. Many moralists would allow that a nation could justifiably defend itself against an imminent attack, provided that offensive military action has begun or is at least clearly intended. From this perspective, in December 1941 the United States would have been morally justified to intercept the Japanese naval convoy even before its planes had had a chance to bomb Pearl Harbor. In 2003, however, the evidence that Iraq was about to invade any of its neighbors was not convincing to most of the world's governments, which is why fewer than a third of them supported the call to war by President Bush and Prime Minister Blair.[53] Millions of people around the world were likewise unconvinced, and the global protests against the proposed war were the largest in human history.[54]

Critics of the Bush and Blair administrations have charged that the president and the prime minister deliberately lied about the dangers posed by Saddam in order to obtain a "regime change" in Iraq. This is not necessarily the case, for it may also be that the two leaders mistook intelligence for facts. Intelligence is information obtained from spies and other sources of surveillance, interpreted in such a way as to provide a coherent picture of a situation. Intelligence, in other words, is made up of bits and pieces of data arranged in a way that makes sense to the intelligence professionals and policy-makers of a country. It is quite possible that both Bush and Blair, afraid of what Saddam might be able to do if he joined forces with international terrorists, took the intelligence that they received and regarded it as factual when in fact it was not.[55] Although they may not have deliberately intended to deceive, they may have carelessly or even unwittingly exaggerated information from spies and other sources in order to claim that war was necessary and justified.*

Even given this benign interpretation of the U.S. and British claims about the threat that Iraq posed to the world, the recent war cannot be morally justified, for moral justification has to rest on facts, not beliefs and suspicions. If this were not so, then any country that harbored beliefs or suspicions about the sinister intentions of another country would be justified in launching a preemptive strike against that country—which even the most loose interpretation of the just war theory would never allow. Regardless of the president's intentions, the facts were not on his side, and therefore going to war against Iraq was not morally justifiable.[56]

One has reason for suspecting that Vice President Cheney, Secretary of Defense Rumsfeld, and Deputy Secretary of Defense Wolfowitz interpreted the intelligence data as favoring war is that, as members of The Project for the New American Century, they had been considering the possibility of action against Iraq even before the 2000 presidential election.[57] In the aftermath of September 11, they found what they were prepared to find in U.S. intelligence reports, and they saw what they believed they should see going on in Iraq, regardless of what was said by the U.N. weapons inspectors and other sources of information that disagreed with the conclusions that they wanted to reach.[58]

To be sure, it does not help the president's credibility that he supported his call to war by citing Iraq's aggression against its

---

* The most obvious proof that the reports of Saddam's weapons of mass destruction were false (whether deliberately or mistakenly) is that no weapons were ever found.

neighbors and its use of chemical weapons on its own people. Both of those violations of international law occurred when the United States was an ally of Saddam Hussein and in fact provided him with the means to develop weapons of mass destruction.[59] Nor does it help that Mr. Bush justified the invasion of Iraq by accusing Saddam's undemocratic regime of suppressing human rights, jailing people without trial, torturing prisoners, and assassinating political opponents. All of these crimes are regularly committed by other countries with which the United States continues to maintain friendly relations.[60] Moreover, the claims that Iraq was capable of launching weapons of mass destruction within forty-five minutes, and that it had been trying to purchase uranium from Africa, have both been discredited.[61] In the end, all of President Bush's reasons for overthrowing Saddam Hussein by military force have proven to be mistaken, questionable, or misleading.[62]

Looking finally at what happened in light of the teaching of Jesus and the Christian tradition of nonviolence, it is obvious that the war violated the literal meaning of many gospel passages concerning the love of enemies and treating others as oneself, and that it ran counter to the deliberate pacifism of the early Christian centuries. Even though many Christians supported the war because they believed the government's claims to be true, if the New Testament reveals how God wants people to behave, then many Christians behaved badly. And even though American forces fought for what they believed to be a just cause, they apparently did not stop to consider the possibility that God's way to peace is not through violence but through love, as Jesus taught.

In the months since the official ending of the war on May 1, 2003, more Americans have died than were killed during the six weeks of combat. Almost every day, people in the U.S. read and hear about soldiers and civilians being bombed or shot, leading some to wonder what is going wrong.

Perhaps what is going on are the unintended consequences of violence, the effects that occur after a military action, when people sit back and assess what it did to them and their loved ones. It is clear that the attacks against U.S. and U.N. personnel are not random acts of violence but are organized assaults, whether perpetrated by Iraqis loyal to Saddam or by "holy warriors" from other countries. It is also equally clear to military strategists that guerilla warfare of this sort cannot be carried on without at least tacit support from many civilians. But why would ordinary Iraqis hate their liberators?

Undoubtedly, some of them were better off under the old regime, and they resent the loss of their privileges. Perhaps, too, some of them were so brainwashed by Saddam's anti-American propaganda that they still believe it to be true. But, perhaps as well, they lost sons among the tens of thousands of Iraqi men and boys killed in the first Gulf war. Or perhaps they lost parents and children among the more than half million who died prematurely during the twelve years of sanctions, which took a disproportionate share of the weak, the elderly, and the very young. Or perhaps they saw friends and relatives fall among the more than thirty thousand soldiers and civilians killed and injured in the most recent invasion of their country.[63] People who are grieving sometimes act emotionally and behave in ways that are not in their best interests. Sometimes they even want revenge.

Might this be one of the reasons that God sent his Son to tell human beings not to hate their enemies?

Responding to the Threat of Terrorism

It may be that for centuries Christians could afford to ignore the teachings of Jesus and hate their enemies. It may also be that this is no longer the case.

With electronic communication as quick as it is, with international travel as easy as it is, the world has become a global village. The rules of war, when war was fought "over there," far away from the home front, seem no longer to apply.

The Law of Moses limited revenge within Israel to an eye for an eye and a tooth for a tooth. The reason for this, as we saw in the last chapter, was to prevent a small society such as Israel from being torn apart by revenge killings.

The world is now as small as Israel was in Jesus' day. But revenge and retaliation cannot be prevented today even in as small a country as Israel.[64] How then can the United States, with four thousand miles of border on land and five thousand miles of waterfront, protect itself from terrorism? And what will the global village look like in ten or twenty years, when the war on terrorism has escalated on both sides, with no end in sight?

The current administration has chosen one strategy, which seems to be far from Christian. It has chosen a defensive strategy, what one might call a very human strategy or a natural strategy. It is what the Bible calls carnal, or of the flesh, or human, or worldly, or sinful, depending on which translation you read.[65] As a result, it has incarcerated innocent foreigners, it has turned away refugees, it has violated people's rights, and it has gone to war not once but twice. Are these things that Jesus would do? Are these actions that he would endorse?

Perhaps the world has grown too small for the traditional strategies. Perhaps we have lived beyond the time when normal human reactions to violence can save us. Perhaps we have arrived at the point where we can no longer protect ourselves by defending ourselves. Perhaps it is time to listen to Jesus and take the offensive in transforming the world.[66]

If we do not demonize our enemies but see them as human beings (sinful human beings, granted, but still human beings with parents and friends and perhaps even children of their own), it begins to become possible to love our enemies. Remember that the word *love* here does not mean to like or to have affection for but to care about and to take care of, for it translates the Greek word *agápe*. One way that Jesus spoke about love of neighbor was simply to treat others the way we would like to be treated.

The September 11 terrorists came from four countries (Saudi Arabia, Egypt, United Arab Emirates, and Lebanon) where many people are deprived of human rights and live without human dignity. Those nineteen extremists believed that they were acting on behalf of Arabs and Muslims who have been wronged—as they see it—by the richest and most powerful country in the world, the United States of America. How they believe America has done wrong is at this point less important than what America could do today that is so right that even its enemies would have to agree that it is doing what is right.

The majority of Arabs and Muslims in the world today are poor—including those who live in oil-producing countries. They have inadequate health care, and many people (especially children) die from diseases that are easily preventable. They have little education, and many of those who do graduate from school cannot do anything with what they have learned. Many of their young people feel deprived when they look around them and compare it to what they see on American television. Many of them discover that they have no future when they get out of school and cannot find a job. They know about the United States and they wonder why the richest country in the world does so little to alleviate the suffering in the world, especially their suffering and that of those around them.

It is the young who are recruited into the Taliban, into Al Qaeda, into Hamas, into Islamic Jihad, and into all of the extremist organizations that see no alternative to the situation of Muslims around the world other than violence against the wealthy and powerful countries that they perceive as oppressive, or at the very least as indifferent to their plight. It is the young who get indoctrinated in the religious schools of these organizations because Arab countries do not provide their children with public education. It is the young, of whom there will be an endless supply into the foreseeable future, for the birth rates in poor countries are always high.

Islam, like Judaism and Christianity, recognizes the virtues of justice and compassion. Even Islamists—as Muslim extremists are sometimes called—have studied enough of the Koran to know that Allah smiles on those who act fairly, and that Allah blesses those who perform works of mercy.* Even Islamists would have to acknowledge that America is not completely evil if it saw the U.S. government doing good in the Muslim world and elsewhere.

What if the United States (and others in a new "coalition of the willing") embarked on a worldwide program to provide health care to the poor? What if the United States worked visibly to alleviate hunger and malnutrition in all countries? What if the United States sponsored educational opportunities for children and adolescents around the world?

What if the United States stopped reacting like a Texas Ranger and started acting like Jesus?

Conclusion

In business ethics it is sometimes called enlightened self-interest. The idea is to help people so that they will like your company and perhaps buy your product. Bill Gates practices enlightened self-interest when he gives away millions of dollars worth of computers and Microsoft software to schools around the United States and around the world.[67] He knows that if children are familiar with his company's software, they will be more likely to purchase Microsoft products when they are adults.

Henry Ford practiced enlightened self-interest when he opened the first assembly-line factory for the Model T and immediately doubled the salary of his plant workers. The purpose, he admitted, was to pay them enough money so that they could buy the cars that they were building.

The United States practiced enlightened self-interest when, in the aftermath of the Second World War it helped Germany and the rest of Europe rebuild their economies. The U.S. did not want Germany to relapse into the kind of depression that led to the rise of Nazism, it wanted to prevent war-torn Europe from turning to

---

* The Arabic word *Allah* is not the name of God but the word for God.

Communism and the Soviet Union to solve its economic ills,* and it was looking to Europe as a market for American products as millions of U.S. servicemen returned home looking for jobs in business and manufacturing. The Marshall Plan was both a courageous act of national benevolence and an ingenious application of enlightened self-interest.[68]

One reason why enlightened self-interest works is because it is a large-scale application of the Golden Rule. Granted, such behavior is always a risk because acting kindly toward others is no guarantee that they will return the favor. The kids who use Microsoft in school might buy Apple products when they get older. The Ford employees could have bought Stanley Steamers with their extra wages. And Europe could have bought cheaper products than those made in the U.S.A. But because human nature is designed to respond with gratitude to benevolence, the odds were high that taking the risks would pay off.

Jesus understood how human nature responds to kindness.

Publicans or tax collectors were among the most despised people in first-century Israel. Not only did they take people's money, as tax collectors still do today, but they took money away from Jews and gave it to the government that had conquered Palestine and held it under military occupation—the Roman Empire. Publicans were therefore collaborators with the enemy and traitors to their country. Moreover, publicans did not earn their money by getting a salary from the Roman government. Rather, they were told how much money they had to turn in to the government, but they were then free to collect as much as they wanted. Publicans made their money, therefore, by extorting as much as they could from the people in their districts and by pocketing everything that they did not have to give to Rome. No wonder they were hated by ordinary Jews in Jesus' time.

Luke (19:1–10) reports that, one day when traveling to Jericho, Jesus encountered a tax collector named Zacchaeus who wanted

---

* At that time, the Soviet Union was one of the allies that helped defeat Nazi Germany.

to see the teacher and healer from Nazareth that everyone was talking about. Without worrying that the self-righteous in the crowd might be scandalized by his behavior, Jesus approached Zacchaeus and said he would like to stay at his house while visiting that city. This was a great honor that no self-respecting Jew had ever before paid this wealthy social outcast, and Zacchaeus was overcome with gratitude. On the spot, the tax collector said he would give half his money to the poor and generously pay back anybody he had cheated. Jesus responded by saying, "Today salvation has come to this house." In other words, by deciding to be honest, Zacchaeus was saved from the evil way he had been living.

Jesus' apparent gamble in showing kindness to a sinner paid off.

Notes

[1] More thorough background information on Saddam Hussein and the Middle East is available from the Wikipedia, an Internet encyclopedia available at www.wikipedia.org. Service from this ever-expanding project in information sharing is free, but you must log in if you want to discuss or edit articles. For additional information about Iraq since 1963, type "Saddam Hussein" in the Search line.

[2] See President Bush's speech to the United Nations September 12, 2002, available at www.bushcountry.org. Click on Bush Speeches in the left margin, then scroll down to the date.

[3] For background on Afghanistan and the Taliban, go to the Afghan Info Center at www.afghan-info.com, which does not seem to have been updated since the war but which is still online, supported by Afghan expatriates. See also the 1998 special report of the United States Institute of Peace, "The Taliban and Afghanistan: Implications for Regional Security and Options for International Action," available at www.usip.org by typing "Taliban and Afghanistan" in the Search line. Also, A. J. Abdurasulov, "Civil War in Afghanistan," a research paper

written by an international student in the United States, available at http://jalik.host.net.kg/afghanistan.htm.

[4] The most thorough and easily available summary of the war is available from the online Wikipedia, mentioned above. Look for the article titled "U.S. Invasion of Afghanistan."

[5] See "President George Bush Discusses Iraq in National Press Conference," available at www.whitehouse.gov or www.bushcountry.org.

[6] For detailed information about the invasion, including day-by-day events, see the Wikipedia article, "2003 Invasion of Iraq," available at www.wikipedia.org by typing the title in the Search line.

[7] See Frederick H. Russell, *The Just War in the Middle Ages* (Cambridge University Press, 1975), p. 18.

[8] The Pew Forum on Religion and Public Life provides a good summary of the just war theory at its website, www.pewforum.org; click on Issues, then on Just War Tradition. The BBC has a more thorough treatment at www.bbc.co.uk/religion/ethics/war; under the Ethics of War, click on Just War. Both sites provide links to additional resources.

[9] See Lisa Sowle Cahill, *Love Your Enemies: Discipleship, Pacifism, and the Just War Theory* (Fortress Press, 1994), chapters 9 and 10. Also Roland H. Bainton, *Christian Attitudes Toward War and Peace: A Historical Survey and Critical Re-evaluation* (Abingdon Press, 1960), chapter 14; and Arthur F. Holmes (ed.), *War and Christian Ethics* (Baker Book House, 1975), chapter VII.

[10] Perhaps the most famous story related to early Christian pacifism is that of Martin of Tours, a Roman soldier who lived in the mid-fourth century. After his conversion to Christianity, he is reported to have said in his letter of resignation, "Hitherto I have served you as a soldier. Allow me now to become a soldier to God. . . . It is not lawful for me to fight." Quoted in Jean-Michel Hornus, *It Is Not Lawful For Me To Fight: Early Christian Attitudes Toward War, Violence, and the State* (Herald Press, 1980), p. 144.

[11] Church policies were not uniform throughout the Roman Empire, but what is said here was generally the case. There are stories, for example, of Christians being discovered in the military and then martyred for

their faith. Other exceptions could also be cited. See C. John Cadoux, *The Early Christian Attitude to War: A Contribution to the History of Christian Ethics* (Gordon Press, 1975; originally published in 1940). Also Bainton, mentioned above, chapter 5. For translations of early Christian documents on this topic, see Louis J. Swift, *The Early Fathers on War and Military Service* (Michael Glazier, 1983).

[12] Luke (19:45–46) just says that Jesus drove peddlers out of the temple. Mark (11:15–17) and Matthew (21:12–13) add that he overturned some tables and chairs. Only John (2:13–16) adds the details memorialized in Christian art—the whip made out of cord, money being scattered, and all sorts of animals being chased out of the temple.

[13] For an explanation of this concept in greater detail, see Glen H. Stassen, *Just Peacemaking: Transforming Initiatives for Justice and Peace* (Westminster/John Knox, 1992), chapters 2–4.

[14] See Matthew 21:5. The Gospel of John (12:15) also alludes to this prophecy.

[15] The Gospel of Luke (19:38) makes a connection with the prophecy of Zechariah by quoting the crowd as saying, "Blessed is the king who comes in the name of the Lord! Peace in heaven, and glory in the highest heaven!"

[16] See Exodus 17:8–16; Numbers 21:21–35; Deuteronomy 2:14–37; Joshua 1–12; Judges 4–12; 18–21. Scripture scholars suggest that the early history of Israel may not have been one of military conquest but one of gradual settlement, and that the glorious victories in the Pentateuch reflect Israel's confidence in God rather than events that actually happened as described. See Norman K. Gottwald, *The Tribes of Yahweh: A Sociology of the Religion of Liberated Israel 1250–1050 BCE* (Orbis Books, 1979).

[17] See 1 Samuel 8 for Israel's request for a king; 1 Samuel 11–15 and 30 for Saul's battles; 1 Samuel 17 and 30 for David's early military career.

[18] See 1 Kings 11–16 for the schism between Israel and Judah, their battles with each other and early wars with their enemies. Chapters 20–22 recount the wars of King Ahab, who receives advice from God's prophets at the beginning but who eventually loses God's favor. 2 Kings 3, 6 and 7 describe campaigns in which God is sometimes mentioned, and sometimes not. God is hardly an actor in the wars mentioned in chapters

10–18, and chapter 24 recounts the fall of Judah as a punishment from God.

[19] See 1 Chronicles 18–20 for the wars of David, some of which is taken from 2 Samuel. 2 Chronicles 20 describes a battle for the protection of Jerusalem and the temple, and chapter 32 recounts a miraculous rescue from an invasion by the Assyrians.

[20] Later revolts of the Jews against occupying forces in the second century BC are found in the apocryphal books of 1 and 2 Maccabees. Although battles described are fought in the name of political and religious freedom, their treatment is much more secular than in the canonical books of the Bible.

[21] See William Klassen, *Love of Enemies: The Way to Peace* (Fortress Press, 1984), especially chapter 2, "Love Your Enemy and Peace in the Hebrew Bible."

[22] See 1 Samuel 23–26. Even so, David did not trust Saul and so he stayed away until after the king had died in battle.

[23] See also 1 Samuel 7:14 and 1 Kings 5:4 for references to peace as the absence of war.

[24] See Claus Westerman, "Peace (*Shalom*) in the Old Testament," in Perry B. Yoder and Willard M. Swartley (eds.), *The Meaning of Peace: Biblical Studies* (Westminster/John Knox Press, 1992), pp. 16–48; also Randall T. Ruble, "The Gift of Shalom in the Old Testament," in Thomas D. Parker and Brian J. Fraser (eds.), *Peace, War and God's Justice* (United Church of Christ Publishing House, 1989), pp. 3–15.

[25] See Jeremiah 6:14 and 8:11. Judah was relying on unholy alliances, thinking it could avoid war. The prophet is saying that war is coming anyway, and it will be God's punishment for injustice in the land.

[26] See Walter Brueggemann, *Peace* (Chalice Press, 2001), especially chapter 2: "*Shalom* for 'Haves' and 'Have-Nots.'"

[27] Speech to the Joint Session of Congress, September 20, 2001. Note that this interpretation of the attackers' motives was made just nine days after September 11, long before anyone from the Arab and Muslim communities had had an opportunity to suggest what the deeper motives of Osama bin Laden and the Al Qaeda organization might have been. For

bin Laden's own words on the topic, go to the PBS Frontline website at www.pbs.org/wgbh/pages/frontline/shows/binladen and click on Interviews.

[28] Better known CIA coups during the Cold War include Iran (1953), Guatemala (1954), Greece (1967), and Chile (1973). For a detailed history, see William Blum, *Killing Hope: U.S. Military and CIA Interventions Since World War II* (Common Courage Press, 1995). For more information about CIA involvement in the Middle East, see Said K. Aburish, *A Brutal Friendship: The West and the Arab Elite* (St. Martin's Press, 1998); also Mohamoud A. Shaikh, "How West helped Saddam gain power and decimate the Iraqi elite" (1998), available from Muslimedia International at www.muslimedia.com; click on Search Archives, then type in the first four words of the title.

[29] See Michael Dobbs, "U.S. Had Key Role in Iraq Buildup," *Washington Post* (December 30, 2002), p. A1; available at www.washingtonpost.com; click on Archives, then type in the name of the author and the year of publication in the website's search engine.

[30] See Russ W. Baker, "Iraqgate," *Columbia Journalism Review* (March/April 1993), available at www.cjr.org or by going directly to http://archives.cjr.org/year, scrolling down to 1993, and clicking on the title of the article. Also "The Teicher Affidavit: Iraqgate," available from the Real History Archives, but most easily accessed by typing the title in an Internet search engine. Original government documents are also available at the National Security Archive of George Washington University, electronically accessible by typing "Iraqgate 1980–1994" into a search engine.

[31] See Kenneth R. Timmerman, *The Death Lobby: How the West Armed Iraq* (Houghton Mifflin, 1991), a book review of which is available from *The Bulletin of the Atomic Scientists* website, www.thebulletin.org > Back Issues > September 1992 > The Death Lobby. Also Mark Phythian, *Arming Iraq: How the U.S. and Britain Secretly Built Saddam's War Machine* (Northwestern University Press, 1996). Also Norm Dixon, "How the US armed Saddam Hussein with chemical weapons," *Green Left Weekly* (August 28, 2002); available at www.greenleft.org.au; click on Back Issues, then type key words of the title in the Search line.

32 See Alex Atroushi, "Halabja: Bloody Friday," a photo essay available on the Internet through the website of the Kurdistan Democratic Party (KDP), www.kdp.pp.se; click on Halabja. Also "Nerve Gas used in Northern Iraq on Kurds," a report of Physicians for Human Rights, available at www.phrusa.org; enter key words from the title in the search line on the home page. Also "Foreign Suppliers to Iraq's Biological Weapons Program," a report of the Center for Nonproliferation Studies (CNS) at the Monterey Institute for International Studies, most readily accessed on the Internet by typing the title into a search engine.

33 The two primary grievances were, first, Kuwait's refusal to forgive (as other Arab countries had done) the millions lent to Iraq (with U.S. loan guarantees) to fight the war against Iran, and second, the practice of slant drilling that enabled Kuwait to siphon oil from oil deposits inside Iraq. See the Wikipedia article, "Saddam Hussein," available at www.wikipedia.com. Scroll down to "Conflict with Kuwait, Persian Gulf War."

34 At least three good articles are available on the Internet as of 2003, including a transcript of the ambassador's meeting with Saddam Hussein on July 25, 1990. To find them, type "April Glaspie" into a search engine.

35 See Scott Peterson, "In war, some facts less factual," *Christian Science Monitor* (September 6, 2002), available at www.csmonitor.com; click on Archive, then type the headline in the keyword search box; or more directly, type the headline in a search engine. Also "No casus belli? Invent one!" a story from *The Guardian* dated February 5, 2003, and available from the Freedom of Information Center in the University of Missouri School of Journalism , but most readily accessible by typing the title into an Internet search engine.

36 For bin Laden's life and other details, see the entry under his name in the Wikipedia, available at www.wikipedia.org.

37 See "The Highway of Death," posted by Free Speech TV and available at www.freespeech.org, but more easily accessed by typing the title into a search engine. This site also contains a link to the War Crimes Report of the International War Crimes Tribunal, which concluded that this military action violated the Geneva Protocols. See also the testimony of Joyce Chediac, "The Massacre of Withdrawing Soldiers on 'The Highway of Death'," given to the Commission of Inquiry for the International War

Crimes Tribunal in 1992, and most easily accessed by typing the title into a search engine.

[38] See Barton Gellman, "Allied Air War Struck Broadly in Iraq; Officials acknowledge strategy went beyond purely military targets," *Washington Post* (June 23, 1991), p. A1, and available at www.washingtonpost.com by typing the first three words of the title and the year 1991 into the Archives search engine. The Wikipedia article on Operation Desert Storm reports the bombardment reduced electricity production to 4 percent of its pre-war level. See www.wikipedia.org > Operation Desert Storm > Air Campaign.

[39] While the effects of the sanctions were not widely reported in the United States, information about them was readily available from a variety of sources. See, for example, "Evaluation of food & nutrition situation in Iraq," a 1995 statement by the Food and Agricultural Organization of the United Nations, available from the International Action Center at www.iacenter.org; "Iraq surveys show 'humanitarian emergency,'" a 1999 UNICEF Newsline article, available at www.unicef.org/media > Press Releases > Search this site for title of article; "Iraq: People Come First," a report of Amnesty International, available at www.amnesty.org > Search title; "Iraq Crisis," a website of the Global Policy Forum, available at www.globalpolicy.org > Iraq Crisis. These items can also be directly accessed through an Internet search engine.

[40] Albright made the statement on the television program "60 Minutes" on May 12, 1996. See Douglas E. Hill, "Albright's Blunder," *Irvine Review* Online (December 2002), available at www.irvinereview.org by typing the title in the Search line on the homepage. Items banned by the sanctions included baby food, bandages, blankets, chlorine, cotton swabs, disinfectants, incubators, medical gauze, medical journals, notebooks, oxygen tents, paper, pencils, school books, soap, surgical gloves, syringes, tissues, toilet paper, tooth brushes, toothpaste, and X-ray equipment. See "The Sanctions War," an article on the Iraq Resource Information Site at www.geocities.com, but more quickly accessed by typing the title into a search engine.

[41] Estimates from 1991 to 1998 ranged from 2,690 to 5,357 children's deaths per month. See "Effects of the Iraq sanctions," *Seattle Post Intelli-*

gencer (May 11, 1999), available at www.seattlepi.nwsource.com; click on P-I Archives, then type in the name of the article.

[42] See, for example, "Statement on the Morality of the War in the Persian Gulf by American Catholic Theologians and Professors of Religious Studies" in *Horizons* (Spring 1993), pp. 118–126.

[43] The organization was responsible for or implicated in the bombings of four U.S. embassies, three attacks against American military personnel in the Middle East, and the bombing of the USS Cole. See the article on Al Qaeda in the Wikipedia at www.wikipedia.org.

[44] This is one of the more conservative estimates. See Carl Conetta, "Operation Enduring Freedom: Why a Higher Rate of Civilian Bombing Casualties," a briefing report of the Project of Defense Alternatives, available from the Commonwealth Institute at www.comw.org; type the first three words of the title in the Search line on the home page.

[45] See Phil Zabriskie and Spin Boldak, "Undefeated: On the Afghanistan-Pakistan border, the Taliban are regrouping, bent on spreading terror," *Time* (July 21, 2003), available online at www.time.com/time/asia/magazine and typing the first word in the Search line; also Mike Boettcher and Henry Schuster, "Al Qaeda terror strategy turns to assassination," CNN Online (January 22, 2003), available at www.cnn.com, but more quickly accessed by typing the title into a search engine. For an overview, see the entry on Afghanistan in Amnesty International's Annual Report, available at www.amnesty.org > Library > Annual Reports > Report 2003 > Afghanistan.

[46] For critiques of Western manipulation of military factions and indifference to humanitarian issues in Afghanistan, see Nafeez Mosaddeq Ahmed, "Afghanistan, the Taliban and the United States: The Role of Human Rights in Western Foreign Policy," first published by the Online Center for Afghan Studies (January 12, 2001) and now available on a number of websites that can be reached by typing the title of the article into an Internet search engine. For a more extensive analysis, see Carl Conetta, "Strange Victory: A Critical Appraisal of Operation Enduring Freedom and the Afghanistan War," a briefing report of the Project of Defense Alternatives, available from the Commonwealth Institute at www.comw.org by typing the two-word title in the Search line on the home page.

[47] See, for example, Richard Bernstein, "U.S. is losing the sympathy of the world," *International Herald Tribune* (September 11, 2003), p. 1.

[48] From the Statement of Principles of the Project for the New American Century, dated June 3, 1997 and signed by, among others, Dick Cheney, Donald Rumsfeld and Paul Wolfowitz; available at www.newamericancentury.org by clicking on Statement of Principles.

[49] See "Rebuilding America's Defenses: Strategy, Forces and Resources for a New Century," a report of The Project for the New American Century (September 2000), p. 10; available at www.newamericancentury.org > Defense and National Security > Rebuilding America's Defenses.

[50] From "Rebuilding America's Defenses," p. iv.

[51] From the Statement of Principles, cited above. See also a letter dated September 20, 2001 and signed by 41 members of The Project for the New American Century, which said, "It may be that the Iraqi government provided assistance in some form to the recent attack on the United States. But *even if evidence does not link Iraq directly to the attack*, any strategy aiming at the eradication of terrorism and its sponsors must include a determined effort to remove Saddam Hussein from power in Iraq. Failure to undertake such an effort will constitute an early and perhaps decisive surrender in the war on international terrorism" (emphasis added). Available at www.newamericancentury.org > Letters/Statements > Letter to President Bush on the War on Terrorism.

[52] One reason why the U.S. Congress voted overwhelmingly to support the president's call for war is that they were led to believe that the threat from Iraq was imminent. See John McCarthy, "Senators were told Iraqi weapons could hit U.S.," *Florida Today* (December 15, 2003). Available at www.floridatoday.com but most easily accessed by typing the title into a search engine.

[53] The Bush administration had supporters among just war theorists, most notably conservative Catholic Michael Novak, who argued the case for war in Rome on February 10, 2003. The Vatican, however, was not persuaded by Novak's argument, and to the very end the pope insisted that war was not the answer to the perceived crises. See Michael Novak, " 'Asymmetrical Warfare' and Just War," *National Review Online* (Febru-

ary 10, 2003), available at www.nationalreview.com; click on Find an Article, then type in the first two words of the title. See also Bill Haynes, "Just War Theory and Iraq," an analysis of the American Center for Law and Justice, available at www.aclj.org by typing the title in the Search line of the home page, which was supportive of the president's advocacy of war. On the other side, see Michael Gannon, "Is This a Just War?" *Gainesville Sun* (February 25, 2003), best accessed by typing the Advanced Search option in Google and typing the title in the Exact Phrase line and Gainesville in the All of the Words line. All of the arguments favoring a justifiable invasion of Iraq were based in part on assumptions which subsequent events showed to be erroneous, e.g., the existence of large stockpiles of chemical and biological weapons in Iraq.

[54] The largest crowds were not in the United States but in other countries. See "Movement Against War and Occupation in Iraq," a compilation of stories by the Global Policy Forum available at www.globalpolicy.org; click on Site Search, then enter the title of the report. See also the entries on "Global protests against war on Iraq" and "Popular opposition to war on Iraq" available from www.wikipedia.org.

[55] This interpretation of events is supported by the factual analysis of Seymour M. Hersh, "The Stovepipe: How conflicts between the Bush Administration and the intelligence community marred the reporting on Iraq's weapons," *The New Yorker* (October 27, 2003), pp. 77–87.

[56] Questions about the morality of the war can also be raised from the perspective of civilian casualties, which were largely ignored by the government and underreported by the media. See, however, Bradley Graham and Dan Morgan, "U.S. Has No Plans to Count Civilian Casualties," *Washington Post* (April 15, 2003), p. A13; also Derrick Z. Jackson, "Burying the Number of Civilian Deaths in Iraq," *Chicago Tribune* (June 16, 2003); both articles are most readily accessible by typing the title into an Internet search engine. See also the Amnesty International report, "Iraq: Civilians under fire," available at www.amnesty.org by clicking on Library and then typing the title in the Search line. John Sloboda and Hamit Dardagan, "Counting the Human Cost: A Survey of Projects Counting Civilians Killed by the War in Iraq" conclude that between 6,073 and 7,782 people were killed or died from injuries by June 12, 2003; available from www.iraqbodycount.org > Comment & Analysis > title of report. The same organization reports that at least 20,000 non-

combatants were injured during the war. A more recent report by International Physicians for the Prevention of Nuclear War adds that another 2,000 civilians were killed in Iraq between May and October 2003; "Continuing Collateral Damage: The health and environmental costs of the war on Iraq" is available at www.ippnw.org.

[57] "The current American peace will be short-lived if America becomes vulnerable to rogue powers with small, inexpensive arsenals of ballistic missiles and nuclear weapons or other weapons of mass destruction. We cannot allow North Korea, Iran, Iraq or similar states to undermine American leadership, intimidate American allies or threaten the American homeland itself." From "Rebuilding America's Defenses," p. 75. See above, note 48.

[58] See Matt Kelley, "Ex-intelligence officials say Bush overstated Iraq's link to al-Qaida," Louisville *Courier-Journal* (July 13, 2003), p. A4. On September 17, 2003, President Bush himself admitted, "We've had no evidence that Saddam Hussein was involved in September 11." See Steve Holland, "Bush denies Saddam-9/11 link," a Reuters news story available through Yahoo! UK at http://uk.news.yahoo.com by typing the title in the News Search line.

[59] See above, note 30.

[60] According to Amnesty International, which carefully documents its findings, in 2002, 53 countries arrested and detained people without charging them with a crime or bringing them to trial, 35 countries incarcerated political prisoners and prisoners of conscience, 105 countries allowed the torture and ill-treatment of prisoners by police and security forces, 33 countries permitted state agents to forcibly abduct or "disappear" people, and 42 countries tolerated political assassinations or the killing of undesirables. Of the countries in the Middle East, Iraq was in four out of these five categories, but so also were Kuwait, Lebanon and Israel. Human rights offenses in three of these five categories were committed by Egypt, Jordan, Syria, and Saudi Arabia. See "Amnesty International Report 2003" available at www.ai.org > Library > Annual Reports > Report 2003. For corroboration, see also the "Human Rights Watch World Report 2003" available at www.hrw.org > Publications > World Reports > 2003.

61 See Jo Dillon, "Revealed: last-minute changes to Iraq dossier," *The Independent* (August 17, 2003), available at www.truthout.org by typing the author's name in the archives search line. Also Joseph C. Wilson, "What I Didn't Find in Africa," *New York Times* (July 6, 2003), available from a number of different Internet sites by typing the title into a search engine.

62 Mr. Bush's critics sometimes overstate their case, but in the interest of thoroughness they deserve to be looked at. See, for example, "Bush Iraq Evidence Lies," compiled by Bush Watch and available at www.bushwatch.com but most easily accessed by typing the title in a search engine. For similar criticism of Tony Blair, see Glen Rangwala, "The Thirty-six Lies that Launched a War," available from the Centre for Research on Globalisation at www.globalresearch.ca by typing the title in the Site Search line.

63 The best estimate of Iraqi casualties is about five thousand military killed and injured, at least six thousand civilians killed, and about twenty thousand injured. See note 55 above.

64 For background, see the Wikipedia article, "Israeli-Palestinian Conflict," at www.wikipedia.org. Basic information about the separation barrier can be obtained from the Israeli peace organization, Gush Shalom, at http://gush-shalom.org/thewall.

65 Look up the following passages, for example, in different translations: Romans 8:6–7; 1 Corinthians 3:1–4; 2 Corinthians 10:4. One quick way to do this is by using the Advanced Search feature at www.biblegateway.com.

66 See the suggestions in Glen H. Stassen, ed., *Just Peacemaking: Ten Practices for Abolishing War* (Pilgrim Press, 1998), which could also be subtitled *Ten Practices for Abolishing Terrorism*.

67 See, for example, "Bill Gates gives NYC schools $51 million" (September 17, 2003) at www.cnn.com/education; type the title in the Search line.

68 See Marc Fest, "Enlightened self-interest," *Miami Herald* (September 21, 2001), most easily accessed by typing the title into a search engine.

6

Policies and Consequences

"Keep my commands and you will live." (Proverbs 7:2 NIV)

For centuries, many Christians thought that the reason they should be good was so that they would be rewarded in heaven. Likewise, they thought the reason they should not commit sins was so that they would not be punished in hell. Scripture scholars today question this simple picture of what life is all about.

One clue that the Bible gives for suspecting that ethical living is not about "pie in the sky when you die" is that the Israelites did not believe in life after death. People in the ancient Near East did have a concept of an underworld, a dark region under the earth where people somehow went when they had died. In Greek it was known as *hades*; in Hebrew it was called *she'ol*. But it was not a place of punishment, for everybody went there, regardless of whether they had been upright or wicked. So salvation for them was not a matter of going to heaven.[1]

Salvation, to the Hebrew slaves in Egypt, meant escaping to the land that God had promised them. When they had settled in Canaan, the Israelites thought that salvation might come with having a king, as other countries had. To the tiny northern and southern kingdoms that appeared after Solomon's reign, salvation was thought to be found in alliances with powerful neighbors against even more powerful neighbors. To the Jews during the Babylonian exile, salvation meant returning home to Judah. When the Jews found themselves under Persian, then Greek and finally Roman rule, many of them thought of salvation as freedom from foreign domination, and they prayed for a savior to deliver them from such oppression.

By the time of Jesus, some Jews (notably the Pharisees) had come to believe in life after death and hence the possibility of salvation in a life after this one. Other Jews (led by the Sadducees) held on to the older belief that this life was all that there is. When a group of Sadducees asked Jesus which husband a woman would have in the next life if she had been married more than once, he knew quite well that their question was insincere.*

In the New Testament, salvation is talked about both as something that happens in this life and as something that happens later. When Jesus said to Zacchaeus, "Today salvation has come to this house" (Luke 19:10), he was speaking of salvation in the here and now. On the other hand, when Paul wrote that "salvation is nearer to us now than when we became believers" (Romans 13:11), he was speaking about salvation in the future. Some texts are ambiguous and may refer to salvation in this life or the next.[2]

It appears, then, that biblical morality is much more this-worldly than people often realize. This does not deny that salvation (or its opposite) continues into the next life, but it emphasizes that much of what the Bible says about morality talks about the consequences of human behavior in this life and in this world. This is especially true for what the Bible says about social morality, for there is nothing in the Scriptures that suggests that social entities such as countries go to heaven or hell.

Morality and Sin

Another feature of biblical morality is that some of it is plain common sense. This is certainly not so with regard to the many

---

*See Luke 20:27–38. The gospels say that the Sadducees did not believe in the resurrection of the dead, which is technically correct, but they also did not believe that the souls of the dead were alive in any way. Jesus corrected their thinking by pointing out that if the Scriptures say that God is the God of Abraham, Isaac and Jacob, then those patriarchs must still be alive. See also Mark 12:18–27 and Matthew 22:23–33.

requirements of the Law that deal with worship and diet, but it is true with regard to what we accept today as basic human morality, such as the Ten Commandments.

If the Bible did not contain basic human morality as well as religious and cultural regulations, we would almost have to say that until God gave Moses the commandments of the Law, people had no way of knowing right from wrong. But this is obviously not the case. The Bible itself talks about ethical and unethical people prior to the twentieth chapter of Exodus, referring to them in biblical language as the righteous and the wicked. Furthermore, pagan writings from the ancient Near East contain ethical norms that are similar to many of those in the Old Testament.[3] Finally, Scripture itself says that parts of the Law are in the human heart, and that ignorance of the Law is no excuse for immorality.[4]

Although the Bible often talks about morality in terms of obedience to the Law, biblical morality is better understood as a matter of relationships. In the ancient world, to live a good life and to prosper, one had to be in right relationship with one's parents and siblings, with one's neighbors, and with those in power. It is not so different in the modern world, but our individualistic culture allows us to rebel against our parents, fight with our brothers and sisters, ignore our neighbors, and shirk our civic responsibilities. About the only people we seem to need to get along with are our boss at work and our spouse at home. It seems that we do not even need to get along with our kids, since the culture prompts them at an early age to reject us.

How things seem and how things are, however, can be two very different things. A lot of people who have bought into modern culture's values and ideals are not as happy as they think they should be. The divorce rate is high, children are abused, teenagers run away from home, people drown their sorrows in alcohol and forget their troubles with drugs, and now that the senior population is aging we hear more about elder abuse. The ways in which our society is dysfunctional seem to be growing. Could it be that by accepting modern secular principles and ignoring biblical principles, people on the whole are becoming less adept at forming and maintaining those human relationships that make life worthwhile and enjoyable?

The biblical principles involved here seem to be fairly basic ones, rather on the level of honoring one's parents, being honest in word and deed, not betraying the trust of others, and not giving in to temptations that would destroy relationships—to paraphrase a few of the Ten Commandments.* Such biblical principles appear to be fundamental principles of human morality, principles that are in accordance with our nature as human beings. If they are, this would account for why these principles are always found (in one form or another) in every traditional culture around the world. Since God is both the creator of human nature and the author of the Bible, it stands to reason that the morality which sages discover when they reflect on human nature is in many respects the same as the morality which we discover when we read the Scriptures. Both ultimately come from the same source.

One question raised by philosophers is whether people's actions are morally good and bad because God commands and prohibits them, or whether God commands and prohibits things according to whether they are good and bad. Some thinkers in the Middle Ages who thought that all morality was based on God's will went so far as to suggest that if God changed his mind, then morality would change. It is possible, they thought, that God could change the moral law so that lying would be virtuous and honesty would be sinful, or so that sexual promiscuity would be good and fidelity would be bad.[5]

The medieval philosophers who proposed such theories understood the nature of law but they did not understand much about human nature. It could never be good to be constantly lying

---

* The commandments to honor and serve God alone are the foundation of the rest of biblical morality, inasmuch as one best honors and serves God, as the prophets pointed out, by living the way God wants. Jesus also said that if we love him we will keep his commandments (John 14:15).

because in such a society people could not trust one another, and without some level of trust there can be no such thing as society. The same could be said of stealing, murder, and other crimes that tear the fabric of society. Anthropologists have found some primitive societies that are relatively relaxed about sexual morality, but there has never been any society that did not prize fidelity and family responsibility, which are the foundation of any human society.*

The basic human morality that is found in the Bible therefore seems to be based on human nature, and especially on the human need for good human relationships in order to have a satisfying and rewarding life. You could say that God gave the Israelites (and ultimately the human race) the moral code that is found in the Bible because he knew that it would help people to be happy if they knew the rules of life. The unwritten laws that govern good human relationships are operative whether people know about them or not, so it is better for people to know about them. The Law of Moses was given in part to help people live a better life by living according to the basic principles that arise from human nature and that govern any good society.†

As Moses said to the Israelites about the Law before they entered the Promised Land,

> See, I have set before you today life and prosperity, death and adversity. If you obey the commandments of the Lord your God that I am commanding you today, by loving the Lord your God, walking in his ways, and observing his commandments, decrees, and ordinances, then you shall live and become numerous, and the Lord your God will bless you in the land that you are entering to possess. But if your

---

* The patriarchs Isaac and Jacob, who had more than one sexual partner, were not being simply promiscuous. They had family responsibilities to those women and to their children.
† In the Epistle to the Romans, Paul initially gives the Law a somewhat negative appraisal, but in the end he agrees that the Law of Moses is better than the law of sin. See Romans 7:7-25.

> heart turns away and you do not hear, but are led astray to bow down to other gods and serve them, I declare to you today that you shall perish; you shall not live long in the land that you are crossing the Jordan to enter and possess. I call heaven and earth to witness against you today that I have set before you life and death, blessings and curses. Choose life that you and your descendants may live.
> (Deuteronomy 30:15-19)[6]

Life and prosperity result when people follow God's commands to live in accordance with what is needed for good relationships between people. Conversely, disaster and death result when people serve other gods and do not live the way they are supposed to live.

If morality is not primarily a matter of obeying laws, then immorality or unethical behavior is not primarily a matter of disobeying laws or breaking written commandments. The commandments were given by God to codify or make explicit the demands of human nature, especially with regard to social relationships. If it was possible to be immoral before the giving of the Torah,[*] it is because it was possible to act contrary to what is required for good human relationships.

Neither the Hebrew word for sin in the Old Testament nor the Greek word for sin in the New Testament means breaking a law. Rather, they both mean to miss the mark or to fall short; the image is one of an arrow that flies wide or fails to reach its target.[7] In this respect, sin is more of a failure and a failing than an act of disobedience or defiance. What is wrong about disobeying God's law is not only that such behavior shows disrespect for God, but also that it shows disrespect for other people. That is, those who disregard God's moral laws always disrespect human beings (or other creatures of God) in some manner or another. Such behavior falls short of what God expects, which is why God issued a law

---

[*] Certainly the story of the Flood assumes that human beings were generally wicked while Noah was a man of integrity even before the revelation of the Torah.

Policies and Consequences

about it. But it is always possible to sin by falling short of what is required for good human relationships even if there is not an explicit law about it in the Bible.*

Blessings and Curses

In the Bible, both individuals and groups are said to be blessed and cursed. God blesses people with long life, children, possessions, prosperity, and peace. Curses include childlessness, enslavement, illness, suffering, defeat, disaster, and death. In all these cases, the blessings and curses mentioned are rewards and punishments that occur in this life, not in the next.[8]

When most people think about God's punishment, they probably imagine God in heaven noticing something bad that someone has done, and then deciding to punish that person by making something bad happen to him or her. To some extent, this is in fact the way Israelites thought about punishment for sin. Not having a concept of a real afterlife, but knowing that God is a just God, they believed that moral behavior would be rewarded and immoral behavior would be punished in this life.

Things did not always turn out that way, however. Certainly the Israelites noticed that sometimes "the wicked prosper,"[9] and that sometimes bad things happen to good people. Most Scripture scholars interpret the book of Job as a theological essay, written in the form of a poetic drama, by someone who was wrestling with this very problem.[10] By the end of the drama, however, the author has not yet arrived at the revelation that good and bad behavior

---

* For example, marriage counselors say that a significant cause of most divorces today is a failure in communication, but there are no commandments covering communication between spouses in the Bible. Good communication skills are needed for close relationships, due to the nature and requirements of human intimacy. Christian marriage counselors derive many insights about marriage from the Bible, but they do not find any scriptural instructions about intimate communication between husbands and wives comparable to the detailed instructions one finds about ritual sacrifices, for example.

may be rewarded and punished in a life after death. This is why the upright Job has all of his blessings (property, children and health) restored to him at the end, and the only theological answer provided to the problem of undeserved suffering is that God in his infinite wisdom knows why it happens.[11]

Why would the Israelites have believed that good behavior is rewarded and bad behavior is punished in this life? And why would it say in so many parts of the Bible that this is the way things are? The most plausible reason is that it is often true.

To a great extent, acting in accordance with the laws of nature (including human nature and the nature of society) is a formula for success. A potter who understands the nature of clay, the requirements for molding and glazing it, the function and subtleties of a kiln, and the uses to which ceramic products can be put is going to be a more successful potter than one who does not know these things. A farmer who understands the cycle of the seasons, the nutrition and water needs of the crop being planted, various methods of weed and pest control, and the best ways to harvest and store the crop is going to be more successful than one who ignores these facts. A computer technician who thoroughly knows the programming language being used and is careful to write accurate lines of text is going to be more successful than one who is sloppy and disregards the demands of a working program. A company president who knows the company from top to bottom, who is familiar with employees, who has a good sense of the competition, and who understands how to build and work with a management team is going to be more successful than someone with less knowledge of the ever-changing realities of the business world.

Religious people who experience success in life, and who acknowledge that it was not entirely of their doing, are apt to say that they have been blessed by God. At the very least, many things that could have gone wrong did not go wrong, for there is always an element of chance in any venture. Nonreligious people who realize that they are not fully in control are apt to say that they are lucky rather than blessed. In our culture, then, we have two ways of talking about the same benefits, one that is theological and one that is not theological.

When things do not go our way, however, we tend to say that we are unfortunate or we ran into some bad luck. In our culture, we have only a secular way of talking about misfortune. The ancient world, however, had primarily a religious way of talking about it. They described misfortune as being cursed by the gods. If they were monotheists, like the Israelites, they called it being cursed or punished by God. A Jewish potter, farmer or merchant whose efforts failed would most likely have called it a punishment. Much of the book of Job is devoted to a dialogue between Job and three visitors who keep trying to get him to admit that his troubles must be God's punishment for his sins. Job's problem, since he has always been a very ethical person, is that he cannot think of any sins for which God would be punishing him so severely.

Success and Failure

In every walk of life, knowledge is power—the power to accomplish what one sets out to do, and the power to succeed. The more one understands the nature of the task at hand, the nature of techniques and equipment needed, the nature of the process from initiation to completion, the nature of the possible pitfalls and downfalls, and so on, the more one is likely to succeed. Conversely, the more one overlooks relevant information, the more one ignores pertinent facts, the more one does not comprehend, the more one refuses to think logically and act reasonably, the more one is likely to fail—to fall short, to miss the mark. This is true in crafts and trades, in science and industry, in business and government.

It is also true in human relationships. Couples who know how to listen, who are sensitive to one another's needs, who understand the value of cooperation, who are willing to forgive, and so on, are more likely to experience successful marriages than couples who do not. Parents who have a sense of the ever-changing needs of growing children, who are affirming and supportive, who understand when and how to discipline, and who know when to let go are more likely to be successful parents than people with fewer parenting skills. Individuals who can be honest and frank with one another, who can trust one another, who have a feeling for each other's likes and dislikes, and who are willing to spend time doing what the other likes to do are more likely to succeed as friends than individuals who do not know what it takes to be a true friend.

Putting the requirements for success in the world together with the requirements for success in relationships, we discover something like the requirements of basic human morality. Every successful businessperson understands the importance of maintaining good human relationships for the success of the enterprise. Working with colleagues, superiors, and subordinates, pleasing clients, and satisfying customers, demands moral qualities such as honesty and fairness, trust and cooperation. The most important business is repeat business, and a sound way to grow a business is through referrals, but these do not come to people who do not keep their word, who do not offer solid value for payment received, or who are dishonest and unreliable in other ways. People who are backstabbers, gossips, or overly aggressive and competitive are not likely to do well within an organization or help a business succeed. Moral qualities are not the only requirements for success in business, but they are important baseline qualities on which achievement can be based.

What, then, about the honest and hard-working person who does not succeed? Or the ethical and reliable person who gets bypassed for promotion? Or even the good person with a prospering business who goes bankrupt due to market or social forces beyond his or her control—such as happened to many people in downtown New York after September 2001? This was Job's question. Why do bad things happen to good people?

Morality and Probability

Doing things right increases the likelihood of success, but it does not guarantee success. Moral laws, like the rules for success in business, are statistical in nature rather than mechanical, as are many of the laws in physics and chemistry.* Doing the right thing increases the probability of success, but it gives no assurance of success. Job and other people in the ancient world did not understand the mathematics of probability. Statistics is a twentieth-century science.

By the same token, doing the wrong thing does not guarantee failure but only increases its likelihood. Unethical people often succeed in the short run, but in the long run their unethical behavior tends to catch up with them, especially if it is also illegal. Again here, though, this is only a probability. Some people get caught the first time they do something wrong. Other people get away with murder, so to speak, all their lives. The laws here are statistical rather than mechanical. All things being equal (that is, in the absence of a natural disaster, an economic meltdown or a social cataclysm), most people who are morally good and good at their trade will succeed, and most people who are morally bad or poor at their trade will fail. But some good people will fail and some bad ones will succeed. That is the nature of the statistical bell curve.

Without a knowledge of statistics, the human authors of the Bible observed what happened in the world and talked about it using words that they had in their vocabulary. Moreover, the words in their vocabulary were often theological, and their mode of perception was often moralistic. For this reason, when they observed what we would call success, they called it a blessing, and when they saw people failing or having a hard time, they

---

* Today many of the laws of physics and chemistry are understood as statistical regularities rather than as the absolute rules they were once thought to be, but basic physical and chemical processes can still be treated as though their outcomes were mechanically certain.

called it a curse or a punishment. Blessings and punishments were theologically understood as coming from God—as indeed all things come from God—but the Bible does not explain *how* they come from God.

God's Design and Natural Laws

One explanation is that God observes what people do, he approves or disapproves of it, and on that basis he doles out blessings or punishments. This explanation is simple enough that even a child can understand it, for every child has had the experience of doing something and being rewarded or punished by a parent. A somewhat more sophisticated explanation is that, in creating the universe, God gave it a design that covers everything in creation from the largest cluster of galaxies to the smallest subatomic particle. The nonhuman realities in the universe blindly follow God's design because they have no choice; they have to follow the laws of nature. But human beings have free will, and so they should follow God's laws, but they do not necessarily have to.

Well, actually, human beings do have to follow most of God's laws. There is no escaping the law of gravity, at least not on earth. Our bodies have to follow all the other mechanical laws of physics and chemistry as well. Biological laws tend to be statistical, which is why human beings come in different sizes and shapes, why they have a variety of talents and handicaps, why they have differing degrees of health and illness, and why they do not all have exactly the same lifespan. Psychological laws are likewise statistical, and they are somewhat more elusive, but we still distinguish between mental health and mental illness, between emotional well-being and emotions out of control, between normal perceptions and distorted perceptions, and so on. Social laws, if we can call them that, are very dependent on culture and custom, but nonetheless there are social realities and regularities that are found in all the nations of the world and all the ages of history—realities such as family and fidelity, and regularities such as nurturing the young, caring for the sick, cooperating in maintaining food and shelter, protecting the group from danger, and honoring the dead. A large amount of human living follows laws, about which most people are only dimly aware. But the laws are operative, nonetheless.

Freedom and Consequences

At the same time, there is room for freedom. There is a certain range of human behavior that is not predetermined. We all have to eat, but we can eat fast food or health food. We all have to speak, but we can tell the truth or we can lie. We all have material needs and wants, but we can satisfy them honestly or dishonestly. We all have to live with others, but we can do so in ways that are cooperative or uncooperative. We all have to interact with others, but we can do so in ways that are constructive or destructive. The room for freedom in human life is the space in which morality occurs.

In that space, we can behave in ways that are fair or unfair, that are just or unjust, that are life-giving or life-draining, that are helpful or hurtful, that are honest or dishonest, that are compassionate or uncompassionate, that are caring or uncaring. In that space, we can act in ways that benefit ourselves and others, or we can act in ways that are harmful to ourselves and others, or some mixture of both. In that space, however, we are not free from the laws of nature and their consequences. Those laws—God's design—are still operative.

In a very important sense, living according to God's laws is not an option. If one disregards the laws of physics, one suffers the consequences. For example, if one disregards the law of gravity and jumps out of an open window, one will suffer injury or death. Likewise, if one disregards the laws of chemistry or biology as they affect the human body, and if one consumes too much alcohol or ingests a poisonous substance, one will get sick and perhaps die. Similarly, if one disregards the psychological requirements for healthy human relationships, one will find oneself in dysfunctional, unhappy, and perhaps destructive relationships. Finally, if one disregards the social demand for justice in dealing generally with others, one will be subjected to reactions of retaliation and revenge.

If God's laws apply to human beings in general, they also apply to collections of human beings, or human societies. If a society disregards the laws of physics or chemistry or biology and pollutes its natural environment, people in that society will suffer the consequences in terms of disease and perhaps early death. If a society through unregulated advertising and uninhibited media promotes socially destructive relationships, that society will increase the likelihood of physical and emotional abuse, family breakdown, crime, and other pathological behavior. If a society endows a privileged few with enormous wealth while great numbers suffer deprivation and have no hope for themselves or their children, that society is setting the stage for violent eruptions and perhaps even revolution.

Actions, in other words, have consequences, and the consequences follow certain laws which, in the area of human freedom, are not mechanical certainties but statistical probabilities. As the proverb has it, what goes around comes around. In biblical language, we reap what we sow.[12]

Principles and Consequences

If actions have consequences, then it stands to reason that repeated actions also have consequences. The more we behave in a certain way, the more we are likely to experience the natural consequences of that behavior, even if the consequences are not certain but only probable. A musician who practices every day is more likely to become very accomplished and succeed in the entertainment world. A technician who keeps up with developments through reading and seminars has a better chance of getting promoted than one who just goes to work every day. A politician who visits constituents and gets to know what they are thinking will represent them better in the legislature and will have a good shot at being reelected.

The same is true in the area of moral behavior. People who are frank and honest get a reputation for being that way—as do people who are shady and secretive—and their reputation opens some doors and closes others. People who get into drugs and alcohol as teenagers find it hard to get out of that lifestyle, but people who stay clean and sober through adolescence find it relatively easy to stay away from drugs later on. People who are faithful spouses and caring parents are more likely to have a long marriage and a happy family life than those who do not.

Fortunately or unfortunately, we do not have to make a new moral decision every time we are faced with a new moral choice. We get into patterns of action, ways of behaving, habits and routines that get pretty well established over the course of time. Sometimes we get into such patterns by deciding that this is what we want to do, or this is the kind of person we want to be. More often we get into our habits by sliding into them, almost unnoticed, almost unthinkingly, led there by our parents, our peers and other strong influences on our ideas and values.

Once we get into a certain way of behaving, though, we can be said to be following certain principles. As was noted in chapter 1, principles motivate our actions and guide our behavior even when we do not notice them, even without consciously adverting to them. Principles give a certain consistency to our actions. Principles increase the likelihood that we will experience the consequences of our actions because they lead us to perform the same types of actions over and over again. Principles ensure, for good or for ill, that we will reap what we sow.

The Future of America

This book has been making the argument that, in some very important areas of public policy, the principles that motivate and guide the Bush administration are not those of the Bible. This in itself would not be noteworthy, were it not for the way that the president and others in government have led to Americans to believe that, since they are Christians, they are acting according to

Christian principles, and since they hold the Bible in high esteem, their policies are consistent with biblical principles. While they may be right about this in some areas of government policy, it has become clear that they are wrong in the four areas examined by this book.

People who believe that God's word is true can be understandably concerned when they discover that their government is not being true to God's word. The Scriptures teach that those who follow God's law will be blessed, and that those who do not will be punished. Moreover, we have seen that punishment in the Bible is not a divine afterthought but something that is built into the nature of sinful behavior. It is a way of talking about the negative consequences of sin, and sin does not have to be the breaking of one of the Ten Commandments, but it can be any missing of the mark that God has set for us. Any time we fall short of how God wants human beings to treat the rest of his creation, especially those made in his image and likeness, we sin.* And the more repeatedly we sin, the more likely we are to experience sin's negative consequences.

Translated from a personal to a social level, this means that policies which fall short of God's design, and which run counter to God's will, are sinful. And as such they will not yield the blessings for which Mr. Bush fervently prays.

For what are the blessings that America enjoys?

Are they not half a continent of natural resources? How then will America be blessed by seriously depleting those resources?

Are they not clean air and safe drinking water? How then will America be blessed by increasing the pollution of our air and water supplies?

Is not wealth a blessing? How then will America be blessed if more of its people are driven deeper into poverty?

---

* When Paul in Romans 3:23 declares that "all have sinned and fall short of the glory of God," he is speaking about sin in the way in which we have been discussing it.

Is not health a blessing? How then will America be blessed if many of its citizens, especially its children, do not have access to decent health care?

What of the blessings of knowledge and education? How will America be blessed if it does not adequately fund its schools?

What of the blessings of housing and employment? How will America be blessed if it annually increases the ranks of the homeless and the unemployed?

What of immigrants and refugees, who have contributed so much to making this country as great as it is? How will we be blessed by closing our doors to them?

What of freedom and liberty? How will we be blessed by passing laws that diminish the civil rights of citizens and deny human rights to others?

What of the blessing of justice? How will we be blessed if we incarcerate millions without rehabilitating them?

What of the blessing of security? How will we be blessed if our policies and actions abroad inspire hatred of Americans?

Is not peace a blessing? How will America be blessed if it embarks on a policy of unending war?

Is not respect a blessing? How will America be blessed if it does not respect the community of nations and seeks to impose its will upon the world?

In the light of biblical teaching, it appears that if the present administration continues its current policies, the United States will experience consequences that are very different from the ones its president expects.

Prophetic Hope

We noted in chapter 3 that prophets in Israel and Judah saw the injustice of using oppressive taxes to pay for military alliances, and they foresaw the eventual destruction of both kingdoms. Some of them also foresaw that the Babylonian exile would not last forever, and that the Jews would be allowed to return to their homeland. These were not prophets of doom, but prophets of hope.

Prophetic hope can perceive the direction that needs to be taken if a nation is to be blessed with the rewards that come from living according to God's plan. Some Evangelicals are fond of saying that God has a wonderful plan for each person's life, and when people hear this they sometimes imagine a heavenly blueprint that is unique to each and every individual. God's plan for individuals, however, is the same for every person. As the pamphlet used by Campus Crusade for Christ puts it, God's plan for each and every person is an abundant life, that is, a full and meaningful life.[13] The way to reach that goal is to stop being self-directed and to turn one's life over to Christ, which means deciding in faith to follow his word as it comes to us through the Scriptures, through spiritual mentoring, through books and sermons, and most importantly, through personal prayer. The decision to follow Christ is the beginning, not the end, of salvation.

It would be naïve to expect that an entire nation and its leaders would step out in faith to follow Christ on the road of discipleship. George W. Bush claims to have taken that step himself, and although others may believe he is hypocritical, it is possible that he has taken only the first steps in his spiritual journey and does not perceive its ultimate goal. In that respect, he would not be unusual. Most Christians do not ever become saints, and even saints are people of their times. Some saints have been misogynists, others have owned slaves, and still others have gone to war. Even saints are not perfect. In any case, it is clear that Mr. Bush does not fully appreciate what is written in the Bible about social morality and its implications for national policy.

Is it naïve, however, to expect the leaders of a nation to live according to the principles on which it was founded, the principles it claims to represent, and the principles that are invoked in public speeches? The principles found in the Declaration of Independence and the Constitution are not the heroic demands of the New Testament but the basic morality of the Old Testament first enunciated in the Law of Moses and later reiterated by the prophets. Although an argument can be made for offering humanitarian assistance to the people in countries with governments hostile to the United States, as was done above in chapter 5, it may be impossible to muster the political will for such a revolutionary policy of enlightened self-interest. But should it be impossible to persuade the Congress and the American people to implement domestic and foreign policies that represent the interests of most people rather than those of a privileged few?

Such policies would be based on the biblical principle of stewardship, so that environmental laws and regulations would enhance the quality of life, conserve the balance of nature, and preserve resources for the future.

Such policies would be based on the principle of social justice, showing concern for the common good both in the United States and around the world, both in the present and in the future. Instead of following ideologies from the left or right, social legislation would be preceded by sound research, authorize pilot programs before implementing sweeping changes, and adjust to the changing needs of people over time.

Such policies would be based on the principle of distributive justice, ensuring that the benefits of health and education reach all Americans, that the spread between the highest and lowest incomes is narrowing rather than widening, that everyone has a place to call home, and that no one has to go to bed hungry.

Such policies would be based on the principle of commutative justice, making sure that working people receive a wage that they and their families can live on, and reforming the penal system to put more emphasis on restorative justice, rehabilitation, and other forms of punishment that fit the crime and enable offenders to contribute to society when they are released.

Such policies would acknowledge that human rights are not negotiable, and that the security of the country is not enhanced by denying basic rights to anyone within our borders or overseas.

Such policies would be based on the understanding that peace is not simply the absence of war but a condition of cooperation and harmony among nations and between peoples.

Perhaps most importantly, such policies would exhibit truth and honesty in their formulation, in their presentation to the people, and in their implementation.

Personal Religion and Public Life

As was said at the beginning of this book, George W. Bush is a religious man. He is sincere when he talks about God, he believes what he says about the Bible, and he is committed to doing what he thinks is right. About his sexual ethics, his fidelity to his wife, and his abstinence from alcohol there is little doubt. Although he does not talk about it openly, it appears that at some point in his adult life, Mr. Bush accepted Jesus as his savior and turned his life over to Christ. In doing that, he experienced an inner spiritual renewal—what Evangelicals call being born again.

It is somewhat paradoxical, then, that the president's policies and actions are questioned and attacked by individuals and groups that are also religious. Protestants who believe in the social gospel and Catholics who believe in social justice decry the Bush administration's proposed changes in welfare, health care, and other social programs. Christians who believe that public policy should create a more equitable society object to tax cuts that widen the gap between the rich and the poor. Quakers, Mennonites, and other churches committed to Christian peacemaking deplore the president's rush to war not once but twice.

Increasingly, too, the president and his administration have come under attack for deceiving the public: for lying about Iraq's possession of and ability to deploy weapons of mass destruction, for not being truthful about the benefits of tax cuts, for deceptive labeling of legislation, for claiming that the administration's nominees for federal judgeships are not ideologically conservative, and so on. Whether or not these accusations are correct, they give the appearance of high-level disregard for the commandment prohibiting false witness. And whether or not Mr. Bush is aware of the discrepancies between the words of his speechwriters and the actions of his administration is something that historians will have to judge.

Nevertheless, many such discrepancies exist in the four areas of public policy to which this book has been devoted. More important, however, are the discrepancies that exist between the policies of the Bush administration and the ethical principles revealed in the Bible. Perhaps the president's study of the Bible has not led him to see the contradictions between the responsibilities of stewardship and his administration's environmental policies, between the Law of Moses and its violations of human rights, between the teaching of the prophets and its disregard for social justice, between the commands of Jesus and its pursuit of war. Even so, those discrepancies exist and those contradictions are not difficult to document.

At this point, therefore, it is legitimate to inquire about the president's principles—not his private principles but the principles according to which he acts in public life. If George W. Bush espouses the policies of his administration—and he is certainly the most consistent defender of those policies—then he also embraces the principles on which they are based. Those principles, as we have seen over and over again, are the principles of political and social conservatism. They are not the social principles of the Bible. They are not the ethical principles of the Law and the prophets. They are not the moral principles that Jesus taught his disciples to follow.

George W. Bush may be a Christian, then, but he is not yet a follower of Christ.

Notes

[1] See, for example, Gary W. Light, "Salvation, Save, Savior" (pp. 1153–1155), and Jim West, "Sheol" (pp. 1206–1207) in David Noel Freedman (ed.), *Eerdmans Dictionary of the Bible* (William B. Eerdmans, 2000).

[2] See, for example, Matthew 19:25 and 24:13; Mark 8:35 and 16:16; John 10:9; Romans 5:9–10 and 10:10; 1 Corinthians 10:33 and 15:2.

[3] See, for example, the Code of Hammurabi (Babylonia) and the Book of the Dead (Egypt). Articles about both can be found on the Internet.

[4] See Deuteronomy 30:11–14; Romans 1:18–32.

[5] William of Ockham was one of these medieval thinkers. See Frederick Copleston, *A History of Philosophy* (Newman Press, 1959), Vol. 3, p. 105.

[6] For a lengthier set of blessings and curses, see Leviticus 26.

[7] See, for example, Clayton N. Jefford, "Sin," in *Eerdmans Dictionary of the Bible*, pp. 1224–1226.

[8] See, for example, Genesis 9:1, 9:25, and 24:35; Exodus 23:25; Leviticus 25:21; Numbers 5:18–22; Deuteronomy 7:13–14, 16:10–17, 28:18, and 28:45; 1 Chronicles 4:10; Job 1:10 and 5:3; Psalms 29:1, 67:6, 128:2, and 132:15; Proverbs 10:22 and 22:9; Isaiah 24:6 and 32:20; Jeremiah 11:8 and 23:10.

[9] See, for example, Jeremiah 12:1; Psalm 94:3–7.

[10] See Marvin H. Pope, *Job* (Doubleday, 1965), p. xxix; J. Gerald Janzen, *Job* (John Knox, 1985), pp. 12–22; James H. Wharton, *Job* (Westminster John Knox, 1999), pp. 1–6.

[11] See Job 38:1 – 42:6.

[12] See Job 4:8; Proverbs 11:18 and 22:8; Hosea 8:7 and 10:12; 2 Corinthians 9:6; Galatians 6:7–8.

[13] See John 10:10. For "The Four Spiritual Laws" online, go to www.greatcom.org/laws.

Conclusion

Arnold Toynbee in *A Study of History* counted twenty-eight civilizations, including our own, that have left records of their existence across thousands of years.[1] Twenty-seven of those civilizations have come and gone. It is possible that ours will be the next to go.

During the decades of the Cold War, people feared that the end might come in a nuclear war. Scientists estimated that if the United States and the Soviet Union exploded only a tenth of their atomic arsenals in the atmosphere, all but the lowest forms of life would soon disappear from the face of the planet.[2] The immediate threat of a nuclear cataclysm has passed, but the two greatest nuclear powers on the planet have not yet dismantled most of these deadly weapons. It is still possible that nuclear weapons will be used in a war. And now we also face the possibility of nuclear terrorism.

Something was said in the last chapter that bears reiterating, perhaps in slightly different terms. The claim was made that living according to God's design is a blueprint for success, and that living contrary to God's laws is a recipe for failure. This is not a terribly sophisticated insight, especially if it is formulated in nonreligious terms. Put in more secular language, the claim is that, all other things being equal, living according to the requirements of nature (including the individual and social nature of human beings) leads to progress, and failing to live according to those requirements leads to decline. Put even more simply, it is better to be in touch with reality than to be out of touch with reality.

This principle is so general that it is applicable to any area of human activity. For this reason, examples from crafts, business, politics, and relationships were used to illustrate it. Additional examples could have been easily provided, but once the basic idea was communicated, they would have been superfluous. The claim was also made that the law of consequences, if it may be called a law, is statistical in nature. That is, doing something or acting in a certain way does not guarantee that something else will happen, but it creates a probability that it will happen. Moreover, doing something often or over a long period of time increases the probability that the related consequence will eventually happen. Not everyone who smokes gets ill from it, but the more one smokes and the longer one does it, the more it is likely that one will contract emphysema or lung cancer.

Next, it can be observed that advance knowledge or awareness of consequences is not required for them to happen. Scientists and businesspeople understand that human actions are just as likely to have unintended consequences as well as intended ones. This is partly because human knowledge and foresight are limited, but consequences are not. Actions can set off an unintended chain of events, or they can spread in many directions like the circle of ripples caused when a stone is thrown into a calm body of water.[3]

The law of unintended consequences, as it is sometimes called, can have both beneficial and detrimental effects. Schoolchildren who do their homework in order to pass tests probably do not envision that they are thereby developing mental skills that will stand them in good stead later in their lives. Conversely, adults who regularly engage in criminal behavior increase the likelihood that they will spend time in prison even though they do not intend to get arrested.

American sociologist Robert K. Merton pointed out long ago that the two most pervasive causes of adverse unintended consequences are ignorance and error.[4] In chapter 5 we saw that the war against Saddam Hussein's regime need not have been based on lies and deception but only on poorly interpreted intelligence

Conclusion 237

reports in order to have resulted in the many unintended consequences of that war. Likewise, we can say that ignoring world opinion about the need for that war and disregarding the lack of consensus in the United Nations led to America's having to bear a much greater cost for the war than its planners anticipated.

Merton noted two additional causes of the unintended consequences, which he named immediacy of interest and basic values.[5] By these he meant that the desire to do something quickly can lead one to overlook what might happen afterward, and that acting in accordance with strongly-held values and deep-seated ideals can lead one to overlook the practical consequences of one's actions. This holds true for individuals and for institutions such as corporations and governments.

Both of President Bush's wars were impelled by immediacy. Also, as this book has argued, some conservative values and ideals of the Bush administration are at odds with biblical principles, that is, with the values and ideals presented in the Bible. The final chapter carried the argument further and suggested that this contradiction should be of concern not only for ethical reasons but also for practical reasons. For if the ethical principles revealed in the Scriptures are not arbitrary but are based on human nature and the nature of human relationships, then acting contrary to biblical principles is the equivalent of acting contrary to nature. Acting contrary to nature, however, can have—and in the long run, will have—adverse unintended consequences.

Moreover, acting contrary to the way things are (or being out of touch with reality) is not a formula for success but a prescription for disaster. For to the extent that conservative values and ideals do not reflect the way the way things are but the way that conservatives would like them to be, to that extent conservatives will tend to act in ignorance and refuse to admit the possibility of error. To be sure, the same could be said of liberal values and ideals, but at the present time the United States is in little danger of implementing liberal policies.

Some of what the Bush administration has done and proposed since September 2001 has been in response to the threat of terrorism. The response of the president and his advisors, however, has been anything but biblical, unless one regards the military atrocities of the Old Testament as providing an ethical justification for the killing of civilians in modern warfare. The response has rather been what one might expect when any nation is attacked and is capable of counterattacking. It was not a response that Jesus would have made, even though Christians in the U.S. military services may have behaved honorably and bravely in the war.

Moreover, there is one significant difference between wars in the past and the war on terrorism. Wars in the past were fought between nations, and they were able to be fought until one side claimed victory and the other side admitted defeat. The war on terrorism is not that type of war, if for no other reason than that the enemy is not a nation. And if there is no nation that can be conquered, no nation that can admit defeat, then there is good reason for suspecting that a military war on terrorism cannot be won. Without a decisive defeat there is no way to achieve ultimate victory. An oversight of this magnitude could lead to terrible unintended consequences for the United States.

Christians believe that the Bible reveals God's truth and, as we have seen, much of what the Bible says about morality is pretty basic, almost common sense. It is basic human morality, or what Christian philosophers sometimes call natural law, since it is grounded in the way human beings naturally behave and interact with one another. One could say that the law of unintended consequences is a natural law (although not a moral law) since it is grounded in the natural behavior of individuals and institutions. Although not revealed in the Bible, this law does not contradict the Scriptures, and in fact it could be illustrated with examples taken from the Bible.*

---

* Adam and Eve eating the forbidden fruit; Joseph being sold into Egypt by his brothers; the Israelites asking God for a king to rule them; the social injustice, political corruption and foreign alliances denounced by the prophets; etc.

Christians also believe that God's revelation in the New Testament went far beyond what the Old Testament revealed, but in the area of morality this may not be the case. As we have seen, Jesus was concerned about the fulfillment of the Law and the prophets, and his command to treat others the way one would like to be treated was not much more than a restatement of the biblical precept to love one's neighbor as oneself.[6] If anything, Jesus extended the range of that precept by telling his followers to regard everyone, including their enemies, as their neighbors.

Today it is true that no one is safe from terrorism. It may also be true that a war on terrorism is an unwinnable war. And if this is the case, then we may at last be forced to love our enemies, for only by being a neighbor to them are they likely to become neighbors to us.

Notes

[1] See Arnold J. Toynbee, *A Study of History* (Oxford University Press, 1957). This two-volume edition is an abridgment by D. C. Somervell of the original work, which appeared in twelve volumes.

[2] See Jonathan Schell, *The Fate of the Earth* (William Morrow, 1982).

[3] See Rob Norton, "Unintended Consequences" in *The Concise Encyclopedia of Economics*, part of The Library of Economics and Liberty, available at www.econlib.org; click on Encyclopedia, then type the title in the Search Encyclopedia line.

[4] See Robert K. Merton, "The Unanticipated Consequences of Purposive Social Action," *American Sociological Review*, (December 1936), pp. 894-904; available through the Compleat World Copyright Website at www.compilerpress.atfreeweb.com but most easily accessed by typing the title into a search engine.

[5] See Merton, pp. 900–902.

[6] "You shall not take vengeance or bear a grudge against any of your people, but you shall love your neighbor as yourself: I am the Lord" (Leviticus 19:18).

About the Author

JOSEPH J. MARTOS, PhD, is a retired professor of philosophy and religion. Deeply committed to biblical Christianity and living the Gospel, he has taught and lectured in the United States, Canada, Australia, and Europe. He currently resides in Louisville, Kentucky.

Correspondence can be addressed to PO Box 775, Louisville KY 40201-0775, or to biblicalchristian@yahoo.com.

More information about the author, as well as an electronic version of this book (an earlier edition with a different title), can be found at www.biblicalchristian.us.

Printed in the United States
65783LVS00009B/85-90